THE PROSE WRITINGS OF HEINRICH HEINE

Table of Contents

I.

HEINE gathers up and focuses for us in one vivid point all those influences of his own time which are the forces of to-day. He appears before us, to put it in his own way, as a youthful and militant Knight of the Holy Ghost, tilting against the spectres of the past and liberating the imprisoned energies of the human spirit. His interest from this point of view lies, largely, apart from his interest as a supreme lyric poet, the brother of Catullus and Villon and Burns; we here approach him on his prosaic—his relatively prosaic—side.

One hemisphere of Heine's brain was Greek, the other Hebrew. He was born when the genius of Goethe was at its height; his mother had absorbed the frank earthliness, the sane and massive Paganism, of the Roman elegies, and Heine's ideals in all things, whether he would or not, were always Hellenic—using that word in the large sense in which Heine himself used it—even while he was the first in rank and the last in time of the Romantic poets of Germany. He sought, even consciously, to mould the modern emotional spirit into classic forms. He wrought his art simply and lucidly, the aspirations that pervade it are everywhere sensuous, and yet it recalls oftener the turbulent temper of Catullus than any serener ancient spirit.

For Heine arose early in active rebellion against a merely passive classicism; just as fiercer and more ardent cries, as from the Orient, pierce through the songs of Catullus. The mischievous Hermes was irritated by the calm and quiet activities of the aged Zeus of Weimar. And then the earnest Hebrew nature within him, liberated by Hegel's favourite thought of the divinity of man, came into play with its large revolutionary thirsts. Thus it was that he appeared before the world as the most brilliant leader of a movement of national or even world-wide emancipation. The greater part of his prose works, from the youthful *Reisebilder* onwards, and a considerable portion of his poetic work, record the energy with which he played this part.

But whether the Greek or the Hebrew element happened to be most active in Heine, the ideal that he set up for life generally was the equal activity of both sides—in other words, the harmony of flesh and spirit. It is this thought which dominates *The History of Religion and Philosophy in Germany*, his finest achievement in this kind. That book was written at the moment when Heine touched the highest point of his enthusiasm for freedom and his faith in the possibility of human progress. It is a sort of programme for the immediate future of the human spirit, in the form of a brief and bold outline of the spiritual history of Germany and Germany's great emancipators, Luther, Lessing, Kant, and the rest. It sets forth in a fresh and fascinating shape that Everlasting Gospel which, from the time of Joachim of Flora downwards, has always gleamed in dreams before the minds of men as the successor of Christianity. Heine's vision of a democracy of cakes and ale, founded on the heights of religious, philosophical, and political freedom, still spurs and thrills us—even now-a-days, when we have wearied of stately bills of fare for a sulky humanity that will not feed at our bidding, no, not on cakes and ale. Heine is wise enough to see, however imperfectly, that it is unreasonable to expect the speedy erection of any New Jerusalem; for, as he expresses it in his own way, the holy vampires of the middle ages have sucked away so much of our life-blood that the world has become a hospital. A sudden revolution of fever-stricken or hysterical invalids can effect little of permanent value; only a long and invigorating course of the tonics of life can make free from danger the open-air of nature. "Our first duty," he asserted in this book, "is to become healthy."

Heine confesses that he too was among the sick and decrepit souls. In reality he was at no period so full of life and health, so harmoniously inspired and upborne by a great enthusiasm. He laughs a little at Goethe; he fails to see that the Phidian Zeus, at whose confined position he jests, was the greatest liberator of them all; but for the most part his mocking sarcasm is here silent. It was not until ten years later, when the subtle seeds of disease had begun to appear, and when, too, he had perhaps gained a clearer insight into the possibilities of life, that Heine realised that the practical reforming movements of his time were not those for which his early enthusiasm had been aroused. And then he wrote *Atta Troll*.

With the slow steps of that consuming disease, and after the revolution of 1848, Heine ceased to recognise as of old any common root for his various activities, or to insist on the fundamental importance of religion. Everything in the world became the sport of his intelligence. The brain still functioned brilliantly in the atrophied body; the lightning-like wit still struck unerringly; it spared not even himself. The *Confessions* are full of irony, covering all things with laughter that is half reverence, or with reverence that is more than half laughter—and woe to the reader who is not at every moment alert! In the romantic, satirical poem of *Atta Troll*, written at the commencement of this last period, this, his final altitude, is most completely revealed. It needs a little study to-day, even for a German, but it is well worth that study.

Atta Troll, the history of a dancing bear who escapes from servitude, is a protest against the radical party, with their narrow conceptions of progress, their tame ideal of *bourgeois* equality, their little watchwords, their solemnity, their indignation at the human creatures who smile "even in their enthusiasm." All these serious concerns of the tribunes of the people are bathed in soft laughter as we listen to the delicious childlike monotonous melody in which the old bear, surrounded by his family, mumbles or mutters of the future. *Atta Troll* is not, as many have thought, a sneer at the most sacred ideals of men. It is, rather, the assertion of those ideals against the individuals who would narrow them down to their own petty scope. There are certain mirrors, Heine said, so constructed that they would present even Apollo as a caricature. But we laugh at the caricature, not at the god. It is well to show, even at the cost of some misunderstanding, that above and beyond the little ideals of our political progress, there is built a yet larger ideal city, of which also the human spirit claims citizenship. The defence of the inalienable rights of the spirit, Heine declares, had been the chief business of his life.

6

In the history of Germany it was her two great intellectual liberators, Luther and Lessing, to whom Heine looked up with the most unqualified love and reverence. By his later vindication of the rights of the spirit, not less than by his earlier fight for religious and political progress, he may be said to have earned for himself a place below, indeed, but not so very far below, those hearty and sound-cored iconoclasts.

II.

To reach the root of the man's nature we must glance at the chief facts of his life. He was born at Düsseldorf on the Rhine, then occupied by the French, probably on the 13th of December 1799.[1] He came, by both parents, of that Jewish race which is, as he said once, the dough whereof gods are kneaded. The family of his mother, Betty van Geldern, had come from Holland a century earlier; Betty herself received an excellent education; she shared the studies of her brother, who became a physician of repute; she spoke and read English and French; her favourite books were Rousseau's *Emile* and Goethe's elegies. Some letters written during her twenty-fourth year reveal a frank, brave and sweet nature; she was a bright, attractive little person, and had many wooers. In the summer of 1796 Samson Heine, bearing a letter of introduction, entered the house of the Van Gelderns. He was the son of a Jewish merchant settled in Hanover, and he had just made a campaign in Flanders and Brabant, in the capacity of commissary with the rank of officer, under Prince Ernest of Cumberland. He was a large and handsome man, with soft blond hair and beautiful hands; there was something about him, said his son, a little characterless and feminine. After a brief courtship he married Betty and settled at Düsseldorf as an agent for English velveteens. Harry (so he was named after an Englishman) was the first child. While from his rather weak and romantic father came whatever was loose and unbalanced in Heine's temperament, it was his mother, with her strong and healthy nature, well developed both intellectually and emotionally, who, as he himself said, played the chief part in the history of his evolution.

Harry was a quick child; his senses were keen, though he was not physically strong; he loved reading, and his favourite books were *Don Quixote* and *Gulliver's Travels*. He used to make rhymes with his only and much-loved sister Lotte, and at the age of ten he wrote a ghost-poem which his teachers considered a masterpiece. At the Lyceum he worked well, at night as well as by day. Only once, at the public ceremony at the end of a school year, he came to grief; he was reciting a poem, when his eyes fell on a beautiful, fair-haired girl in the audience; he hesitated, stammered, was silent, fell down fainting. So early he revealed the extreme cerebral irritability of a nature absorbed in dreams and taken captive by visions. It was not long after this, at the age of seventeen, when his rich uncle at Hamburg was trying in vain to set him forward on a commercial career, that Heine met the woman who aroused his first and last profound passion, always unsatisfied except in so far as it found exquisite embodiment in his poems. He never mentioned her name; it was not till after his death that the form standing behind this Maria, Zuleima, Evelina of so many sweet, strange, or melancholy

7

songs was known to be that of his cousin, Amalie Heine.

With his uncle's help he studied law at Bonn, Göttingen and Berlin. At Berlin he fell under the dominant influence of Hegel, the vanquisher of the romantic school of which Schelling was the philosophic representative. Heine afterwards referred to this period as that in which he "herded swine with the Hegelians;" it is certain that Hegel exerted great and permanent influence over him. At Berlin, in 1821, appeared his first volume of poems, and then he began to take his true place.

At this period Heine is described as a good-natured and gentle youth, but reserved, not caring to show his emotions. He was of middle height and slender, with rather long light brown hair (in childhood it was red, and he was called "Rother Harry") framing the pale and beardless oval face, the bright blue short-sighted eyes, the Greek nose, the high cheek-bones, the large mouth, the full—half cynical, half sensual—lips. He was not a typical German; like Goethe, he never smoked; he disliked beer, and until he went to Paris he had never tasted *sauerkraut*.

For some years he continued, chiefly at Göttingen, to study law. But he had no liking and no capacity for jurisprudence, and his spasmodic fits of application at such moments as he realised that it was not good for him to depend on the generosity of his rich and kind-hearted uncle Solomon, failed to carry him far. A new idea, a sunny day, the opening of some flower-like *lied*, a pretty girl—and the Pandects were forgotten.

Shortly after he had at last received his doctor's diploma he went through the ceremony of baptism in hope of obtaining an appointment from the Prussian Government. It was a step which he immediately regretted, and which, far from placing him in a better position, excited the enmity both of Christians and Jews, although the Heine family had no very strong views on the matter; Heine's mother, it should be said, was a Deist, his father indifferent, but the Jewish rites were strictly kept up. He still talked of becoming an advocate, until, in 1826, the publication of the first volume of the *Reisebilder* gave him a reputation throughout Germany by its audacity, its charming and picturesque manner, its peculiarly original personality. The second volume, bolder and better than the first, was received with delight very much mixed with horror, and it was prohibited by Austria, Prussia, and many minor states. At this period Heine visited England;[2] he was then disgusted with Germany and full of enthusiasm for the "land of freedom," an enthusiasm which naturally met with many rude shocks, and from that time dates the bitterness with which he usually speaks of England. He found London—although, owing to a clever abuse of uncle Solomon's generosity, exceedingly well supplied with money—"frightfully damp and uncomfortable;" only the political life of England attracted him, and there were no bounds to his admiration of Canning. He then visited Italy, to spend there the happiest days of his life; and having at length realised that his efforts to obtain any government appointment in Germany would be fruitless, he emigrated to Paris. There, save for brief periods, he remained until his death.

This entry into the city which he had called the New Jerusalem was an important epoch in Heine's life. He was thirty-one years of age, still youthful, and eager to receive new impressions; he was apparently in robust health, notwithstanding constant headaches; Gautier describes him as in appearance a sort of German Apollo. He was still developing, as he continued to develop, even up to the end; the ethereal loveliness of the early poems vanished, it is true, but only to give place to a closer grasp of reality, a larger laughter, a keener cry of pain. He was now heartily welcomed by the extraordinarily brilliant group then living and working in Paris, including Victor Hugo, George Sand, Balzac, Michelet, Alfred de Musset, Gautier, Chopin, Louis Blanc, Dumas, Sainte-Beuve, Quinet, Berlioz, and many others, and he entered with eager delight into their manifold activities. For a time also he attached himself rather closely to the school of Saint-Simon, then headed by Enfantin; he was especially attracted by their religion of humanity, which seemed the realisation of his own dreams. Heine's book on *Religion and Philosophy in Germany* was written at Enfantin's suggestion, and the first edition dedicated to him; Enfantin's name was, he said, a sort of Shibboleth, indicating the most advanced party in the "liberation war of humanity." In 1855 he withdrew the dedication; it had become an anachronism; Enfantin was no longer ransacking the world in search of *la femme libre*; the martyrs of yesterday no longer bore a cross—unless it were, he added characteristically, the cross of the Legion of Honour.

A few years after his arrival in Paris Heine entered on a relationship which occupied a large place in his life. Mathilde Mirat, a lively grisette of sixteen, was the illegitimate daughter of a man of wealth and position in the provinces, and she had come up from Normandy to serve in her aunt's shoe-shop. Heine often passed this shop, and an acquaintance, at first carried on silently through the shop window, gradually ripened into a more intimate relationship. Mathilde could neither read nor write; it was decided that she should go to school for a time; after that they established a little common household, one of those *ménages parisiens*, recognised as almost legitimate, for which Heine had always had a warm admiration, because, as he said, he meant by "marriage" something quite other than the legal coupling effected by parsons and bankers. As in the case of Goethe, it was not until some years later that he went through the religious ceremony, as a preliminary to a duel in which he had become involved by his remarks on Börne's friend, Madame Strauss; he wished to give Mathilde an assured position in case of his death. After the ceremony at St. Sulpice he invited to dinner all those of his friends who had contracted similar relations, in order that they might be influenced by his example. That they were so influenced is not recorded.

It is not difficult to understand the strong and permanent attraction that drew the poet, who had so many intellectual and aristocratic women among his friends, to this pretty, laughter-loving grisette. It lay in her bright and wild humour, her childlike impulsiveness, not least in her charming ignorance. It was delightful to Heine that Mathilde had never read a line of his books, did not even know what a poet was, and loved him only for himself. He found in her a continual source of refreshment.

9

He had need of every source of refreshment. In the years that followed his formal marriage in 1841, the dark shadows, within and without, began to close round him. Although he was then producing his most mature work, chiefly in poetry— *Atta Troll, Romancero, Deutschland*—his income from literary sources remained small. Mathilde was not a good housekeeper; and even with the aid of a considerable allowance from his uncle Solomon, Heine was frequently in pecuniary difficulties, and was consequently induced to accept a small pension from the French government, which has sometimes been a matter of concern to those who care for his fame. As years passed, the enmities that he suffered from or cherished increased rather than diminished, and his bitterness found expression in his work. Even Mathilde was not an unalloyed source of joy; the charming child was becoming a middle-aged woman, and was still like a child. She could not enter into Heine's interests; she delighted in theatres and circuses, to which he could not always accompany her; and he experienced the pangs of an unreasonable jealousy more keenly than he cared to admit. Then uncle Solomon died, and his son refused, until considerable pressure was brought to bear on him, to continue the allowance which his father had intended Heine to receive. This was a severe blow, and the excitement it produced developed the latent seeds of his disease. It came on with alarming symptoms of paralysis, which even in a few months gave him, he says, the appearance of a dying man. During the next two years, although his brain remained clear, the long pathological tragedy was unfolded.

He went out for the last time in May 1848. Half blind and half lame, he slowly made his way out of the streets, filled with the noise of revolution, into the silent Louvre, to the shrine dedicated to "the goddess of beauty, our dear lady of Milo." There he sat long at her feet; he was bidding farewell to his old gods; he had become reconciled to the religion of sorrow; tears streamed from his eyes, and she looked down at him, compassionate but helpless: "Dost thou not see, then, that I have no arms, and cannot help thee?"

On eût dit un Apollon germanique—so Gautier said of the Heine of 1835; twenty years later an English visitor wrote of him—"He lay on a pile of mattresses, his body wasted so that it seemed no bigger than a child under the sheet which covered him—his eyes closed, and the face altogether like the most painful and wasted 'Ecce Homo' ever painted by some old German painter."

His sufferings were only relieved by ever larger doses of morphia; but although still more troubles came to him, and the failure of a bank robbed him of his small savings, his spirit remained unconquered. "He is a wonderful man," said one of his doctors; "he has only two anxieties—to conceal his condition from his mother, and to assure his wife's future." His literary work, though it decreased in amount, never declined in power; only, in the words of his friend Berlioz, it seemed as though the poet was standing at the window of his tomb, looking around on the world in which he had no longer a part.

He saw a few friends, of whom Ferdinand Lassalle, with his exuberant power and enthusiasm, was the most interesting to him, as the representative of a new age

10

and a new social faith; and the most loved, that girl-friend who sat for hours or days at a time by the "mattress-grave" in the Rue d' Amsterdam, reading to him or writing his letters or correcting proofs. To the last the loud, bright voice of Mathilde, when he chanced to hear it, scolding the servants or in other active exercise, often made him stop speaking, while a smile of delight passed over his face. He died on the 16th of February 1856. He was buried, silently, in Montmartre, according to his wish; for, as he said, it is quiet there.

III.

Throughout and above all Heine was a poet. From first to last he was led by three angels who danced for ever in his brain, and guided him, singly or together, always. They were the same as in *Atta Troll* he saw in the moonlight from the casement of Uraka's hut—the Greek Diana, grown wanton, but with the noble marble limbs of old; Abunde, the blond and gay fairy of France; Herodias, the dark Jewess, like a palm of the oasis, and with all the fragrance of the East between her breasts: "O, you dead Jewess, I love you most, more than the Greek goddess, more than that fairy of the North."[3]

Those genii of three ideal lands danced for ever in his brain, and that is but another way of indicating the opposition that lay at the root of his nature. From one point of view, it may well be, he continued the work of Luther and Lessing, though he was less great-hearted, less sound at core, though he had not that element of sane Philistinism which marks the Shakespeares and Goethes of the world. But he was, more than anything else, a poet, an artist, a dreamer, a perpetual child. The practical reformers among whom at one time he placed himself, the men of one idea, were naturally irritated and suspicious; there was a flavour of aristocracy in such idealism. In the poem called "Disputation" a Capuchin and a Rabbi argued before the King and Queen at Toledo concerning the respective merits of the Christian and Jewish religions. Both spoke at great length and with great fervour, and in the end the King appealed to the beautiful Queen by his side. She replied that she could not tell which of them was right, but that she did not like the smell of either; and Heine was generally of the Queen's mind. He sighed for the restoration of Barbarossa, the long-delayed German Empire, and his latest biographer asserts that he would have greeted the discovery of Barbarossa under the disguise of the King of Prussia, with Bismarckian insignia of blood and iron, as the realisation of all his dreams. It is doubtful, however, whether the meeting would be very cordial on either side. It would probably be the painful duty of the Emperor, as of the Emperor of the vision in *Deutschland*, to tell Heine, in very practical language, that he was wanting in respect, wanting in all sense of etiquette; and Heine would certainly reply to the Emperor, as under the same circumstances he replied to the visionary Barbarossa, that that venerable gentleman had better go home again, that during his long absence Emperors had become unnecessary, and that, after all, sceptres and crowns made admirable playthings for monkeys.

"We are founding a democracy of gods," he wrote in 1834, "all equally holy, blessed and glorious. You desire simple clothing, ascetic morals, and unseasoned enjoyments; we, on the contrary, desire nectar and ambrosia, purple mantles, costly perfumes, pleasure and splendour, dances of laughing nymphs, music and plays.—Do not be angry, you virtuous republicans; we answer all your reproaches in the words of one of Shakespeare's fools: 'Dost thou think that because thou art virtuous there shall be no more cakes and ale?'" What could an austere republican, a Puritanic Liberal, who scorned the vision of roses and myrtles and sugar-plums all round, say to this? Börne answered, "I can be indulgent to the games of children, indulgent to the passions of a youth, but when on the bloody day of battle a boy who is chasing butterflies gets between my legs; when at the day of our greatest need, and we are calling aloud on God, the young coxcomb beside us in the church sees only the pretty girls, and winks and flirts—then, in spite of all our philosophy and humanity, we may well grow angry.... Heine, with his sybaritic nature, is so effeminate that the fall of a roseleaf disturbs his sleep; how, then, should he[Pgxix] rest comfortably on the knotty bed of freedom? Where is there any beauty without a fault? Where is there any good thing without its ridiculous side? Nature is seldom a poet and never rhymes; let him whom her rhymeless prose cannot please turn to poetry!" Börne was right; Heine was not the man to plan a successful revolution, or defend a barricade, or edit a popular democratic newspaper, or represent adequately a radical constituency— all this was true. Let us be thankful that it was true; Börnes are ever with us, and we are grateful: there is but one Heine.

The same complexity of nature that made Heine an artist made him a humorist. But it was a more complicated complexity now, a cosmic game between the real world and the ideal world; he could go no further. The young Catullus of 1825, with his fiery passions crushed in the wine-press of life and yielding such divine ambrosia, soon lost his faith in passion. The militant soldier in the liberation-war of humanity of 1835 soon ceased to flourish his sword. It was only with the full development of his humour, when his spinal cord began to fail and he had taken up his position as a spectator of life, that Heine attained the only sort of unity possible to him—the unity that comes of a recognised and accepted lack of unity. In the lambent flames of this unequalled humour he bathed all the things he counted dearest; to its service he brought the secret of his poet's nature, the secret of speaking with a voice that every heart leaps up to answer. It is scarcely the humour of Aristophanes, though it is a greater force, even in moulding our political and social ideals, than Börne knew; it is oftener a modern development of the humour of the mad king and the fool in *Lear*—that humour which is the last concentrated word of the human organism under the lash of Fate.

And if it is still asked why Heine is so modern, it can only be said that these discords out of which his humour exhaled are those which we have nearly all of us known, and that he speaks with a voice that seems to arise from the depth of our own souls. He represents our period of transition; he gazed, from what[Pgxx] appeared the vulgar Pisgah of his day, behind on an Eden that was for ever closed, before on a promised land he should never enter. While with clear sight he announced things to come, the music of the past floated up to him; he brooded wistfully over the vision of the old Olympian gods, dying, amid faint music of cymbals and flutes, forsaken, in the mediæval wilderness; he heard strange sounds of psaltries and harps, the psalms of Israel, the voice of Princess Sabbath, sounding across the remote waters of Babylon.—In a few years this significance of Heine will be lost; that it is not yet lost the eagerness with which his books are read and translated sufficiently testifies.

HAVELOCK ELLIS.

HEINE'S PROSE WORKS.

REISEBILDER.

IDEAS, OR THE BOOK LE GRAND.

[The *Ideas*, of which the chief portion is here presented, was published in 1826 in the second volume of the *Reisebilder*, or *Travel-Pictures*. The German title has been retained, as Heine himself retained it in the French translation. The translation here given is founded on Mr. Leland's; it has been carefully revised.]

CHAPTER I.

She was lovable, and he loved her. But he was not lovable, and she
did not love him.—*Old Play.*

MADAME, do you know the old play? It is quite an extraordinary play, only a little too melancholy. I once played the leading part in it myself, so that all the ladies wept; only one did not weep, not even a single tear, and that was the point of the play, the whole catastrophe.

Oh, that single tear! it still torments my thoughts. When Satan wishes to ruin my soul, he hums in my ear a ballad of that unwept tear, a deadly song with a more deadly tune. Ah! such a tune is only heard in Hell!

You can readily form an idea, Madame, of what life is like in Heaven, the more readily as you are married. There people amuse themselves altogether superbly, every sort of entertainment is provided, and one lives in mere desire and delight. One eats from morning to night, and the cookery is as good as Jagor's; roast geese fly round with gravy-boats in their bills, and feel flattered if any one eats them; tarts gleaming with butter grow wild like sunflowers; everywhere there are brooks of *bouillon* and champagne, everywhere trees on which napkins flutter, and you eat and wipe your lips and eat again without injury to your stomach; you sing psalms, or flirt and joke with the dear, delicate little angels, or take a walk on the green Hallelujah-Meadow, and your white flowing garments fit very comfortably, and nothing disturbs the feeling of blessedness, no pain, no vexation—even when one accidentally treads on another's corns and exclaims,

13

"*Excusez!*" he smiles as if enraptured, and assures, "Thy foot, brother, did not hurt in the least, quite *au contraire*, a deeper thrill of heavenly rapture shoots through my heart!"

But of Hell, Madame, you have no idea. Of all the devils you know, perhaps, only the little Amor, the pretty *Croupier* of Hell, Beelzebub, and you know him only from *Don Juan*, and doubtless think that for such a betrayer of innocence Hell can never be made hot enough, though our praiseworthy theatre directors spend upon him as much flame, fiery rain, powder, and colophonium as any Christian could desire in Hell.

But things in Hell look much worse than our theatre directors know, or they would not bring out so many bad plays. For in Hell it is infernally hot, and when I was there, in the dog-days, it was past endurance. Madame, you can have no idea of Hell! We have very few official returns from that place. Still, it is rank calumny to say that down there all the poor souls are compelled to read, the whole day long, all the dull sermons that are printed on earth. Bad as Hell is, it has not come to that; Satan will never invent such refinements of torture. On the other hand, Dante's description is too mild on the whole, too poetic. Hell appeared to me like a great kitchen, with an endlessly long stove, on which stood three rows of iron pots, and in these sat the damned, and were cooked. In one row were placed Christian sinners, and, incredible as it may seem, their number was anything but small, and the devils poked the fire up under them with especial good-will. In the next row were Jews, who continually screamed and cried, and were occasionally mocked by the fiends, which sometimes seemed very amusing, as, for instance, when a fat, wheezy old pawnbroker complained of the heat, and a little devil poured several buckets of cold water on his head, that he might realise what a refreshing benefit baptism was. In the third row sat the heathen, who, like the Jews, could take no part in salvation, and must burn forever. I heard one of these, as a burly devil put fresh coals under his kettle, cry out from his pot, "Spare me! I was Socrates, the wisest of mortals. I taught Truth and Justice, and sacrificed my life for Virtue." But the stupid, burly devil went on with his work, and grumbled, "Oh, shut up, there! All heathens must burn, and we can't make an exception for the sake of a single man." I assure you, Madame, the heat was terrible, with such a screaming, sighing, groaning, quacking, grunting, squealing—and through all these terrible sounds rang distinctly the deadly tune of the song of the unwept tear.

CHAPTER II.

"She was lovable, and he loved her. But he was not lovable, and she did not love him."—*Old Play.*

Madame! that old play is a tragedy, though the hero in it is neither killed nor commits suicide. The eyes of the heroine are beautiful—very beautiful—Madame, do you smell the perfume of violets?—very beautiful, and yet so piercing that they struck like poignards of glass through my heart and probably came out through my back—and yet I was not killed by those treacherous, murderous eyes.

14

The voice of the heroine was also sweet—Madame, did you hear a nightingale just then?—a soft, silken voice, a sweet web of the sunniest tones, and my soul was entangled in it, and choked and tormented itself. I myself—it is the Count of Ganges who now speaks, and the story goes on in Venice—I myself soon had enough of these tortures, and had thoughts of putting an end to the play in the first act, and of shooting myself through the head, fool's-cap and all. I went to a fancy shop in the Via Burstah, where I saw a pair of beautiful pistols in a case—I remember them perfectly well—near them stood many pleasant playthings of mother-of-pearl and gold, steel hearts on gilt chains, porcelain cups with delicate devices, and snuff-boxes with pretty pictures, such as the divine history of Susannah, the Swan Song of Leda, the Rape of the Sabines, Lucretia, a fat, virtuous creature, with naked bosom, in which she was lazily sticking a dagger; the late Bethmann, *la belle Ferronière*—all enrapturing faces—but I bought the pistols without much ado, and then I bought balls, then powder, and then I went to the restaurant of Signor Somebody, and ordered oysters and a glass of Hock.

I could eat nothing, and still less could I drink. The warm tears fell in the glass, and in that glass I saw my dear home, the holy, blue Ganges, the ever-gleaming Himalaya, the giant banyan woods, amid whose broad arcades calmly wandered wise elephants and white-robed pilgrims, strange dream-like flowers gazed on me with meaning glance, wondrous golden birds sang wildly, flashing sun-rays and the sweet, silly chatter of monkeys pleasantly mocked me, from far pagodas sounded the pious prayers of priests, and amid all rang the melting, wailing voice of the Sultana of Delhi—she ran impetuously around in her carpeted chamber, she tore her silver veil, with her peacock fan she struck the black slave to the ground, she wept, she raged, she cried. I could not, however, hear what she said; the restaurant of Signor Somebody is three thousand miles distant from the Harem of Delhi, besides the fair Sultana had been dead three thousand years—and I quickly drank up the wine, the clear, joy-giving wine, and yet my soul grew darker and sadder—I was condemned to death.

As I left the restaurant I heard the "bell of poor sinners" ring, a crowd of people swept by me; but I placed myself at the corner of the Strada San Giovanni, and recited the following monologue:—

"In ancient tales they tell of golden castles,
Where harps are sounding, lovely ladies dance,
And gay attendants gleam, and jessamine,
Myrtle, and roses spread their soft perfume—
And yet a single word of sad enchantment
Sweeps all the glory of the scene to naught,
And there remain but ruins old and grey,
And screaming birds of night and foul morass.
Even so have I, with but a single word,
Enchanted Nature's blooming loveliness.
There lies she now, lifeless and cold and pale,
Just like a monarch's corse laid out in state,
The royal deathly cheeks fresh stained with rouge,

And in his hand the kingly sceptre laid,
Yet still his lips are yellow and most changed,
For they forgot to dye them, as they should,
And mice are jumping o'er the monarch's nose,
And mock the golden sceptre in his grasp."

It is everywhere agreed, Madame, that one should deliver a soliloquy before shooting himself. Most men, on such occasions, use Hamlet's "To be, or not to be." It is an excellent passage, and I would gladly have quoted it—but charity begins at home, and when a man has written tragedies himself, in which such farewell-to-life speeches occur, as, for instance, in my immortal *Almansor*, it is very natural that one should prefer his own words even to Shakespeare's. At any rate, the delivery of such speeches is a very useful custom; one gains at least a little time. And so it came to pass that I remained a rather long time standing at the corner of the Strada San Giovanni—and as I stood there like a condemned criminal awaiting death, I raised my eyes, and suddenly beheld *her*.

She wore her blue silk dress and rose-red hat, and her eyes looked at me so mildly, so death-conqueringly, so life-givingly—Madame, you well know, out of Roman history, that when the vestals in ancient Rome met on their way a malefactor led to death, they had the right to pardon him, and the poor rogue lived. With a single glance she saved me from death, and I stood before her revived, and dazzled by the sunbeams of her beauty, and she passed on—and left me alive.

CHAPTER III.

And she left me alive, and I live, which is the main point.

Others may, if they choose, enjoy the good fortune of having their lady-love adorn their graves with garlands and water them with the tears of fidelity. Oh, women! hate me, laugh at me, jilt me—but let me live! Life is all too laughably sweet, and the world too delightfully bewildered; it is the dream of an intoxicated god, who has taken French leave of the carousing multitude of immortals, and has laid himself down to sleep in a solitary star, and knows not himself that he creates all that he dreams—and the dream images form themselves in such a mad variegated fashion, and often so harmoniously reasonable—the Iliad, Plato, the battle of Marathon, Moses, Medician Venus, Strasburg Cathedral, the French Revolution, Hegel, the steamboat, etc., etc., are single good thoughts in this divine dream—but it will not last long, and the god awakes and rubs his sleepy eyes, and smiles—and our world has run to nothing—yes, has never been.

No matter! I live. If I am but a shadowy image in a dream, still this is better than the cold, black, void annihilation of Death. Life is the greatest good and death the worst evil. Berlin lieutenants of the guard may sneer and call it cowardice, because the Prince of Homburg shudders when he beholds his open grave. Henry Kleist[4] had, however, as much courage as his high-breasted, tightly-laced colleagues, and has, alas! proved it. But all strong men love life. Goethe's Egmont does not part willingly from "the cheerful wont of being and working."

16

Immermann's Edwin clings to life "like a little child to its mother's breast," and though he finds it hard to live by stranger mercy, he still begs for mercy: "For life and breath is still the highest."

When Odysseus in the under-world sees Achilles as the leader of dead heroes, and extols his renown among the living, and his glory even among the dead, Achilles answers:—

"No more discourse of death, consolingly, noble Odysseus!
Rather would I in the field as daily labourer be toiling,
Slave to the meanest of men, a pauper and lacking possessions,
Than mid the infinite host of long-vanished mortals be ruler."

Yes, when Major Duvent challenged the great Israel Lyon to fight with pistols and said to him, "If you do not meet me, Mr. Lyon, you are a dog;" the latter replied, "I would rather be a live dog than a dead lion!" and he was right. I have fought often enough, Madame, to dare to say this—God be praised! I live! Red life pulses in my veins, earth yields beneath my feet, in the glow of love I embrace trees and statues, and they live in my embrace. Every woman is to me the gift of a world. I revel in the melody of her countenance, and with a single glance of my eye I can enjoy more than others with their every limb through all their lives. Every instant is to me an eternity. I do not measure time with the ell of Brabant or of Hamburg, and I need no priest to promise me a second life, for I can live enough in this life, when I live backwards in the life of those who have gone before me, and win myself an eternity in the realm of the past.

And I live! The great pulsation of nature beats too in my breast, and when I carol aloud, I am answered by a thousand-fold echo. I hear a thousand nightingales. Spring has sent them to awaken Earth from her morning slumber, and Earth trembles with ecstasy; her flowers are hymns, which she sings in inspiration to the sun—the sun moves far too slowly; I would fain lash on his steeds that they might advance more rapidly. But when he sinks hissing in the sea, and the night rises with her great passionate eyes, oh! then true pleasure first thrills through me, the evening breezes lie like flattering maidens on my wild heart, and the stars wink to me, and I rise and sweep over the little earth and the little thoughts of men.

CHAPTER IV.

But a day will come when the fire in my veins will be quenched, when winter will dwell in my heart, when his snow flakes will whiten my locks, and his mists will dim my eyes. Then my friends will lie in their lonely graves, and I alone shall remain like a solitary stalk forgotten by the reaper. A new race will have sprung up with new desires and new ideas; full of wonder I shall hear new names and listen to new songs, for the old names will be forgotten, and I myself forgotten, perhaps still honoured by a few, scorned by many and loved by none! And then the rosy-cheeked boys will spring around me and place the old harp in my trembling hand, and say, laughing, "You have been long silent, you greybeard; sing us again songs of your youthful dreams!"

17

Then I will grasp the harp, and my old joys and sorrows will awake, tears will again spring from my dead eyes; there will be Spring again in my breast, sweet tones of sorrow will tremble on the harpstrings, I shall see again the blue stream and the marble palaces and the lovely faces of women and girls—and I will sing a song of the flowers of Brenta.

It will be my last song; the stars will gaze on me as in the nights of my youth, the loving moonlight will once more kiss my cheeks, the spirit chorus of nightingales long dead will sound from afar, my sleep-drunken eyes will close, my soul will echo with the notes of my harp; I shall smell the flowers of Brenta.

A tree will shadow my grave. I would gladly have it a palm, but that tree will not grow in the North. It will be a linden, and on summer evenings lovers will sit there and caress; the green-finch, who rocks himself on the branches, will be listening silently, and my linden will rustle tenderly over the heads of the happy ones, who will be so happy that they will have no time to read what is written on the white tombstone. But when later the lover has lost his love, then he will come again to the well-known linden, and sigh, and weep, and gaze long and oft upon the stone, and read the inscription—"He loved the flowers of Brenta."

CHAPTER V.

Madame! I have deceived you. I am not the Count of the Ganges. Never in my life have I seen the holy stream, nor the lotus flowers which are mirrored in its sacred waves. Never did I lie dreaming under Indian palms, nor in prayer before the Diamond Deity Juggernaut, who with his diamonds might have easily aided me out of my difficulties. I have no more been in Calcutta than the turkey, of which I ate yesterday at dinner, had ever been in the realms of the Grand Turk. Yet my ancestors came from Hindostan, and therefore I feel so much at my ease in the great forest of song of Valmiki. The heroic sorrows of the divine Ramo move my heart like familiar griefs; from the flower lays of Kalidasa the sweetest memories bloom; and when a few years ago a gentle lady in Berlin showed me the beautiful pictures which her father, who had been Governor in India, had brought from thence, the delicately-painted, holy, calm faces seemed as familiar to me as though I were gazing at my own family gallery.

Franz Bopp—Madame, you have of course read his *Nalus* and his System of Sanscrit Conjugations—gave me much information relative to my ancestry, and I now know with certainty that I am descended from Brahma's head, and not from his corns. I have also good reason to believe that the entire *Mahabarata*, with its two hundred thousand verses, is merely an allegorical love-letter which my first fore-father wrote to my first fore-mother. Oh! they loved dearly, their souls kissed, they kissed with their eyes, they were both but one single kiss.

An enchanted nightingale sits on a red coral bough in the silent sea, and sings a song of the love of my ancestors; the pearls gaze eagerly from their shells, the wonderful water-flowers tremble with sorrow, the cunning sea-snails, bearing on their backs many-coloured porcelain towers, come creeping onwards, the ocean-roses blush with shame, the yellow, sharp-pointed starfish, and the thousand-

18

hued glassy jelly-fish quiver and stretch, and all swarm and listen.

Unfortunately, Madame, this nightingale song is far too long to be set down here; it is as long as the world itself, even its dedication to Anangas, the God of Love, is as long as all Scott's novels, and there is a passage referring to it in Aristophanes, which in German[5] reads thus:—

"Tiotio, tiotio, tiotinx,
Totototo totototo tototinx."
(Voss's *Translation*.)

No, I was not born in India. I first beheld the light of the world on the shores of that beautiful stream, in whose green hills folly grows and is plucked in Autumn, laid away in cellars, poured into barrels, and exported to foreign lands. In fact, only yesterday I heard some one speaking a piece of folly which, in the year 1811, was imprisoned in a bunch of grapes, which I myself then saw growing on the Johannisburg. But much folly is also consumed at home, and men are the same there as everywhere: they are born, eat, drink, sleep, laugh, cry, slander each other, are greatly troubled about the propagation of their race, try to seem what they are not and to do what they cannot, never shave until they have a beard, and often have beards before they get discretion, and when they at last have discretion, they drink it away in white and red folly.

Mon dieu! if I had faith, so that I could remove mountains—the Johannisburg would be just the mountain which I would carry with me everywhere. But as my faith is not strong enough, imagination must aid me, and she quickly sets me by the beautiful Rhine.

Oh, that is a fair land, full of loveliness and sunshine. In the blue stream are mirrored the mountain shores, with their ruined towers, and woods, and ancient towns. There, before the house-door, sit the good townspeople, of a summer evening, and drink out of great cans, and gossip confidentially about how the wine—the Lord be praised!—thrives, and how justice should be free from all secrecy, and how Marie Antoinette's being guillotined is none of our business, and how dear the tobacco tax makes tobacco, and how all mankind are equal, and what a glorious fellow Gœrres is.

I have never troubled myself about such conversation, and sat rather with the maidens in the arched window, and laughed at their laughter, and let them throw flowers in my face, and pretended to be ill-natured until they told me their secrets, or some other important stories. Fair Gertrude was half wild with delight when I sat by her. She was a girl like a flaming rose, and once, as she fell on my neck, I thought that she would burn away into perfume in my arms. Fair Katharine flamed into sweet music when she talked with me, and her eyes were of a pure, internal blue, which I have never seen in men or animals, and very seldom in flowers—one gazed so gladly into them, and could then think such sweet things. But the beautiful Hedwig loved me, for when I came to her she bowed her head till her black curls fell down over her blushing face, and her bright eyes shone like stars from the dark heaven. Her bashful lips spoke not a

19

word, and I too could say nothing to her. I coughed and she trembled. She often begged me, through her sisters, not to climb the rocks so rashly, or to bathe in the Rhine when I was hot with running or drinking wine. Once I overheard her pious prayer before the Virgin Mary, which she had adorned with gold leaf and illuminated with a lamp, and which stood in a corner at the entrance. I plainly heard her pray to the Mother of God to keep him from climbing, drinking, and bathing. I should certainly have been desperately in love with her if she had been indifferent to me, and I was indifferent to her because I knew that she loved me. —Madame, to win my love, I must be treated *en canaille*.

Johanna was the cousin of the three sisters, and I was glad to be with her. She knew the most beautiful old legends, and when she pointed with her white hand through the window out to the mountains where all had happened which she narrated, I became enchanted; the old knights rose visibly from the ruined castles and hewed away at each other's iron clothes, the Lorely sat again on the mountain summit, singing a-down her sweet, seductive song, and the Rhine rippled so reasonably soothing—and yet so mockingly horrible—and the fair Johanna looked at me so strangely, with such enigmatic tenderness, that she seemed herself one with the legend that she told. She was a slender, pale girl, sickly and musing, her eyes were clear as truth itself, her lips piously arched, in her face lay a great story—was it a love legend? I know not, and I never had the courage to ask. When I looked at her long, I grew calm and cheerful—it seemed to me as though it was Sunday in my heart and the angels held service there.

In such happy hours I told her tales of my childhood, and she listened earnestly, and, strangely, when I could not think of the names she remembered them. When I then asked her with wonder how she knew the names, she would answer with a smile that she had learned it of the birds that had built a nest on the sill of her window—and she tried to make me believe that these were the same birds which I once bought with my pocket-money from a hard-hearted peasant boy, and then let fly away. But I believed that she knew everything because she was so pale, and really soon died. She knew, too, when she would die, and wished that I would leave Andernach the day before. When I bade her farewell she gave me both her hands—they were white, sweet hands, and pure as the Host—and she said, You are very good, and when you are not, think of the little dead Veronica.

Did the chattering birds also tell her this name? Often in hours of remembrance I had wearied my brain in trying to think of that dear name, but could not.

And now that I have it again, my earliest infancy shall bloom into memory again —and I am again a child, and play with other children in the Castle Court at Düsseldorf on the Rhine.

CHAPTER VI.

Yes, Madame, there was I born, and I am particular in calling attention to the fact, lest after my death seven cities—those of Schilda, Krähwinkel, Polkwitz, Bockum, Dülken, Göttingen, and Schöppenstadt[6]—should contend for the honour of being my birthplace. Düsseldorf is a town on the Rhine; sixteen thousand people live there, and many hundred thousands besides are buried there. And among them are many of whom my mother says it were better if they were still alive—for example, my grand-father and my uncle, the old Herr von Geldern, and the young Herr von Geldern, who were both such celebrated doctors, and saved the lives of so many men, and yet must both die themselves. And pious Ursula, who carried me as a child in her arms, also lies buried there, and a rose-bush grows over her grave—she loved rose-perfume so much in her life, and her heart was all rose-perfume and goodness. And the shrewd old Canonicus also lies there buried. Lord, how miserable he looked when I last saw him! He consisted of nothing but soul and plasters, and yet he studied night and day as though he feared lest the worms might find a few ideas missing in his head. Little William also lies there—and that is my fault. We were schoolmates in the Franciscan cloister, and were one day playing on that side of the building where the Düssel flows between stone walls, and I said, "William, do get the kitten out, which has just fallen in!" and he cheerfully climbed out on the board which stretched over the brook, and pulled the cat out of the water, but fell in himself, and when they took him out he was cold and dead. The kitten lived to a good old age.

The town of Düsseldorf is very beautiful, and if you think of it when in foreign lands, and happen at the same time to have been born there, strange feelings come over the soul. I was born there, and feel as if I must go directly home. And when I say *home*, I mean the Volkerstrasse and the house where I was born. This house will be some day very remarkable, and I have sent word to the old lady who owns it, that she must not for her life sell it. For the whole house she would now hardly get as much as the present which the green-veiled distinguished English ladies will give the servant when she shows them the room where I was born, and the hen-house wherein my father generally imprisoned me for stealing grapes, and also the brown door on which my mother taught me to write with chalk. Ah me! should I ever become a famous author, it has cost my poor mother trouble enough.

But my fame still slumbers in the marble quarries of Carrara; the waste paper laurel with which they have bedecked my brow has not yet spread its perfume through the wide world, and when the green-veiled distinguished English ladies visit Düsseldorf, they leave the celebrated house unvisited, and go direct to the Market Place, and there gaze on the colossal black equestrian statue which stands in its midst. This represents the Prince Elector, Jan Wilhelm. He wears black armour and a long, hanging wig. When a boy, I was told that the artist who made this statue observed with terror while it was being cast that he had not metal enough, and then all the citizens of the town came running with all their silver spoons, and threw them in to fill the mould; and I often stood for hours before the statue puzzling my head as to how many spoons were sticking in it, and how many apple-tarts all that silver would buy. Apple-tarts were then my passion—now it is love, truth, freedom, and crab-soup—and not far from the statue of the Prince Elector, at the theatre corner, generally stood a curiously constructed sabre-legged rascal with a white apron, and a basket girt around him full of smoking apple-tarts, which he knew how to praise with an irresistible treble voice. "Apple tarts! quite fresh! so delicious!" Truly, whenever in my later years the Evil One sought to win me, he always cried in just such an enticing treble, and I should certainly have never remained twelve hours by the Signora Giulietta, if she had not thrilled me with her sweet, fragrant, apple-tart-tones. And, in fact, the apple-tarts would never have so enticed me, if the crooked Hermann had not covered them up so mysteriously with his white apron—and it is aprons, you know, which—but I wander from the subject. I was speaking of the equestrian statue which has so many silver spoons in its body and no soup, and which represents the Prince Elector, Jan Wilhelm.

He must have been a brave gentleman, very fond of art, and skilful himself. He founded the picture gallery in Düsseldorf, and in the observatory there they show a very artistic piece of woodwork, which he, himself, had carved in his leisure hours, of which latter he had every day four-and-twenty.

In those days princes were not the persecuted wretches which they now are; the crowns grew firmly on their heads, and at night they drew their night-caps over it and slept peacefully, and their people slumbered peacefully at their feet, and when they awoke in the morning they said, "Good morning, father!" and he replied, "Good morning, dear children!"

But there came a sudden change over all this. One morning when we awoke in Düsseldorf and would say, "Good morning, father!" the father had travelled away, and in the whole town there was nothing but dumb sorrow. Everywhere there was a funeral-like expression, and people slipped silently to the market and read the long paper on the door of the Town Hall. It was bad weather, yet the lean tailor Kilian stood in his nankeen jacket, which he generally wore only at home, and his blue woollen stockings hung down so that his little bare legs peeped out in a troubled way, and his thin lips quivered as he murmured the placard. An old invalid soldier from the Palatine read it rather louder, and at some words a clear tear ran down his white honourable old moustache. I stood near him, crying too, and asked why we were crying? And he replied "The Prince Elector has abdicated." And then he read further, and at the words, "for the long manifested fidelity of my subjects," "and hereby release you from allegiance," he wept still more. It is a strange sight to see, when an old man, in faded uniform, and scarred veteran's face, suddenly bursts into tears. While we read, the Princely Electoral coat of arms was being taken down from the Town Hall, and everything began to appear as anxiously dreary as though we were waiting for an eclipse of the sun. The town councillors went about at an abdicating, wearisome gait; even the omnipotent beadle looked as though he had no more commands to give, and stood calmly indifferent, although the crazy Aloysius stood upon one leg and chattered the names of French generals with foolish grimaces, while the tipsy, crooked Gumpertz rolled around in the gutter, singing ça ira! ça ira!

But I went home crying and lamenting, "The Prince Elector has abdicated." My mother might do what she would, I knew what I knew, and went crying to bed, and in the night dreamed that the world had come to an end—the fair flower

22

gardens and green meadows of the world were taken up and rolled away like carpets from the floor, the beadle climbed up on a high ladder and took down the sun, and the tailor Kilian stood by and said to himself, "I must go home and dress myself neatly, for I am dead and am to be buried this afternoon." And it grew darker and darker—a few stars glimmered on high, and even these fell down like yellow leaves in autumn, men gradually vanished, and I, poor child, wandered in anguish around, until before the willow fence of a deserted farm-house I saw a man digging up the earth with a spade, and near him an ugly, spiteful-looking woman, who held something in her apron like a human head, but it was the moon, and she laid it carefully in the open grave—and behind me stood the Palatine soldier sobbing, and spelling, "The Prince Elector has abdicated."

When I awoke the sun shone as usual through the window, there was a sound of drums in the street, and as I entered our sitting-room and wished my father—who sat in his white dressing-gown—good morning, I heard the little light-footed barber, as he made up his hair, narrate very minutely that homage would that morning be offered at the Town Hall to the Arch Duke Joachim. I heard, too, that the new ruler was of excellent family, that he had married the sister of the Emperor Napoleon, and was really a very respectable man, that he wore his beautiful black hair in curls, that he would shortly enter the town, and would certainly please all the ladies. Meanwhile, the drumming in the streets continued, and I stood before the house-door and looked at the French troops marching, those joyous and famous people who swept over the world, singing and playing, the merry, serious faces of the grenadiers, the bearskin shakoes, the tri-coloured cockades, the glittering bayonets, the *voltigeurs* full of vivacity and *point d'honneur*, and the giant-like silver-laced Tambour Major, who cast his *bâton* with the gilded head as high as the first storey, and his eyes to the second, where pretty girls gazed from the windows. I was so glad that soldiers were to be quartered in our house—my mother was not glad—and I hastened to the market-place. There everything looked changed; it was as though the world had been new whitewashed. A new coat of arms was placed on the Town Hall, its iron balconies were hung with embroidered velvet drapery, French grenadiers stood as sentinels, the old town councillors had put on new faces and Sunday coats, and looked at each other French fashion, and said, "*Bon jour!*" ladies peeped from every window, inquisitive citizens and soldiers filled the square, and I, with other boys, climbed on the shining Prince Elector's great bronze horse, and looked down on the motley crowd.

Neighbour Peter and Long Conrad nearly broke their necks on this occasion, and that would have been well, for the one afterwards ran away from his parents, enlisted as a soldier, deserted, and was finally shot in Mayence, while the other, having made geographical researches in strange pockets, became a working member of a public tread-mill institute. But having broken the iron bands which bound him to his fatherland, he passed safely beyond sea, and eventually died in London, in consequence of wearing a much too long cravat, one end of which happened to be firmly attached to something, just as a royal official removed a plank from beneath his feet.

23

Long Conrad told us there was no school to-day on account of the homage. We had to wait a long time till this was over. At last the balcony of the Council House was filled with gay gentlemen, flags and trumpets, and our burgomaster, in his celebrated red coat, delivered an oration, which stretched out like India rubber, or like a night-cap into which one has thrown a stone—only that it was not the stone of wisdom—and I could distinctly understand many of his phrases, for instance, that "we are now to be made happy"—and at the last words the trumpets and drums sounded, and the flags waved, and the people cried Hurrah! —and as I myself cried Hurrah! I held fast to the old Prince Elector. And that was necessary, for I began to grow giddy; it seemed to me that the people were standing on their heads while the world whizzed around, and the Prince Elector, with his long wig, nodded and whispered, "Hold fast to me!"—and not till the cannon re-echoed along the wall did I become sobered, and climbed slowly down from the great bronze horse.

As I went home I saw crazy Aloysius again dancing on one leg, while he chattered the names of French generals, and crooked Gumpertz was rolling in the gutter drunk, and growling *ça ira, ça ira*—and I said to my mother that we were all to be made happy, and so there was no school to-day.

CHAPTER VII.

The next day the world was again all in order, and we had school as before, and things were got by heart as before—the Roman kings, chronology—the *nomina* in *im*, the *verba irregularia*—Greek, Hebrew, geography, German, mental arithmetic —Lord! my head is still giddy with it!—all must be learnt by heart. And much of it was eventually to my advantage. For had I not learnt the Roman kings by heart, it would subsequently have been a matter of perfect indifference to me whether Niebuhr had or had not proved that they never really existed. And had I not learnt chronology, how could I ever, in later years, have found out anyone in Berlin, where one house is as like another as drops of water, or as grenadiers, and where it is impossible to find a friend unless you have the number of his house in your head. Therefore I associated with every friend some historical event which had happened in a year corresponding to the number of his house, so that the one recalled the other, and some curious point in history always occurred to me whenever I met an acquaintance. For instance, when I met my tailor I at once thought of the Battle of Marathon; if I saw the well-dressed banker, Christian Gumpel, I remembered the destruction of Jerusalem; if a Portuguese friend, deeply in debt, of the flight of Mahomet; if the University Judge, a man whose probity is well known, of the death of Haman; and if Wadzeck, I was at once reminded of Cleopatra.—Ach, *lieber Himmel*! the poor creature is dead now, our tears are dry, and we may say of her, with Hamlet, "Take her for all in all, she was a hag—we oft shall look upon her like again!" As I said, chronology is necessary. I know men who have nothing in their heads but a few years, yet who know exactly where to look for the right houses, and are, moreover, regular professors. But oh, the trouble I had at school with dates!— and it went even worse with arithmetic. I understood *subtraction* best, and for

24

this I had a very practical rule—"Four from three won't go, I must borrow one"—but I advise everyone, in such a case, to borrow a few extra shillings, for one never knows.

But as for the Latin, Madame, you can really have no idea how muddled it is. The Romans would never have found time to conquer the world if they had been obliged first to learn Latin. Those happy people knew in their cradles the nouns with an accusative in *im*. I, on the contrary, had to learn them by heart, in the sweat of my brow, but still it is well that I knew them. For if, for example, when I publicly disputed in Latin, in the College Hall of Göttingen, on the 20th of July 1825—Madame, it was well worth while to hear it—if, I say, I had said *sinapem* instead of *sinapim*, the blunder would have been evident to the Freshmen, and an endless shame for me. *Vis, buris, sitis, tussis, cucumis, amussis, cannabis, sinapis*—these words, which have attracted so much attention in the world, effected this, because they belonged to a determined class, and yet were exceptions; on that account I value them highly, and the fact that I have them ready at my finger's ends when I perhaps need them in a hurry affords me in many dark hours of life much internal tranquillity and consolation. But, Madame, the *verba irregularia*—they are distinguished from the *verbis regularibus* by the fact that in learning them one gets more whippings—are terribly difficult. In the damp arches of the Franciscan cloister near our school-room there hung a large crucified Christ of grey wood, a dismal image, that even yet at times marches through my dreams and gazes sorrowfully on me with fixed bleeding eyes—before this image I often stood and prayed, "Oh thou poor and equally tormented God, if it be possible for thee, see that I get by heart the irregular verbs!"

I will say nothing of Greek; I should irritate myself too much. The monks of the Middle Ages were not so very much in the wrong when they asserted that Greek was an invention of the Devil. Lord knows what I suffered through it. It went better with Hebrew, for I always had a great predilection for the Jews, although they to this very hour have crucified my good name; but I never could get so far in Hebrew as my watch, which had an intimate intercourse with pawnbrokers, and in consequence acquired many Jewish habits—for instance, it would not go on Saturday—and learned the holy language, and was subsequently occupied with its grammar, for often when sleepless in the night I have to my amazement heard it industriously repeating: *katal, katalta, katalki—kittel, kittalta, kittalti—pokat, pokadeti—pikat—pik—pik.*

Meanwhile I learned much more German, and that is not such child's play. For we poor Germans, who have already been sufficiently plagued with soldiers quartered on us, military duties, poll-taxes, and a thousand other exactions, must needs, over and above all this, torment each other with accusatives and datives. I learned much German from the old Rector Schallmeyer, a brave, clerical gentleman, whose protégé I was from childhood. Something of the matter I also learned from Professor Schramm, a man who had written a book on Eternal Peace, and in whose class my school-fellows fought with especial vigour.

And while thus dashing on in a breath, and thinking of everything, I have unexpectedly found myself back among old school stories, and I avail myself of this opportunity to show you, Madame, that it was not my fault if I learned so little geography, that later in life I could not make my way in the world. For in those days the French had deranged all boundaries, every day countries were recoloured; those which were once blue suddenly became green, many even blood-red; the old established rules were so confused and confounded that no Devil would recognise them. The products of the country also changed, chickory and beets now grew where only hares and hunters running after them were once to be seen; even the characters of different races changed—the Germans became pliant, the French paid compliments no longer, the English ceased making ducks and drakes of their money, and the Venetians were not subtle enough; there was promotion among princes, old kings obtained new uniforms, new kingdoms were cooked up and sold like hot cakes, many potentates, on the other hand, were chased from house and home, and had to find some new way of earning their bread, while others went at once at a trade, and manufactured, for instance, sealing-wax, or—Madame, this sentence must be brought to an end, or I shall be out of breath—in short, it is impossible in such times to advance far in geography.

I succeeded better in natural history, for there we find fewer changes, and we always have standard engravings of apes, kangaroos, zebras, rhinoceroses, etc. And having many such pictures in my memory, it often happens that at first sight many mortals appear to me like old acquaintances.

I did well in mythology; I took real delight in the mob of gods and goddesses who ruled the world in joyous nakedness. I do not believe that there was a schoolboy in ancient Rome who knew the chief articles of his catechism—that is, the loves of Venus—better than I. To tell the truth, it seems to me that if we must learn all the heathen gods by heart, we might as well have kept them from the first, and we have not perhaps made so much out of our New Roman Trinity or even our Jewish monotheism. Perhaps that mythology was not in reality so immoral as we imagine, and it was, for example, a very decent thought of Homer's to give the much-loved Venus a husband.

But I succeeded best of all in the French class of the Abbé d'Aulnoi, a French *emigré* who had written a number of grammars, and wore a red wig, and jumped about very nervously when he recited his *Art poétique*, and his *Histoire Allemande*. He was the only one in the whole gymnasium who taught German history. Still French has its difficulties, and to learn it there must be much quartering of troops, much drumming in, much *apprendre par cœur*, and above all, no one should be a *bête allemande*. Thus many bitter words came in. I remember still, as though it happened yesterday, the scrapes I got into through *la réligion*. Six times came the question:—"Henry, what is the French for 'the faith?'" And six times, ever more tearfully, I replied, "It is called *le crédit*." And at the seventh question, with a deep cherry-red face, my furious examiner cried, "It is called *la réligion*"—and there was a rain of blows, and all my school-fellows laughed. Madame!—since that day I can never hear the word *réligion* but my back turns pale with terror, and my cheeks red with shame. And to speak truly, *le crédit* has during my life stood me in better stead than *la réligion*. It occurs to me at this moment that I still owe the landlord of the Lion, in Bologna, five thalers. And I pledge you my word of honour that I would owe him five thalers more if I could only be certain that I should never again hear that unlucky word, *la réligion*.

Parbleu, Madame! I have succeeded well in French! I understand not only *patois*, but even aristocratic nurse-maid French. Not long ago, when in noble society, I understood full one-half of the conversation of two German countesses, each of whom could count at least sixty-four years, and as many ancestors. Yes, in the *Café Royal*, at Berlin, I once heard Monsieur Hans Michel Martens talking French, and understood every word, though there was no understanding in it. We must know the spirit of a language, and this is best learned by drumming. *Parbleu!* how much do I not owe to the French Drummer who was so long quartered in our house, who looked like a Devil, and yet had the heart of an angel, and who drummed so excellently.

He was a little, nervous figure, with a terrible black moustache, beneath which the red lips turned suddenly outwards, while his fiery eyes glanced around.

I, a youngster, stuck to him like a burr, and helped him to rub his military buttons like mirrors, and to pipe-clay his vest—for Monsieur Le Grand liked to look well—and I followed him to the watch, to the roll-call, to the parade—in those times there was nothing but the gleam of weapons and merriment—*les jours de fête sont passés!* Monsieur Le Grand knew only a little broken German, only the chief expressions—"Bread," "Kiss," "Honour"—but he could make himself very intelligible with his drum. For instance, if I did not know what the word *liberté* meant, he drummed the *Marseillaise*—and I understood him. If I did not understand the word *egalité*, he drummed the march, "Ca ira, ... *les aristocrats à la lanterne!*" and I understood him. If I did not know what *bêtise* meant, he drummed the Dessauer March, which we Germans, as Goethe also declares, have drummed in Champagne—and I understood him. He once wanted to explain to me the word *l'Allemagne*, and he drummed the all too simple primeval melody, which on market days is played to dancing dogs—namely, *dum—dum—dum*.[7] I was vexed, but I understood him.

In the same way he taught me modern history. I did not understand the words, it is true, but as he constantly drummed while speaking, I knew what he meant. At bottom this is the best method. The history of the storming of the Bastille, of the Tuilleries, and the like, we understand first when we know how the drumming was done. In our school compendiums of history we merely read: "Their excellencies, the Baron and Count, with the most noble spouses of the aforesaid, were beheaded. Their highnesses the Dukes, and Princes, with the most noble spouses of the aforesaid, were beheaded. His Majesty the King, with his most sublime spouse, the Queen, was beheaded." But when you hear the red guillotine march drummed, you understand it correctly, for the first time, and you know the how and the why. Madame, that is indeed a wonderful march! It thrilled through marrow and bone when I first heard it, and I was glad that I forgot it. One forgets so much as one grows older, and a young man has now-a-days so much other knowledge to keep in his head—whist, Boston, genealogical tables, parliamentary data, dramaturgy, the liturgy, carving—and yet, notwithstanding all jogging up of my brain, I could not for a long time recall that tremendous tune! But, only think, Madame! not long ago I sat at table with a whole menagerie of Counts, Princes, Princesses, Chamberlains, Court-marshallesses, Seneschals, Upper Court Mistresses, Court-keepers-of-the-royal-plate, Court-hunters' wives, and whatever else these aristocratic domestics are termed, and their under-domestics ran about behind their chairs and shoved full plates before their mouths—but I, who was passed by and neglected, sat without the least occupation for my jaws, and I kneaded little bread-balls, and drummed for *ennui* with my fingers—and, to my astonishment, I suddenly drummed the red, long-forgotten guillotine march!

"And what happened?" Madame, the good people were not disturbed in their eating, nor did they know that other people, when they have nothing to eat, suddenly begin to drum, and that, too, very queer marches, which people thought long forgotten.

Is drumming, now, an inborn talent, or was it early developed in me?—enough, it lies in my limbs, in my hands, in my feet, and often manifests itself involuntarily. I once sat at Berlin in the lecture-room of the Privy Councillor Schmaltz, a man who had saved the state by his book on the "Red and Black Coat Danger."—You remember, perhaps, Madame, out of Pausanias, that by the braying of an ass an equally dangerous plot was once discovered, and you also know from Livy, or from Becker's *History of the World*, that geese once saved the capitol, and you must certainly know from Sallust that a loquacious *putain*, the Lady Livia, brought the terrible conspiracy of Cataline to light. But to return to the mutton aforesaid. I listened to international law in the lecture-room of the Herr Privy Councillor Schmaltz, and it was a sleepy summer afternoon, and I sat on the bench and heard less and less—my head had gone to sleep—when all at once I was wakened by the noise of my own feet, which had stayed awake, and had probably observed that the exact opposite of international law and constitutional tendencies was being preached, and my feet which, with the little eyes of their corns, had seen more of how things go in the world than the Privy Councillor with his Juno-eyes—these poor dumb feet, incapable of expressing their immeasurable meaning by words, strove to make themselves intelligible by drumming, and they drummed so loudly, that I thereby nearly came to grief.

Cursed, unreflecting feet! They once played me a similar trick, when I on a time in Göttengen sponged without subscribing on the lectures of Professor Saalfeld, and as, with his angular activity, he jumped about here and there in his pulpit, and heated himself in order to curse the Emperor Napoleon in regular set style, —no, my poor feet, I cannot blame you for drumming then; indeed, I would not have blamed you if in your dumb naïveté you had expressed yourselves by still more energetic movements. How could I, the scholar of Le Grand, hear the Emperor cursed? The Emperor! the Emperor! the great Emperor!

When I think of the great Emperor, my thoughts again grow summer-green and golden; a long avenue of lindens rises blooming around, on the leafy twigs sit singing nightingales, the water-fall rustles, flowers are growing from full round beds, dreamily nodding their fair heads—I was once wondrously intimate with them; the rouged tulips, proud as beggars, condescendingly greeted me, the nervous sick lilies nodded with melancholy tenderness, the drunken red roses laughed at me from afar, the night-violets sighed—with the myrtles and laurels I was not then acquainted, for they did not entice with a shining bloom, but the mignonette, with whom I now stand so badly, was very intimate. I am speaking of the court garden of Düsseldorf, where I often lay upon the bank, and piously listened while Monsieur Le Grand told of the warlike feats of the great Emperor, beating meanwhile the marches which were drummed during the deeds, so that I saw and heard all to the life. I saw the passage over the Simplon—the Emperor in advance and his brave grenadiers climbing on behind him, while the scream of frightened birds of prey sounded around, and avalanches thundered in the distance—I saw the Emperor with flag in hand on the bridge of Lodi—I saw the Emperor in his grey cloak at Marengo—I saw the Emperor mounted in the battle of the Pyramids—naught around save powder-smoke and Mamelukes—I saw the Emperor in the battle of Austerlitz—ha! how the bullets whistled over the smooth, icy road!—I saw, I heard the battle of Jena—*dum, dum, dum.*—I saw, I heard the battles of Eylau, of Wagram—— ah, I could hardly bear it! Monsieur Le Grand drummed so that the drums of my ears nearly burst.

CHAPTER VIII.

But what were my feelings when I saw with my own highly-graced eyes himself? Hosannah! the Emperor!

It was in that very avenue of the Court Garden at Düsseldorf. As I pressed through the gaping crowd, thinking of the doughty deeds and battles which Monsieur Le Grand had drummed to me, my heart beat the "general march"—yet at the same time I thought of the police regulation, that no one should dare ride through the avenue under penalty of a fine of five thalers. And the Emperor with his retinue rode directly down the avenue. The trembling trees bowed towards him as he advanced, the sunbeams quivered, frightened, yet curious, through the green leaves, and in the blue heaven above there swam visibly a golden star. The Emperor wore his invisible-green uniform and the little world-renowned hat. He rode a white steed, which stepped with such calm pride, so confidently, so nobly —had I then been Crown Prince of Prussia I would have envied that steed. Carelessly, almost lazily, sat the Emperor, holding his rein with one hand, and with the other good-naturedly patting the horse's neck. It was a sunny, marble hand, a mighty hand—one of those two hands which bound fast the many-headed monster of anarchy, and ordered the war of races—and it good-naturedly patted the horse's neck. Even the face had that hue which we find in the marble of Greek and Roman busts; the traits were as nobly cut as in the antique, and on that face was written, "Thou shalt have no Gods before me." A smile, which warmed and soothed every heart, flitted over the lips—and yet all knew that those lips needed but to whistle—*et la Prusse n'existait plus*—those lips needed but to whistle—and the entire clergy would have stopped their ringing and singing—those lips needed but to whistle—and the entire holy Roman empire would have danced. And those lips smiled and the eye smiled too. It was an eye clear as Heaven; it could read the hearts of men, it saw at a glance all the things of this world, while we others see them only one by one and by their coloured shadows. The brow was not so clear, the phantoms of future battles were nestling there; there was a quiver which swept over that brow, and those were the creative thoughts, the great seven-mile-boot thoughts, wherewith the spirit of the Emperor strode invisibly over the world—and I believe that every one of those thoughts would have given to a German author full material wherewith to write, all the days of his life.

The Emperor rode quietly straight through the avenue. No policeman opposed him; proudly, on snorting horses and laden with gold and jewels, rode his retinue; the drums were beating, the trumpets were sounding; close to me the wild Aloysius was muttering his general's name; not far away the drunken Gumpertz was grumbling, and the people shouted with a thousand voices, "Long live the Emperor!"

CHAPTER IX.

The Emperor is dead. On a waste island in the Atlantic ocean is his lonely grave, and he for whom the world was too narrow lies quietly under a little hillock, where five weeping willows hang their green heads, and a little brook, murmuring sorrowfully, ripples by. There is no inscription on his tomb; but Clio, with a just pen, has written thereon, invisible words, which will resound, like spirit-tones, through thousands of years.

Britannia! the sea is thine. But the sea has not water enough to wash away the shame with which the death of that Mighty One has covered thee. Not thy windy Sir Hudson—no, thou thyself wert the Sicilian bravo with whom perjured kings bargained, that they might revenge on the man of the people that which the people had once inflicted on one of themselves.—And he was thy guest, and had seated himself by thy hearth.

Until far ages the boys of France will sing and tell of the terrible hospitality of the *Bellerophon*, and when those songs of mockery and tears resound across the Channel, the cheeks of every honourable Briton will blush. Some day, however, this song will ring thither, and Britannia will be no more; the people of pride will be humbled to the earth, Westminster's monuments will be broken, and the royal dust which they enclosed forgotten.—And St. Helena is the Holy Grave, whither the races of the East and of the West will make their pilgrimage in ships with flags of many a colour, and their hearts will grow strong with great memories of the deeds of the worldly Saviour, who suffered and died under Hudson Lowe, as it is written in the evangelists, Las Cases, O'Meara, and Autommarchi.

Strange! A terrible destiny has already overtaken the three greatest enemies of the Emperor. Londonderry has cut his throat, Louis XVIII. has rotted away on his throne, and Professor Saalfeld is still Professor in Göttingen.

CHAPTER X.

On a clear, frosty autumn morning, a young man of student-like appearance slowly loitered through the avenue of the Düsseldorf Court Garden, often, with childlike pleasure, kicking aside the leaves which covered the ground, and often sorrowfully gazing towards the bare trees, on which a few golden-hued leaves still hung. As he thus gazed up, he thought on the words of Glaucus—

"Like the leaves in the forests, so are the races of mortals;
Leaves are blown down to the earth by the wind, while others are shooting
Again in the green budding wood, when fresh up-liveth the spring-tide;
So are the races of man—this grows and the other departeth."

In earlier days the youth had gazed with far different eyes on the same trees. He was then a boy, and sought birds' nests or summer insects, which delighted him as they merrily hummed around, and were glad in the beautiful world, and contented with a sap-green leaf and a drop of water, with a warm sunbeam and the sweet perfumes of the grass. In those times the boy's heart was as gay as the fluttering insects. But now his heart had grown older, its little sunbeams were quenched, all its flowers had faded, even its beautiful dream of love had grown dim; in that poor heart was nothing but pride and care, and, saddest of all, it was my heart.

I had returned that day to my old father-town, but I would not remain there over night, and I longed for Godesberg, that I might sit at the feet of my girl-friend and tell of the little Veronica. I had visited the dear graves. Of all my living friends I had found but an uncle and an aunt. Even when I met once known forms in the street they knew me no more, and the town itself gazed on me with strange glances. Many houses were coloured anew, strange faces gazed on me through the window-panes, worn-out old sparrows hopped on the old chimneys, everything looked dead and yet fresh, like a salad growing in a graveyard; where French was once spoken I now heard Prussian; even a little Prussian court had taken up its retired dwelling there, and the people bore court titles. My mother's old hair dresser had now become the Court Hair dresser, and there were Court-Tailors, Court-Shoemakers, Court-Bed-Bug-Destroyers, Court-Grog-Shops—the whole town seemed to be a Court-Asylum for Court-lunatics. Only the old Prince Elector knew me, he still stood in the same old place; but he seemed to have grown thinner. For just because he stood in the Market Place, he had had a full view of all the miseries of the time, and people seldom grow fat on such sights. I was in a dream, and thought of the legend of the enchanted city, and hastened out of the gate, lest I should awake too soon. I missed many a tree in the Court Garden, and many had grown crooked with age, and the four great poplars, which once seemed to me like green giants, had become smaller. Pretty girls were walking here and there, dressed as gaily as wandering tulips. And I had known these tulips when they were but little buds; for ah! they were the neighbours' children with whom I had once played "Princes in the Tower." But

31

the fair maidens, whom I had once known as blooming roses, were now faded roses, and in many a high brow whose pride had once thrilled my heart, Saturn had cut deep wrinkles with his scythe. And now for the first time, and alas! too late, I understood what those glances meant, which they had once cast on the adolescent boy; for I had meanwhile in other lands fathomed the meaning of similar glances in other lovely eyes. I was deeply moved by the humble bow of a man whom I had once known as wealthy and respectable, and who had since become a beggar. Everywhere in the world we see that men when they once begin to fall, do so according to Newton's law, ever faster and faster as they descend to misery. One, however, who did not seem to be in the least changed was the little baron, who tripped merrily as of old through the Court Garden, holding with one hand his left coat-skirt on high, and with the other swinging hither and thither his light cane;—he still had the same genial face as of old, its rosy bloom now somewhat concentrated towards the nose, but he had the same comical hat and the same old queue behind, only that the hairs which peeped from it were now white instead of black. But merry as the old baron seemed, it was still evident that he had suffered much sorrow—his face would fain conceal it, but the white hairs of his queue betrayed him behind his back. Yet the queue itself seemed striving to lie, so merrily did it shake.

I was not weary, but a fancy seized me to sit once more on the wooden bench, on which I had once carved the name of my love. I could hardly discover it there, so many new names were cut around. Ah! once I slept upon this bench, and dreamed of happiness and love. "Dreams are foam." And the old games of childhood came again to my memory, and with them old and beautiful stories; but a new treacherous game, and a new terrible tale ever resounded through them, and it was the story of two poor souls who were untrue to each other, and went so far in their untruth, that they were at last untrue to the dear God himself. It is a sad story, and when one has nothing better to do, one can weep over it. Oh, Lord! once the world was so beautiful, and the birds sang thy eternal praise, and little Veronica looked at me with silent eyes, and we sat by the marble statue before the castle court; on one side lies an old ruined castle, wherein ghosts wander, and at night a headless lady in long, trailing black-silken garments sweeps around, and on the other side is a high, white dwelling, in whose upper rooms gay pictures gleamed beautifully in their golden frames, while below stood thousands of mighty books, which Veronica and I beheld with longing when the good Ursula lifted us up to the window. In later years, when I had become a great boy, I climbed every day to the very top of the library ladder, and brought down the topmost books, and read in them so long, that finally I feared nothing— least of all ladies without heads—and became so wise that I forgot all the old games and stories and pictures and little Veronica, even her name.

But while I sat upon the old bench in the Court Garden, and dreamed my way back into the past, there was a sound behind me of the confused voices of men lamenting the ill-fortune of the poor French soldiers, who, having been taken prisoners in the Russian war and sent to Siberia, had there been kept prisoners for many a long year, though peace had been re-established, and who now were returning home. As I looked up, I beheld in reality these orphan children of Fame. Through their tattered uniforms peeped naked misery, deep sorrowing eyes were couched in their desolate faces, and though mangled, weary, and mostly lame, something of the military manner was still visible in their mien. Singularly enough, they were preceded by a drummer who tottered along with a drum, and I shuddered as I recalled the old legend of soldiers, who had fallen in battle, and who by night rising again from their graves on the battle-field, and with the drummer at their head, marched back to their native city. And of them the old ballad sings thus—

"He beat on the drum with might and main,
To their old night-quarters they go again;
Through the lighted street they come;
Trallerie—trallerei—trallera,
They march before Sweetheart's home.

And their bones lie there at break of day,
As white as tombstones in cold array,
And the drummer he goes before;
Trallerie—trallerei—trallera,
And we see them come no more."

Truly the poor French drummer seemed to have risen but half repaired from the grave. He was but a little shadow in a dirty patched grey capote, a dead yellow countenance, with a great moustache which hung down sorrowfully over his faded lips, his eyes were like burnt-out tinder, in which but a few sparks still gleamed, and yet by one of those sparks I recognised Monsieur Le Grand.

He too recognised me and drew me to the turf, and we sat down together as of old, when he taught me French and Modern History on the drum. He had still the well-known old drum, and I could not sufficiently wonder how he had preserved it from Russian plunderers. And he drummed again as of old, but without speaking a word. But though his lips were firmly pressed together, his eyes spoke all the more, flashing fiercely and victoriously as he drummed the old marches. The poplars near us trembled, as he again thundered forth the red guillotine march. And he drummed as before the old war of freedom, the old battles, the deeds of the Emperor, and it seemed as though the drum itself were a living creature which rejoiced to speak out its inner soul. I heard once more the thunder of cannon, the whistling of balls, the riot of battle; I saw once more the death rage of the Guards,—the waving flags, again, the Emperor on his steed— but little by little there fell a sad tone in amid the most stirring confusion, sounds rang from the drum, in which the wildest hurrahs and the most fearful grief were mysteriously mingled; it seemed a march of victory and a march of death. Le Grand's eyes opened spirit-like and wide, and I saw in them nothing but a broad white field of ice covered with corpses—it was the battle of Moscow.

I had never thought that the hard old drum could give forth such wailing sounds as Monsieur Le Grand had drawn from it. They were tears which he drummed, and they sounded ever softer and softer, and, like a troubled echo, deep sighs broke from Le Grand's breast. And he became ever more languid and ghost-like, his dry hands trembled, as if from frost, he sat as in a dream, and stirred with his drum-stick nothing but the air, and seemed listening to voices far away, and at last he gazed on me with a deep, entreating glance—I understood him—and then his head sank down on the drum.

In this life Monsieur Le Grand never drummed more. And his drum never gave forth another sound; it was not destined to serve the enemies of liberty for their servile roll calls. I had well understood Le Grand's last entreating glance, and at once drew the sword from my cane, and pierced the drum.

CHAPTER XI.

Du sublime au ridicule il n'y a qu'un pas, Madame!

But life is in reality so terribly serious, that it would be insupportable without such union of the pathetic and the comic; as our poets well know. The most harrowing forms of human madness Aristophanes exhibits only in the laughing mirror of wit; Goethe only presumes to set forth the fearful pain of thought comprehending its own nothingness in the doggerel of a puppet show; and Shakespeare puts the most deadly lamentation over the misery of the world into the mouth of a fool, who rattles his cap and bells in agony.

They have all learned from the great First Poet, who, in his World Tragedy in thousands of acts, knows how to carry humour to the highest point, as we see every day. After the departure of the heroes, the clowns and *graciosos* enter with their baubles and wooden swords, and after the bloody scenes of the Revolution there came waddling on the stage the fat Bourbons, with their stale jokes and tender "legitimate" *bon mots*, and the old noblesse with their starved laughter hopped merrily before them, while behind all swept the pious Capuchins with candles, cross, and banners of the Church. Yes, even in the highest pathos of the World Tragedy, bits of fun slip in. The desperate republican, who, like Brutus, plunged a knife to his heart, perhaps smelt it first to see whether some one had not split a herring with it—and on this great stage of the world all passes exactly the same as on our beggarly boards. On it, too, there are tipsy heroes, kings who forget their part, scenes which obstinately stay up in the air, prompters' voices sounding above everything, danseuses who create astonishing effects with the poetry of their legs, and costumes which are the main thing. And high in Heaven, in the first row of the boxes, sit the dear little angels, and keep their *lorgnettes* on us comedians here down below, and the blessed Lord himself sits seriously in his great box, and, perhaps, finds it dull, or calculates that this theatre cannot be kept up much longer because this one gets too high a salary, and that one too little, and that they all play much too badly.

Du sublime au ridicule il n'y a qu'un pas, Madame! As I ended the last chapter, narrating to you how Monsieur Le Grand died, and how I conscientiously executed the *testamentum militaire* which lay in his last glance, some one knocked at my door, and there entered a poor old lady, who asked if I were not a

Doctor. And as I assented, she kindly asked me to go home with her and cut her husband's corns.

LAST WORDS (Reisebilder).

Written 29th November 1830.

It was a depressed, an arrested time in Germany when I wrote the second volume of the *Reisebilder*, and had it printed as I wrote. But before it appeared something was whispered about it; it was said that my book would awaken and encourage the cowed spirit of freedom, and that measures were being taken to suppress it. When such rumours were afloat, it was advisable to advance the book as quickly as possible, and drive it through the press. As it was necessary, too, that it should contain a certain number of leaves, to escape the requisitions of the estimable censorship, I followed the example of Benvenuto Cellini, who, in founding his Perseas, was short of bronze, and to fill up the mould threw into the molten metal all the tin plates he could lay his hands on. It was certainly easy to distinguish between the tin—especially the tin termination of the book—and the better bronze; anyone, however, who understands the craft will not betray the workman.

But as everything in this world is liable to turn up again, so it came to pass that, in this very volume, I found myself again in the same scrape, and I have been obliged to again throw some tin into the mould—let me hope that this renewed melting of baser metal will simply be attributed to the pressure of the times.

Alas! the whole book sprang from the pressure of the times, as well as the earlier writings of similar tendency. The more intimate friends of the writer, who are acquainted with his private circumstances, know well how little his own vanity forced him to the tribune, and how great were the sacrifices which he was obliged to make for every independent word which he has spoken since then and —if God will!—which he still means to speak. Now-a-days, a word is a deed whose consequences cannot be measured, and no one knows whether he may not in the end appear as witness to his words in blood.

For many years I have waited in vain for the words of those bold orators, who once in the meetings of the German Burschenschaft so often claimed a hearing, who so often overwhelmed me with their rhetorical talent, and spoke a language spoken so oft before; they were then so forward in noise—they are now so backward in silence. How they then reviled the French and the foreign Babel, and the un-German frivolous betrayers of the Fatherland, who praised French-dom. That praise verified itself in the great week!

Ah, the great week of Paris! The spirit of freedom, which was wafted thence over Germany, has certainly upset the night-lamps here and there, so that the red curtains of several thrones took fire, and golden crowns grew hot under blazing night-caps; but the old catch-polls, in whom the royal police trusted, are already bringing out the fire-buckets, and now scent around all the more suspiciously, and forge all the more firmly their secret chains, and I mark well that a still

35

thicker prison vault is being invisibly arched over the German people.

Poor imprisoned people! be not cast down in your need. Oh, that I could speak catapults! Oh, that I could shoot falarica from my heart!

The distinguished ice-rind of reserve melts from my heart, a strange sorrow steals over me—is it love, and love for the German people? Or is it sickness?—my soul quivers and my eyes burn, and that is an unfortunate occurrence for a writer, who should command his material, and remain charmingly objective, as the art school requires, and as Goethe has done—he has grown to be eighty years old in so doing, and a minister, and portly—poor German people! that is thy greatest man!

I still have a few octavo pages to fill, and I will therefore tell a story—it has been floating in my head since yesterday—a story from the life of Charles the Fifth.[8] But it is now a long time since I heard it, and I no longer remember its details exactly. Such things are easily forgotten, if one does not receive a regular salary for reading them every half-year from his lecture books. But what does it matter if places and dates are forgotten, so long as one holds their significance, their moral meaning, in his memory. It is this which stirs my soul and moves me even to tears. I fear I am getting ill.

The poor emperor was taken prisoner by his enemies, and lay in stern imprisonment. I believe it was in Tyrol. There he sat in solitary sorrow, forsaken by all his knights and courtiers, and no one came to his help. I know not if he had even in those days that cheese-yellow complexion with which Holbein painted him. But the misanthropic under-lip certainly protruded, even more then than in his portraits. He must have despised the people who fawned around him in the sunshine of prosperity, and who left him alone in his bitter need. Suddenly the prison door opened, and there entered a man wrapped in a cloak, and as he cast it aside, the emperor recognised his trusty Kunz von der Rosen, the court-fool. One brought him consolation and counsel—and it was the court-fool.

O, German Fatherland! dear German people! I am thy Kunz von der Rosen. The man whose real office was pastime, and who should only make thee merry in happy days, forces his way into thy prison, in time of need; here, beneath my mantle, I bring thee thy strong sceptre and the beautiful crown—dost thou not remember me, my emperor? If I cannot free thee, I will at least console thee, and thou shalt have some one by thee who will talk with thee about thy most pressing oppressions, and will speak courage to thee, and who loves thee, and whose best jokes and best blood are ever at thy service. For thou, my people, art the true emperor, the true lord of the land—thy will is sovereign and more legitimate than that purple *Tel est notre plaisir*, which grounds itself upon divine right, without any better guarantee than the quackery of shaven jugglers—thy will, my people, is the only righteous source of all power. Even though thou liest down there in fetters, thy good right will arise in the end, the day of freedom draws near, a new time begins—my emperor, the night is over, and the dawn shines outside.

"Kunz von der Rosen, my Fool, thou errest. Thou hast perhaps mistaken a bright axe for the sun, and the dawn is nothing but blood."

"No, my Emperor, it is the sun, though it rises in the west—for six thousand years men have always seen it rise in the east—it is high time that it for once made a change in its course."

"Kunz von der Rosen, my Fool, thou hast lost the bells from thy red cap, and it now has such a strange look, that red cap!"

"Ah, my Emperor, I have shaken my head in such mad earnest over your distress that the fool's bell fell from my cap; but it is none the worse for that!"

"Kunz von der Rosen, my Fool, what is that breaking and cracking outside there?"

"Hush! it is the saw and the carpenter's axe; the doors of your prison will soon be broken in, and you will be free, my Emperor!"

"Am I then really Emperor? Alas! it is only the Fool who tells me so!"

"Oh, do not sigh, my dear lord, it is the air of the dungeon which so dispirits you; when you have once regained your power, you will feel the bold imperial blood in your veins, and you will be proud as an emperor, and arrogant, and gracious, and unjust, and smiling, and ungrateful as princes are."

"Kunz von der Rosen, my Fool, when I am free again, what wilt thou be doing?"

"I will sew new bells on my cap."

"And how shall I reward thy fidelity?"

"Ah! dear master—do not let me be put to death!"

ENGLISH FRAGMENTS.

[The *English Fragments*, from which three chapters have been selected for this volume, were published in 1828 in a German magazine of which Heine was one of the editors. They were collected and published with important additions (including the following chapters) in 1831. Mr. Leland's translation, revised throughout, has been here used.]

LONDON.

I HAVE seen the greatest wonder which the world can show to the astonished spirit; I have seen it, and am more astonished then ever—and still there remains fixed in my memory that stone forest of houses, and amid them the rushing stream of faces, of living human faces, with all their motley passions, all their terrible impulses of love, of hunger, and of hate—I am speaking of London.

Send a philosopher to London, but no poet! Send a philosopher there, and stand him at a corner of Cheapside, he will learn more there than from all the books of the last Leipzig fair; and as the human waves roar around him, so will a sea of new thoughts rise before him, and the Eternal Spirit which moves upon the face of the waters will breathe upon him; the most hidden secrets of social harmony will be suddenly revealed to him, he will hear the pulse of the world beat audibly, and see it visibly—for, if London is the right hand of the world—its active, mighty right hand—then we may regard that that which leads from the Exchange to Downing Street is the world's radial artery.

But send no poet to London! This downright earnestness of all things, this colossal uniformity, this machine-like movement, this moroseness even in pleasure, this exaggerated London, smothers the imagination and rends the heart. And should you ever send a German poet thither—a dreamer, who stands staring at every single phenomenon, even a ragged beggar-woman, or a shining jeweller's shop—why, then he will find things going badly with him, and he will be hustled about on every side, or even be knocked over with a mild "*God damn!*" *God damn!*—the damned pushing! I soon saw that these people have much to do. They live on a large scale, and though food and clothes are dearer with them than with us, they must still be better fed and clothed than we are—as gentility requires. Moreover, they have enormous debts, yet occasionally in a vain-glorious mood they make ducks and drakes of their guineas, pay other nations to fight for their pleasure, give their respective kings a handsome *douceur* into the bargain —and, therefore, John Bull must work day and night to get the money for such expenses; by day and by night he must tax his brain to discover new machines, and he sits and reckons in the sweat of his brow, and runs and rushes without looking about much from the Docks to the Exchange, and from the Exchange to the Strand, and, therefore, it is quite pardonable if, when a poor German poet, gazing into a print-shop window, stands in his way at the corner of Cheapside, he should knock him aside with a rather rough "God damn!"

But the picture at which I was gazing as I stood at the corner of Cheapside, was that of the passage of the French across the Beresina.

And when, jolted out of my gazing, I looked again on the raging street, where a parti-coloured coil of men, women, and children, horses, stage-coaches, and with them a funeral, whirled groaning and creaking along, it seemed to me as though all London were such a Beresina Bridge, where every one presses on in mad haste to save his scrap of life, where the daring rider stamps down the poor pedestrian, where every one who falls is lost forever; where the best friends rush, without feeling, over each other's corpses, and where thousands, weak and bleeding, grasp in vain at the planks of the bridge, and slide down into the ice-pit of death.

How much more pleasant and homelike it is in our dear Germany! How dreamily comfortable, how Sabbatically quiet all things glide along here! Calmly the sentinels are changed, uniforms and houses shine in the quiet sunshine, swallows flit over the flag-stones, fat court-councilloresses smile from the windows, while along the echoing streets there is room enough for the dogs to sniff at each other, and for men to stand at ease and chat about the theatre, and bow low—oh, how low!—when some small aristocratic scamp or vice-scamp, with coloured ribbons on his shabby coat, or some powdered and gilded court-marshal struts by, graciously returning salutations!

I had made up my mind not to be astonished at that immensity of London of which I had heard so much. But it happened to me as to the poor school-boy, who had made up his mind not to feel the whipping he was to receive. The facts of the case were, that he expected to get the usual blows with the usual stick in the usual way on the back, whereas he received a most unusually severe thrashing on an unusual place with a slender switch. I anticipated great palaces, and saw nothing but mere small houses. But their very uniformity and their limitless extent are wonderfully impressive.

These houses of brick, owing to the damp atmosphere and coal smoke, become uniform in colour, that is to say, of a brown olive green; they are all of the same style of building, generally two or three windows wide, three storeys high, and adorned above with small red tiles, which remind one of newly-extracted bleeding teeth; so that the broad and accurately-squared streets seem to be bordered by endlessly long barracks. This has its reason in the fact that every English family, though it consist of only two persons, must still have a house to itself for its own castle, and rich speculators, to meet the demand, build wholesale entire streets of these dwellings, which they retail singly. In the principal streets of the city, where the business of London is most at home, where old-fashioned buildings are mingled with the new, and where the fronts of the houses are covered with names and signs, yards in length, generally gilt, and in relief, this characteristic uniformity is less striking—the less so, indeed, because the eye of the stranger is incessantly caught by the new and brilliant articles exposed for sale in the windows. And these articles do not merely produce an effect because the Englishman completes so perfectly everything which he manufactures, and because every article of luxury, every astral lamp and every boot, every tea kettle and every woman's dress, shines out so invitingly and so "finished;" there is a peculiar charm in the art of arrangement, in the contrast of colours, and in the variety of the English shops; even the most commonplace necessaries of life appear in a startling magic light through this artistic power of setting forth everything to advantage. Ordinary articles of food attract us by the new light in which they are placed, even uncooked fish lie so delightfully dressed that the rainbow gleam of their scales attracts us; raw meat lies, as if painted, on neat and many-coloured porcelain plates, garlanded about with parsley—yes, everything seems painted, reminding us of the brilliant, yet modest pictures of Franz Mieris. Only the people are not so cheerful as in the Dutch paintings; they sell the most delightful playthings with the most serious faces, and the cut and colour of their clothes is as uniform as that of their houses.

At the opposite side of the town, which they call the West End, where the more aristocratic and less-occupied world lives, this uniformity is still more dominant; yet here there are very long and very broad streets, where all the houses are large as palaces, though outwardly anything but distinguished, unless we except the fact that in these, as in all the better class of houses in London, the windows

39

of the first storey are adorned with iron-barred balconies, and also on the ground floor there is a black railing protecting the entrance to certain cellar apartments buried in the earth. In this part of the city there are also great squares, where rows of houses, like those already described, form a quadrangle, in whose centre there is a garden enclosed by a black iron railing, and containing some statue or other. In all of these squares and streets the eye is never shocked by the dilapidated huts of misery. Everywhere we are stared down on by wealth and respectability, while crammed away in retired lanes and dark, damp alleys poverty dwells with her rags and her tears.

The stranger who wanders through the great streets of London, and does not chance right into the regular quarters of the people, sees little or nothing of the misery there. Only here and there, at the mouth of some dark alley, stands a ragged woman with a suckling babe at her wasted breast, and begs with her eyes. Perhaps if those eyes are still beautiful, one glances into them and shrinks back at the world of wretchedness within them. The common beggars are old people, generally blacks, who stand at the corners of the streets cleaning pathways—a very necessary thing in muddy London—and ask for "coppers" in reward. It is in the dusky twilight that Poverty with her mates, Vice and Crime, glide forth from their lairs. They shun daylight the more anxiously, the more cruelly their wretchedness contrasts with the pride of wealth which glitters everywhere; only Hunger sometimes drives them at noonday from their dens, and then they stand with silent, speaking eyes, staring beseechingly at the rich merchant who hurries along, busy and jingling gold, or at the lazy lord who, like a surfeited god, rides by on his high horse, casting now and then an aristocratically indifferent glance at the mob below, as though they were swarming ants, or, at all events, a mass of baser beings, whose joys and sorrows have nothing in common with his feelings. Yes, over the vulgar multitude which sticks fast to the soil, soar, like beings of a higher nature, England's nobility, who regard their little island as only a temporary resting-place, Italy as their summer garden, Paris as their social saloon, and the whole world as their inheritance. They sweep along, knowing nothing of sorrow or suffering, and their gold is a talisman which conjures into fulfilment their wildest wish.

Poor Poverty! how agonising must thy hunger be where others swell in scornful superfluity! And when some one casts with indifferent hand a crust into thy lap, how bitter must the tears be wherewith thou moistenest it! Thou poisonest thyself with thine own tears. Well art thou in the right when thou alliest thyself to Vice and Crime. Outlawed criminals often bear more humanity in their hearts than those cold, blameless citizens of virtue, in whose white hearts the power of evil is quenched; but also the power of good. I have seen women on whose cheeks red vice was painted, and in whose hearts dwelt heavenly purity. I have seen women—I would I saw them again!——

WELLINGTON.

This man has the bad fortune to meet with good fortune wherever the greatest men in the world were unfortunate, and that angers us, and makes him hateful. We see in him only the victory of stupidity over genius—Arthur Wellington triumphant where Napoleon Bonaparte was overwhelmed! Never was a man more ironically gifted by Fortune, and it seems as though she would exhibit his empty littleness by raising him high on the shield of victory. Fortune is a woman, and perhaps, in womanly wise, she cherishes a secret grudge against the man who overthrew her former darling, though the very overthrow came from her own will. Now she lets him conquer again on the Catholic Emancipation question —yes, in the very fight in which George Canning was overwhelmed. It is possible that he might have been loved had the wretched Londonderry been his predecessor in the ministry; but he is the successor of the noble Canning, of the much-wept, adored, great Canning—and he conquers where Canning was overwhelmed. Without so unlucky a luck, Wellington would perhaps pass for a great man; people would not hate him, would not measure him too accurately, at least not with the heroic measure with which a Napoleon and a Canning is measured, and consequently it would never have been discovered how small a man he is.

He is a small man, and less than small. The French could say nothing more sarcastic of Polignac than that he was a Wellington without celebrity. In fact, what remains when we strip from a Wellington the field-marshal's uniform of celebrity?

I have here given the best apology for Lord Wellington—in the English sense of the word. My readers will be astonished, however, when I honourably confess that I once clapped on all sail in praise of this hero. It is a good story, and I will tell it here.

My barber in London was a radical named Mr. White, a poor little man in a shabby black dress, worn until it almost shone white; he was so lean that even his full face looked like a profile, and the sighs in his bosom were visible before they rose. These sighs were caused by the misfortunes of Old England, and by the impossibility of paying the National Debt.

"Ah!" I often heard him sigh, "why need the English people trouble themselves as to who reigns in France, and what the French are doing at home? But the nobility, sir, and the Church were afraid of the principles of liberty of the French Revolution, and, to keep down these principles, John Bull must give his gold and his blood, and make debts into the bargain. We've got all we wanted out of the war—the revolution has been put down, the French eagles of liberty have had their wings cut, and the Church may be quite sure that none of them will come flying over the Channel; and now the nobility and the Church ought to pay for the debts which were made for their own good, and not for any good of the poor people. Ah!—the poor people!"

Whenever Mr. White came to the "poor people," he always sighed more deeply than ever, and the refrain then was, that bread and beer were so dear that the poor people must starve to feed fat lords, stag-hounds, and priests, and that there was only one remedy. At these words he was wont to whet his razor, and as

41

he drew it murderously up and down the strop, he muttered grimly to himself, "Lords, priests, hounds."

But his radical rage boiled most fiercely against the Duke of Wellington; he spat gall and poison whenever he alluded to him, and as he lathered me, he himself foamed with rage. Once I was fairly frightened, when he, while barbering just at my neck, burst out against Wellington, murmuring all the while, "If I only had him so under my razor, I'd save him the trouble of cutting his own throat, as his brother in office and fellow-countryman, Londonderry, did, who killed himself that way at North Cray, in Kent—God damn him!"

I felt already that the man's hand trembled, and fearing lest he might imagine in his excitement that I really was the Duke of Wellington, I endeavoured to allay his violence, and in an underhanded manner, to soothe him, I called up his national pride, I represented to him that the Duke of Wellington had advanced the glory of the English, that he had always been an innocent tool in the hands of others, that he was fond of beefsteak, and that he—but the Lord only knows what fine things I said of Wellington as that razor tickled my throat.

What vexes me most is the reflection that Arthur Wellington will be as immortal as Napoleon Bonaparte. It is true that in like manner the name of Pontius Pilate is as little likely to be forgotten as that of Christ. Wellington and Napoleon! It is a wonderful phenomenon that the human mind can at the same time think of both these names. There can be no greater contrast than these two, even in their external appearance. Wellington, the dull ghost, with an ashy grey soul in a buckram body, a wooden smile on his freezing face—and by the side one thinks of the figure of Napoleon, every inch a god!

That figure never disappears from my memory. I still see him, high on his horse, with eternal eyes in his marble, imperial face, gazing down calm as destiny on the Guards defiling past—he was then sending them to Russia, and the old grenadiers glanced up at him, so terribly devoted, so consciously serious, so proud in death—

"Te, Cæsar, morituri salutant!"

There often steals over me a secret doubt whether I ever really saw him, if we were really his contemporaries, and then it seems to me as if his portrait, torn from the little frame of the present, vanished away more proudly and imperiously in the twilight of the past. His name even now sounds to us like a word of the early world, as antique and heroic as those of Alexander and Cæsar. It has become a rallying word among races, and when the East and the West meet, they fraternise through that single name.

How significant and magical that name can sound I once felt in the deepest manner in the harbour of London, at the India Docks, as I stood on board an East Indiaman just arrived from Bengal. It was a giant-like ship, fully manned with Hindoos. The grotesque forms and groups, the singularly variegated dresses, the enigmatical expressions, the strange gestures, the wild and foreign ring of their language, their shouts of joy and their laughter, and the seriousness ever rising and falling on certain soft, yellow faces, their eyes like black flowers which looked at me as with melancholy woe—all this awoke in me a feeling like that of enchantment; I was suddenly as if transported into Scheherezade's story, and I thought that broad-leaved palms, and long-necked camels, and gold-covered elephants, and other fable-like trees and animals, must forthwith appear. The supercargo who was on the vessel, and who understood as little of the language as I myself, could not, in his genuine English narrowness, narrate to me enough of what a ridiculous race they were, nearly all Mahometans collected from every land of Asia, from the limits of China to the Arabian sea, even jet black, woolly-haired Africans.

To one whose whole soul was weary of the spiritless West, and who was as sick of Europe as I then was, this fragment of the East which moved cheerfully and changingly before my eyes was a refreshing solace, my heart enjoyed at least a few drops of that draught which I had so often longed for in gloomy Hanoverian or Prussian winter nights, and it is very possible that the foreigners saw how agreeable the sight of them was to me, and how gladly I would have spoken a kind word to them. It was also plain from the depths of their eyes that I pleased them well, and they would also have willingly said something pleasant to me, and it was a vexation that neither understood the other's language. At length a means occurred to me of expressing to them with a single word my friendly feelings, and stretching forth my hands reverently, as if in loving greeting, I cried the name, "Mahomed!" Joy suddenly flashed over the dark faces of the foreigners; they folded their arms reverently in turn, and greeted me back with the exclamation, "Bonaparte!"

THE LIBERATION.

SHOULD the time for leisurely research ever return to me, I will prove in the most tiresomely fundamental manner that it was not India, but Egypt which originated that system of castes which has for two thousand years disguised itself in the garb of every country, and has deceived every age in its own language, which is now perhaps dead, yet which, counterfeiting the appearance of life, wanders about among us evil-eyed and mischief-making, poisoning our blooming life with its corpse vapour—yes, like a vampire of the Middle Ages, sucking the blood and the light from the heart of nations. From the mud of the Nile sprang not merely crocodiles which well could weep, but also priests who understand it far better, and that privileged hereditary race of warriors, who in their lust of murder and ravenous appetites far surpass any crocodiles.

Two deeply-thinking men of the German nation discovered the soundest counter-charm to the worst of all Egyptian plagues, and by the black art—by gunpowder and the art of printing—they broke the force of that spiritual and worldly hierarchy which had formed itself from the union of the priesthood and the warrior caste—that is to say, from the so-called Catholic Church, and from the feudal nobility, which enslaved all Europe, body and spirit. The printing-press burst asunder the dogma-structure in which the archpriest of Rome had

43

imprisoned souls, and Northern Europe again breathed free, delivered from the nightmare of that clergy which had indeed abandoned the form of Egyptian inheritance of rank, but which remained all the truer to the Egyptian priestly spirit, since it presented itself, with greater sternness and asperity, as a corporation of old bachelors, continued not by natural propagation, but unnaturally by a Mameluke system of recruiting. In like manner we see how the warlike caste has lost its power since the old routine of the business is worth nothing in the modern methods of war. For the strongest castles are now thrown down by the trumpet-tones of the cannon as of old the walls of Jericho; the iron harness of the knight is no better protection against the leaden rain than the linen blouse of the peasant; powder makes men equal; a citizen's musket goes off just as well as a nobleman's—the people rise.

The earlier efforts of which we read in the history of the Lombard and Tuscan republics, of the Spanish communes, and of the free cities in Germany and other countries, do not deserve the honour of being classed as movements on the part of the people; they were not efforts to attain liberty, but merely liberties; not battles for right, but for municipal rights; corporations fought for privileges, and all remained fixed in the bonds of gilds and trades unions.

Not until the days of the Reformation did the battle assume general and spiritual proportions, and then liberty was demanded, not as an imported, but as an aboriginal right; not as inherited, but as inborn. Principles were brought forward instead of old parchments; and the peasants in Germany, and the Puritans in England, fell back on the gospel whose texts then were of as high authority as the reason, even higher, since they were regarded as the revealed reason of God. There it stood legibly written that men are of equal birth, that the pride which exalts itself will be damned, that wealth is a sin, and that the poor are summoned to enjoyment in the beautiful garden of God, the common Father.

With the Bible in one hand and the sword in the other, the peasants swept over South Germany, and announced to the insolent burghers of high-towered Nuremberg, that in future no house should be left standing which was not a peasant's house. So truly and so deeply had they comprehended equality. Even at the present day in Franconia and in Suabia we see traces of this doctrine of equality, and a shuddering reverence of the Holy Spirit creeps over the wanderer when he sees in the moonshine the dark ruins of the days of the Peasant's War. It is well for him, who, in sober, waking mood, sees naught besides; but if one is a "Sunday child"—and every one familiar with history is that—he will also see the high hunt in which the German nobility, the rudest and sternest in the world, pursued their victims. He will see how unarmed men were slaughtered by thousands: racked, speared, and martyred; and from the waving corn-fields one will see the bloody peasant-heads nodding mysteriously, and above one hears a terrible lark whistling, piping revenge, like the Piper of Helfenstein.

The brothers in England and Scotland were rather more fortunate; their defeat was not so disgraceful and so unproductive, and even now we see there the results of their rule. But they did not obtain a firm foundation for their principles, the dainty cavaliers ruled again just as before, and amused themselves with merry tales of the stiff old Roundheads, which a friendly bard had written so prettily to entertain their leisure hours. No social overthrow took place in Great Britain, the framework of civil and political institutions remained undisturbed, the tyranny of castes and of corporations has remained there till the present day, and though drunken with the light and warmth of modern civilisation, England is still congealed in a mediæval condition, or rather in the condition of a fashionable Middle Age. The concessions which have there been made to liberal ideas, have been with difficulty wrested from this mediæval rigidity, and all modern improvements have there proceeded, not from a principle, but from actual necessity, and they all bear the curse of that halfness system which inevitably makes necessary new exertion and new conflicts to the death, with all their attendant dangers. The religious reformation in England is consequently but half completed, and one finds himself much worse off between the four bare prison walls of the Episcopal Anglican Church than in the large, beautifully-painted, and softly-cushioned spiritual dungeon of Catholicism. Nor has the political reformation succeeded much better; popular representation is in England as faulty as possible, and if ranks are no longer distinguished by their coats, they are at least divided by differences in legal standing, patronage, rights of court presentation, prerogatives, customary privileges, and similar misfortunes; and if the rights of person and property depend no longer upon aristocratic caprice, but upon laws, still these laws are nothing but another sort of teeth with which the aristocratic brood seizes its prey, and another sort of daggers wherewith it assassinates people. For in reality, no tyrant upon the Continent squeezes, by his own arbitrary will, so many taxes out of his subjects as the English people are obliged to pay by law; and no tyrant was ever so cruel as England's Criminal Law, which daily commits murder for the amount of one shilling, and that with the coldest formality. Although many improvements have recently been made in this melancholy state of affairs in England; although limits have been placed to temporal and clerical avarice, and though the great falsehood of a popular representation is, to a certain degree, occasionally modified by transferring the perverted electoral voice of a rotten borough to a great manufacturing town; and although the harshest intolerance is here and there softened by giving certain rights to other sects, still it is all a miserable patching up which cannot last long, and the stupidest tailor in England can foresee that, sooner or later, the old garment of state will be rent asunder into wretched rags.

"No man seweth a piece of new cloth on an old garment; else the new piece that filled it up taketh away from the old, and the rent is made worse. And no man putteth new wine into old bottles; else the new wine doth burst the bottles, and the wine is spilled, and the bottles will be marred; but new wine must be put into new bottles."

The deepest truth blooms only out of the deepest love, and hence comes the harmony of the views of the elder Preacher in the Mount, who spoke against the aristocracy of Jerusalem; and those later preachers of the mountain, who, from

45

the summit of the Convention in Paris, preached a tri-coloured gospel, according to which, not merely the form of the State, but all social life should be, not patched, but formed anew, newly founded; yes, born again.

I speak of the French Revolution, that epoch of the world in which the doctrines of freedom and of equality rose so triumphantly from those universal sources of knowledge which we call reason, and which must, as an unceasing revelation which repeats itself in every human head, and founds a distinct branch of knowledge, be far preferable to that transmitted revelation which makes itself known only in a few elect, and which, by the multitude, can only be *believed*. The privileged aristocracy, the caste-system with their peculiar rights, were never able to combat this last-mentioned sort of revelation (which is itself of an aristocratic nature) so safely and surely as reason, which is democratic by nature, now does. The history of the Revolution is the military history of this strife, in which we have all taken a greater or lesser part; it is the death-struggle with Egyptianism.

Though the swords of the enemies grow duller day by day, and though we have already conquered the best positions, still we cannot raise the song of victory until the work is perfected. We can only during the night, when there are armistices, go forth with the lantern on the field of death to bury the dead. Little avails the short burial service! Calumny, the vile insolent spectre, sits upon the noblest graves.

Oh, that the battle were only with those hereditary foes of truth who so treacherously poison the good name of their enemies, and who even humiliated that first Preacher of the Mount, the purest hero of freedom; for as they could no longer deny that he was the greatest of men, they made of him the least of gods. He who fights with priests may make up his mind to have his poor good name torn and befouled by the most infamous lies and the most cutting slanders. But as those flags which are most rent by shot, or blackened by powder-smoke, are more highly honoured than the whitest and soundest recruiting banners, and as they are at last laid up as national relics in cathedrals, so at some future day the names of our heroes, the more they are torn and blackened, will be all the more enthusiastically honoured in the holy St. Geneviève of Freedom.

The Revolution itself has been slandered, like its heroes, and represented as a terror to princes, and as a popular scare-crow, in libels of every description. All the so-called "horrors of the Revolution" have been learned by heart by children in the schools, and at one time nothing was seen in the public fairs but harshly-coloured pictures of the guillotine. It cannot be denied that this machine, which was invented by a French physician, a great world orthopædist, Monsieur Guillotin, and with which stupid heads are easily separated from evil hearts, this wholesome machine has indeed been applied rather frequently, but still only in incurable diseases, in such cases, for example, as treachery, falsehood, and weakness, and the patients were not long tortured, not racked and broken on the wheel as thousands upon thousands of *roturiers* and *vilains*, citizens and peasants were tortured, racked, and broken on the wheel in the good old time. It

46

is, of course, terrible that the French, with this machine, once even amputated the head of their State, and no one knows whether they ought to be accused, on that account, of parricide or of suicide; but on more thorough reflection, we find that Louis of France was less a sacrifice to passion than to circumstances, and that those men who forced the people on to such a sacrifice, and who have themselves, in every age, poured forth princely blood far more abundantly, should not appear solely as accusers. Only two kings, both of them rather kings of the nobility than of the people, were sacrificed by the people, and that not in a time of peace, or to subserve petty interests, but in the extremest needs of war, when they saw themselves betrayed, and when they least spared their own blood. But certainly more than a thousand princes were treacherously slain, on account of avarice or frivolous interests, by the dagger, by the sword, and by the poison of nobility and priests. It really seems as though these castes regarded regicide as one of their privileges, and therefore bewail the more selfishly the death of Louis the XVI. and of Charles I. Oh! that kings at last would perceive that they could live more safely as kings of the people, and protected by the law, than under the guard of their noble body-murderers.

But not only have the heroes of our revolution and the revolution itself been slandered, but even our entire age has been parodied with unheard-of wickedness; and if one hears or reads our vile traducers and scorners, then he will learn that the people are the *canaille*—the vile mob—that freedom is insolence, and with heaven-bent eyes and pious sighs, our enemies complain and bewail that we were frivolous and had, alas! no religion. Hypocritical, sneaking souls, who creep about bent down beneath the burden of their secret vices, dare to vilify an age which is, perhaps, holier than any of its predecessors or successors, an age that sacrifices itself for the sins of the past and for the happiness of the future, a Messiah among centuries, which could hardly endure its bloody crown of thorns and heavy cross, did it not now and then trill a merry vaudeville, and crack a joke at the modern Pharisees and Sadducees. Its colossal pains would be intolerable without such jesting and persiflage! Seriousness shows itself more majestically when laughter leads the way. And the age in this shows itself exactly like its children among the French, who have written very terribly wanton books, and yet have been very strong and serious when strength and seriousness were necessary, as, for instance, Laclos, and even Louvet de Couvray, who both fought for freedom with the self-sacrifice and boldness of martyrs, and yet who wrote in a very frivolous and indecent way, and, alas! had no religion!

As if freedom were not as good a religion as any other! And since it is ours, we may, meeting with the same measure, declare its contemners to be themselves frivolous and irreligious.

Yes, I repeat the words with which I began these pages: freedom is a new religion, the religion of our age. If Christ is not the God of this religion, he is still one of its high-priests, and his name shines consolingly in the hearts of its children. But the French are the chosen people of the new religion, the first gospels and dogmas were penned in their language. Paris is the New Jerusalem, and the Rhine is the Jordan which separates the land of Freedom from the land of the Philistines.

JAN STEEN.

[This fragment—newly translated—is taken from the *Memoiren des Herrn von Schnabelwopski*, which was written in 1831, and published in 1834, in the first volume of the *Salon*. The *Memoirs of Schnabelwopski* consist simply of the hero's light sketches of Hamburg, Amsterdam, and Leyden, and his experiences in those towns; they have generally excited the anger of Heine's German critics and biographers, who appear to detect a tone of irreverent levity about them, which they attribute to Parisian influences. Wagner obtained the story of his *Flying Dutchman* from a chapter of *Schnabelwopski's Memoirs*.]

IN the house I lodged at in Leyden there once lived Jan Steen, the great Jan Steen, whom I hold to be as great as Raphael. Even as a sacred painter Jan was as great, and that will be clearly seen when the religion of sorrow has passed away, and the religion of joy has torn off the thick veil that covers the rose-bushes of the earth, and the nightingales dare at last to sing joyously out their long-concealed raptures.

But no nightingale will ever sing so joyously as Jan Steen painted. No one has understood so profoundly as he that there shall be an eternal festival on the earth; he comprehended that our life is only the pictured kiss of God, and he felt that the Holy Ghost is revealed most gloriously in light and in laughter.

His eye laughed into the light, and the light mirrored itself in his laughing eye. And Jan remained always a dear, good child. The stern old Pastor of Leyden sat near him by the hearth, and delivered a lengthy discourse concerning his jovial life, his laughing, unchristian conduct, his love of drinking, his disorderly domestic affairs, his obdurate gaiety; and Jan listened quietly for two long hours, and betrayed not the slightest impatience at the lengthy sermon; only once he broke in with the words—"Yes, Domine, that light is far better; yes, Domine, I beg of you to draw your stool a little nearer to the fire, so that the flame may cast its red gleam over your whole face, and leave the rest of the figure in shade——"

The Domine stood up wrathful and departed. But Jan seized his palate and painted the stern old man, just as in that sermon on vice he had unconsciously furnished a model. The picture is excellent, and hung in my bed-room at Leyden.

Now that I have seen so many of Jan Steen's pictures in Holland, I seem to know the whole life of the man. I know all his relations, his wife, his children, his mother, all his cousins, his enemies, his various connections—yes, I know them all by sight. These faces greet us out of all his pictures, and a collection of them would be a biography of the painter. He has often with a single stroke revealed the deepest secrets of his soul. As I think, his wife reproached him far too often about drinking too much. For in the picture which represents the bean-feast, where Jan and his family are sitting at table, we see his wife with a large jug of wine in her hand, and eyes beaming like a Bacchante's. I am convinced, however, that the good lady never indulged in too much wine; only the rogue wanted us to believe that it was his wife, and not he, who was too fond of drinking. That is why he laughs so joyously out of the picture. He is happy; he sits in the midst of his family; his little son is bean-king, and, with his tinsel crown, stands upon a stool; his old mother, with the happiest smirk of satisfaction in the wrinkles of her countenance, carries the youngest grandchild upon her arm; the musicians play their maddest dance melodies; and the frugal, sulky housewife is painted in, an object of suspicion to all posterity, as though she were inebriated.

How often, during my stay at Leyden, did I think myself back for whole hours into the household scenes in which the excellent Jan must have lived and suffered. Many a time I thought I saw him bodily, sitting at his easel, now and then grasping the great jug, "reflecting and therewith drinking, and then again drinking without reflecting." It was no gloomy Catholic spectre that I saw, but a modern bright spirit of joy, who after death still visited his old work-room to paint merry pictures and to drink. Only such ghosts will our children sometimes see, in the light of day, while the sun shines through the windows, and from the spire no black, hollow bells, but red, exulting trumpet tones, announce the pleasant hour of noon.

THE ROMANTIC SCHOOL.

[*The Romantic School*, one of Heine's chief works, of which the most interesting portions are here given, was published in 1833. It was first written in French, as a counterblast to Madame de Staël's *De l'Allemagne*, forming a series of articles in the *Europe Littéraire*. Notwithstanding many errors of detail, and some occasional injustice, it remains by far the best account of the most important aspect of German literature. Indirectly Heine wished to lay down the programme of the future, for he regarded himself as the last of the Romantic poets, and the inaugurator of a new school. The following translation is Mr. Fleishman's; it has been carefully revised.]

MADAME de Staël's work, *De l'Allemagne*, is the only comprehensive account of the intellectual life of Germany which has been accessible to the French; and yet since her book appeared a considerable period has elapsed, and an entirely new school of literature has arisen in Germany. Is it only a transitional literature? Has it already reached its zenith? Has it already begun to decline? Opinions are divided concerning it. The majority believe that with the death of Goethe a new literary era begins in Germany; that with him the old Germany also descended to its grave; that the aristocratic period of literature was ended, and the democratic just beginning; or, as a French journal recently phrased it, "The intellectual dominion of the individual has ceased,—the intellectual rule of the many has commenced."

So far as I am concerned, I do not venture to pass so decided an opinion as to the future evolutions of German intellect. I had already prophesied many years in advance the end of the Goethean art-period, by which name I was the first to designate that era. I could safely venture the prophecy, for I knew very well the ways and the means of those malcontents who sought to overthrow the Goethean art-empire, and it is even claimed that I took part in those seditious outbreaks against Goethe. Now that Goethe is dead, the thought of it fills me with an overpowering sorrow.

While I announce this book as a sequel to Madame de Staël's *De l'Allemagne*, and extol her work very highly as being replete with information, I must yet recommend a certain caution in the acceptance of the views enunciated in that book, which I am compelled to characterise as a coterie-book. Madame de Staël, of glorious memory, here opened, in the form of a book, a salon in which she received German authors and gave them an opportunity to make themselves known to the civilised world of France. But above the din of the most diverse voices, confusedly discoursing therein, the most audible is the delicate treble of Herr A. W. Schlegel. Where the large-hearted woman is wholly herself,—where she is uninfluenced by others, and expresses the thoughts of her own radiant soul, displaying all her intellectual fireworks and brilliant follies,—there the book is good, even excellent. But as soon as she yields to foreign influences, as soon as she begins to glorify a school whose spirit is wholly unfamiliar and incomprehensible to her, as soon as through the commendation of this school she furthers certain Ultramontane tendencies which are in direct opposition to her own Protestant clearness, just so soon her book becomes wretched and unenjoyable. To this unconscious partisanship she adds the evident purpose, through praise of the intellectual activity, the idealism, of Germany, to rebuke the realism then existing among the French, and the materialistic splendours of the Empire. Her book *De l'Allemagne* resembles in this respect the *Germania* of Tacitus, who perhaps likewise designed his eulogy of the Germans as an indirect satire against his countrymen. In referring to the school which Madame de Staël glorified, and whose tendencies she furthered, I mean the Romantic School. That this was in Germany something quite different from that which was designated by the same name in France, that its tendencies were totally diverse from those of the French Romanticists, will be made clear in the following pages.

But what was the Romantic School in Germany?

It was nothing else than the reawakening of the poetry of the middle ages as it manifested itself in the poems, paintings, and sculptures, in the art and life of those times. This poetry, however, had been developed out of Christianity; it was a passion-flower which had blossomed from the blood of Christ. I know not if the melancholy flower which in Germany we call the passion-flower is known by the same name in France, and if the popular tradition has ascribed to it the same mystical origin. It is that motley-hued, melancholic flower in whose calyx one may behold a counterfeit presentment of the tools used at the crucifixion of Christ—namely, hammer, pincers, and nails. This flower is by no means unsightly, but only spectral: its aspect fills our souls with a dread pleasure, like those convulsive, sweet emotions that arise from grief. In this respect the passion-flower would be the fittest symbol of Christianity itself, whose most awe-inspiring charm consists in the voluptuousness of pain.

Although in France Christianity and Roman Catholicism are synonymous terms, yet I desire to emphasise the fact, that I here refer to the latter only. I refer to that religion whose earliest dogmas contained a condemnation of all flesh, and not only admitted the supremacy of the spirit over the flesh, but sought to mortify the latter in order thereby to glorify the former. I refer to that religion through whose unnatural mission vice and hypocrisy came into the world, for through the odium which it cast on the flesh the most innocent gratification of the senses were accounted sins; and, as it was impossible to be entirely spiritual, the growth of hypocrisy was inevitable. I refer to that religion which, by teaching the renunciation of all earthly pleasures, and by inculcating abject humility and angelic patience, became the most efficacious support of despotism. Men now recognise the nature of that religion, and will no longer be put off with promises of a Heaven hereafter; they know that the material world has also its good, and is not wholly given over to Satan, and now they vindicate the pleasures of the world, this beautiful garden of the gods, our inalienable heritage. Just because we now comprehend so fully all the consequences of that absolute spirituality, we are warranted in believing that the Christian-Catholic theories of the universe are at an end; for every epoch is a sphinx which plunges into the abyss as soon as its problem is solved.

We by no means deny the benefits which the Christian-Catholic theories effected in Europe. They were needed as a wholesome reaction against the terrible colossal materialism which was developed in the Roman Empire, and threatened the annihilation of all the intellectual grandeur of mankind. Just as the licentious memoirs of the last century form the *pièces justificatives* of the French Revolution; just as the reign of terror seems a necessary medicine when one is familiar with the confessions of the French nobility since the regency; so the wholesomeness of ascetic spirituality becomes manifest when we read Petronius or Apuleius, books which may be considered as *pièces justificatives* of Christianity. The flesh had become so insolent in this Roman world that Christian discipline was needed to chasten it. After the banquet of a Trimalkion, a hunger-cure, such as Christianity, was required.

Or did, perhaps, the hoary sensualists seek by scourgings to stimulate the cloyed flesh to renewed capacity for enjoyment? Did aging Rome submit to monkish flagellations in order to discover exquisite pleasure in torture itself, voluptuous bliss in pain?

Unfortunate excess! it robbed the Roman body-politic of its last energies. Rome was not destroyed by the division into two empires. On the Bosphorus as on the Tiber, Rome was eaten up by the same Judaic spiritualism, and in both Roman history became the record of a slow dying-away, a death agony that lasted for centuries. Did perhaps murdered Judea, by bequeathing its spiritualism to the Romans, seek to avenge itself on the victorious foe, as did the dying centaur, who so cunningly wheedled the son of Jupiter into wearing the deadly vestment poisoned with his own blood? In truth, Rome, the Hercules among nations, was so effectually consumed by the Judaic poison that helm and armour fell from its decaying limbs, and its imperious battle tones degenerated into the prayers of snivelling priests and the trilling of eunuchs.

But that which enfeebles the aged strengthens the young. That spiritualism had a wholesome effect on the over-robust races of the north; the ruddy barbarians became spiritualised through Christianity; European civilisation began. This is a praiseworthy and sacred phase of Christianity. The Catholic Church earned in this regard the highest title to our respect and admiration. Through grand, genial institutions it controlled the bestiality of the barbarian hordes of the North, and tamed their brutal materialism.

The works of art in the middle ages give evidence of this mastery of matter by the spirit; and that is often their whole purpose. The epic poems of that time may be easily classified according to the degree in which they show that mastery. Of lyric and dramatic poems nothing is here to be said; for the latter do not exist, and the former are comparatively as much alike in all ages as are the songs of the nightingales in each succeeding spring.

Although the epic poetry of the middle ages was divided into sacred and secular, yet both classes were purely Christian in their nature; for if the sacred poetry related exclusively to the Jewish people and its history, which alone was considered sacred; if its themes were the heroes of the Old and the New Testaments, and their legends—in brief, the Church—still all the Christian views and aims of that period were mirrored in the secular poetry. The flower of the German sacred poetry of the middle ages is, perhaps, *Barlaam and Josaphat*, a poem in which the dogma of self-denial, of continence, of renunciation, of the scorn of all worldly pleasures, is most consistently expressed. Next in order of merit I would rank *Lobgesang auf den Heiligen Anno*, but the latter poem already evinces a marked tendency towards secular themes. It differs in general from the former somewhat as a Byzantine image of a saint differs from an old German representation. Just as in these Byzantine pictures, so also do we find in *Barlaam and Josaphat* the greatest simplicity; there is no perspective, and the long, lean, statue-like forms, and the grave, ideal countenances, stand severely outlined, as though in bold relief against a background of pale gold. In the *Lobgesang auf den Heiligen Anno*, as in the old German pictures, the accessories seem almost more prominent than the subject; and, notwithstanding the bold outlines, every detail is most minutely executed, and one knows not which to admire most, the giant-like conception or the dwarf-like patience of execution. Ottfried's *Evangeliengedicht*, which is generally praised as the masterpiece of this sacred poetry, is far inferior to both of these poems.

In the secular poetry we find, as intimated above, first, the cycle of legends called the *Nibelungenlied*, and the *Book of Heroes*. In these poems all the ante-Christian modes of thought and feelings are dominant; brute force is not yet moderated into chivalry; the sturdy warriors of the North stand like statues of stone, and the soft light and moral atmosphere of Christianity have not yet penetrated their iron armour. But dawn is gradually breaking over the old

German forests, the ancient Druid oaks are being felled, and in the open arena Christianity and Paganism are battling: all this is portrayed in the cycle of traditions of Charlemagne; even the Crusades with their religious tendencies are mirrored therein. But now from this Christianised, spiritualised brute force is developed the peculiar feature of the middle ages, chivalry, which finally becomes exalted into a religious knighthood. The earlier knighthood is most felicitously portrayed in the legends of King Arthur, which are full of the most charming gallantry, the most finished courtesy, and the most daring bravery. From the midst of the pleasing, though bizarre, arabesques, and the fantastic, flowery mazes of these tales, we are greeted by the gentle Gawain, the worthy Lancelot of the Lake, by the valiant, gallant, and honest, but somewhat tedious, Wigalois. By the side of this cycle of legends we find the kindred and connected legends of the Holy Grail, in which the religious knighthood is glorified, and in which are to be found the three grandest poems of the middle ages, *Titurel*, *Parcival*, and *Lohengrin*. In these poems we stand face to face, as it were, with the muse of romantic poetry; we look deep into her large, sad eyes, and ere we are aware she has ensnared us in her network of scholasticism, and drawn us down into the weird depths of mediæval mysticism. But further on in this period we find poems which do not unconditionally bow down to Christian spirituality; poems in which it is even attacked, and in which the poet, breaking loose from the fetters of an abstract Christian morality, complacently plunges into the delightful realm of glorious sensuousness. Nor is it an inferior poet who has left us *Tristan and Isolde*, the masterpiece of this class. Verily, I must confess that Gottfried von Strasburg, the author of this, the most exquisite poem of the middle ages, is perhaps also the loftiest poet of that period. He surpasses even the grandeur of Wolfram von Eschilbach, whose *Parcival*, and fragments of *Titurel*, are so much admired. At present, it is perhaps permissible to praise Meister Gottfried without stint, but in his own time his book and similar poems, to which even *Lancelot* belonged, were considered Godless and dangerous. Francesca da Polenta and her handsome friend paid dearly for reading together such a book;—the greater danger, it is true, lay in the fact that they suddenly stopped reading.

All the poetry of the middle ages has a certain definite character, through which it differs from the poetry of the Greeks and Romans. In reference to this difference the former is called Romantic, the latter Classic. These names, however, are misleading, and have hitherto caused the most vexatious confusion, which is even increased when we call the antique poetry plastic as well as classic. In this, particularly, lay the germ of misunderstandings; for artists ought always to treat their subject-matter plastically. Whether it be Christian or pagan, the subject ought to be portrayed in clear contours. In short, plastic configuration should be the main requisite in the modern romantic as well as in antique art. And, in fact, are not the figures in Dante's *Divine Comedy* or in the paintings of Raphael just as plastic as those in Virgil or on the walls of Herculaneum?

The difference consists in this,—that the plastic figures in antique art are identical with the thing represented, with the idea which the artist seeks to communicate. Thus, for example, the wanderings of the Odyssey mean nothing else than the wanderings of the man who was a son of Laertes and the husband of Penelope, and was called Ulysses. Thus, again, the Bacchus which is to be seen in the Louvre is nothing more than the charming son of Semele, with a daring melancholy look in his eyes, and an inspired voluptuousness on the soft arched lips. It is otherwise in romantic art: here the wanderings of a knight have an esoteric signification; they typify, perhaps, the mazes of life in general. The dragon that is vanquished is sin; the almond-tree, that from afar so encouragingly wafts its fragrance to the hero, is the Trinity, the God-Father, God-Son, and God-Holy-Ghost, who together constitute one, just as shell, fibre, and kernel together constitute the almond. When Homer describes the armour of a hero, it is naught else than a good armour, which is worth so many oxen; but when a monk of the middle ages describes in his poem the garments of the Mother of God, you may depend upon it, that by each fold of those garments he typifies some special virtue, and that a peculiar meaning lies hidden in the sacred robes of the immaculate Virgin Mary; as her Son is the kernel of the almond, she is quite appropriately described in the poem as an almond-blossom. Such is the character of that poesy of the middle ages which we designate *romantic*.

Classic art had to portray only the finite, and its forms could be identical with the artist's idea. Romantic art had to represent, or rather to typify, the infinite and the spiritual, and therefore was compelled to have recourse to a system of traditional, or rather parabolic, symbols, just as Christ himself had endeavoured to explain and make clear his spiritual meaning through beautiful parables. Hence the mystic, enigmatical, miraculous, and transcendental character of the art-productions of the middle ages. Fancy strives frantically to portray through concrete images that which is purely spiritual, and in the vain endeavour invents the most colossal absurdities; it piles Ossa on Pelion, Parcival on Titurel, to reach heaven.

Similar monstrous abortions of imagination have been produced by the Scandinavians, the Hindoos, and the other races which likewise strive through poetry to represent the infinite; among them also do we find poems which may be regarded as romantic.

Concerning the music of the middle ages little can be said. All records are wanting. It was not until late in the sixteenth century that the masterpieces of Catholic Church music came into existence, and, of their kind, they cannot be too highly prized, for they are the purest expression of Christian spirituality. The recitative arts, being spiritual in their nature, quite appropriately flourished in Christendom. But this religion was less propitious for the plastic arts, for as the latter were to represent the victory of spirit over matter, and were nevertheless compelled to use matter as a means to carry out this representation, they had to accomplish an unnatural task. Hence sculpture and painting abounded with such revolting subjects as martyrdoms, crucifixions, dying saints, and physical sufferings in general. The treatment of such subjects must have been torture for the artists themselves; and when I look at those distorted images, with pious heads awry, long, thin arms, meagre legs, and graceless drapery, which are intended to represent Christian abstinence and ethereality, I am filled with an unspeakable compassion for the artists of that period. It is true the painters were somewhat more favoured, for colour, the material of their representation, in its intangibility, in its varied lights and shades, was not so completely at variance with spirituality as the material of the sculptors; But even they, the painters, were compelled to disfigure the patient canvas with the most revolting representations of physical suffering. In truth, when we view certain picture galleries, and behold nothing but scenes of blood, scourgings, and executions, we are fain to believe that the old masters painted these pictures for the gallery of an executioner.

But human genius can transfigure deformity itself, and many painters succeeded in accomplishing the unnatural task beautifully and sublimely. The Italians, in particular, glorified beauty,—it is true, somewhat at the expense of spirituality,—and raised themselves aloft to an ideality which reached its perfection in the many representations of the Madonna. Where it concerned the Madonna, the Catholic clergy always made some concessions to sensuality. This image of an immaculate beauty, transfigured by motherly love and sorrow, was privileged to receive the homage of poet and painter, and to be decked with all the charms that could allure the senses. For this image was a magnet, which was to draw the great masses into the pale of Christianity. Madonna Maria was the pretty *dame du comptoir* of the Catholic Church, whose customers, especially the barbarians of the North, she attracted and held fast by her celestial smiles.

During the middle ages architecture was of the same character as the other arts; for, indeed, at that period all manifestations of life harmonised most wonderfully. In architecture, as in poetry, this parabolising tendency was evident. Now, when we enter an old cathedral, we have scarcely a hint of the esoteric meaning of its stony symbolism. Only the general impression forces itself on our mind. We feel the exaltation of the spirit and the abasement of the flesh. The interior of the cathedral is a hollow cross, and we walk here amid the instruments of martyrdom itself. The variegated windows cast on us their red and green lights, like drops of blood and ichor; requiems for the dead resound through the aisles; under our feet are gravestones and decay; in harmony with the colossal pillars, the soul soars aloft, painfully tearing itself away from the body, which sinks to the ground like a cast-off garment. When one views from without these Gothic cathedrals, these immense structures, that are built so airily, so delicately, so daintily, as transparent as if carved, like Brabant laces made of marble, then only does one realise the might of that art which could achieve a mastery over stone, so that even this stubborn substance should appear spectrally etherealised, and be an exponent of Christian spiritualism.

But the arts are only the mirror of life; and when Catholicism disappeared from daily life, so also it faded and vanished out of the arts. At the time of the Reformation Catholic poetry was gradually dying out in Europe, and in its place we behold the long-buried Grecian style of poetry again reviving. It was, in sooth, only an artificial spring, the work of the gardener and not of the sun; the trees and flowers were stuck in narrow pots, and a glass sky protected them from the wind and cold weather.

In the world's history every event is not the direct consequence of another, but all events mutually act and react on one another. It was not alone through the Greek scholars who, after the conquest of Constantinople, immigrated over to us, that the love for Grecian art, and the striving to imitate it, became universal among us; but in art as in life, there was stirring a contemporary Protestantism. Leo X., the magnificent Medici, was just as zealous a Protestant as Luther; and as in Wittenburg protest was offered in Latin prose, so in Rome the protest was made in stone, colours, and *ottava rime*. For do not the vigorous marble statues of Michael Angelo, Giulio Romano's laughing nymph-faces, and the life-intoxicated merriment in the verses of Master Ludovico,[9] offer a protesting contrast to the old, gloomy, withered Catholicism? The painters of Italy combated priestdom more effectively, perhaps, than did the Saxon theologians. The glowing flesh in the paintings of Titian,—all that is simple Protestantism. The limbs of his Venus are much more fundamental theses than those which the German monk nailed to the church door of Wittenburg. Mankind felt itself suddenly liberated, as it were, from the thraldom of a thousand years; the artists, in particular, breathed freely again when the Alp-like burden of Christianity was rolled from off their breasts; they plunged enthusiastically into the sea of Grecian mirthfulness, from whose foam the goddess of beauty again rose to meet them; again did the painters depict the ambrosial joys of Olympus; again did the sculptors, with the olden love, chisel the heroes of antiquity from out the marble blocks; again did the poets sing of the house of Atreus and of Laios; a new era of classic poetry arose.

In France, under Louis XIV., this neo-classic poetry exhibited a polished perfection, and, to a certain extent, even originality. Through the political influence of the *grand monarque* this new classic poetry spread over the rest of Europe. In Italy, where it was already at home, it received a French colouring; the Anjous brought with them to Spain the heroes of French tragedy; it accompanied Madame Henriette to England; and, as a matter of course, we Germans modelled our clumsy temple of art after the bepowdered Olympus of Versailles. The most famous high priest of this temple was Gottsched, that old periwigged pate, whom our dear Goethe has so felicitously described in his memoirs.

Lessing was the literary Arminius who emancipated our theatre from that foreign rule. He showed us the vapidness, the ridiculousness, the tastelessness, of those apings of the French stage, which itself was but an imitation of the Greek. But not only by his criticism, but also through his own works of art, did he become the founder of modern German original literature. All the paths of the intellect, all the phases of life, did this man pursue with disinterested enthusiasm. Art, theology, antiquarianism, poetry, dramatic criticism, history,—he studied these all with the same zeal and with the same aim. In all his works breathes the same grand social idea, the same progressive humanity, the same religion of reason, whose John he was, and whose Messiah we still await. This religion he preached always, but alas! often quite alone and in the desert. Moreover, he lacked the skill to transmute stones into bread. The greater portion of his life was spent in poverty and misery—a curse which rests on almost all the great minds of Germany, and which probably will only be overcome by the political emancipation. Lessing was more deeply interested in political questions than was imagined,—a characteristic which we entirely miss in his contemporaries. Only now do we comprehend what he had in view by his description of the petty despotisms in *Emilia Galotti*. At that time he was considered merely a champion of intellectual liberty and an opponent of clerical intolerance; his theological writings were better understood. The fragments "Concerning the Education of the Human race," which have been translated into French by Eugene Rodrigue, will perhaps suffice to give the French an idea of the wide scope of Lessing's genius. His two critical works which have had the most influence on art are his *Hamburger Dramaturgie* and his *Laocoön, or Concerning the Limits of Painting and Poetry.* His best dramatic works are *Emilia Galotti, Minna von Barnhelm,* and *Nathan the Wise.*

Gotthold Ephraim Lessing was born January 22nd, 1729, at Kamenz, in Upper Lusatia, and died February 15th, 1781, at Brunswick. He was a whole man, who; while with his polemics waging destructive battle against the old, at the same time created something newer and better. "He resembled," says a German author, "those pious Jews, who, at the second building of the temple, were often disturbed by the attacks of their enemies, and with one hand would fight against the foe, while with the other hand they continued to work at the house of God." This is not the place to discuss Lessing more fully, but I cannot refrain from saying that, in the whole range of literary history, he is the author whom I most love.

I desire here to call attention to another author, who worked in the same spirit and with the same aim, and who may be regarded as Lessing's most legitimate successor. It is true, a criticism of this author would be out of place here, for he occupies a peculiarly isolated place in the history of literature, and his relation to his epoch and contemporaries cannot even now be definitely pronounced. I refer to Johann Gottfried Herder, born in 1744, at Morungen, in East Prussia; died in 1803, at Weimar, in Saxony.

The history of literature is a great morgue, wherein each seeks the dead who are near or dear to him. And when, among the corpses of so many petty men, I behold the noble features of a Lessing or a Herder, my heart throbs with emotion. How could I pass you without pressing a hasty kiss on your pale lips?

But if Lessing effectually put an end to the servile apings of Franco-Grecian art, yet, by directing attention to the true art-works of Grecian antiquity, to a certain extent he gave an impetus to a new and equally silly species of imitation. Through his warfare against religious superstition he even advanced a certain narrow-minded *jejune* enlightenment, which at that time vaunted itself in Berlin; the sainted Nicolai was its principal mouthpiece, and the German Encyclopædia its arsenal. The most wretched mediocrity began again to raise its head, more disgustingly than ever. Imbecility, vapidity, and the commonplace distended themselves like the frog in the fable.

It is an error to believe that Goethe, who at that time had already appeared upon the scene, had met with general recognition. His *Goetz von Berlichingen* and his *Werther* were received with enthusiasm, but the works of the most ordinary bungler not less so, and Goethe occupied but a small niche in the temple of literature. It is true, as said before, that the public welcomed Goetz and Werther with delight, but more on account of the subject matter than their artistic merits, which few were able to appreciate. Of these masterpieces, *Goetz von Berlichingen* was a dramatised romance of chivalry, which was the popular style at that time. In *Werther* the public saw only an embellished account of an episode in real life—namely, the story of young Jerusalem, a youth who shot himself from disappointed love, thereby creating quite a commotion in that dead-calm period. Tears were shed over his pathetic letters, and it was shrewdly observed that the manner in which Werther had been ostracised from the society of the nobility must have increased his weariness of life. The discussion concerning suicide brought the book still more into notice; a few fools hit upon the idea of shooting themselves in imitation of Werther, and thus the book made a marked sensation. But the romances of August Lafontaine were in equal demand, and as the latter was a voluminous writer, it followed that he was more famous than Wolfgang Goethe. Wieland was the great poet of that period, and his only rival was Herr Ramler of Berlin. Wieland was worshipped idolatrously, more than Goethe ever was. Iffland, with his lachrymose domestic dramas, and Kotzebue's farces, with their stale witticisms, ruled the stage.

It was against this literature that, in the closing years of the last century, there arose in Germany a new school, which we have designated the Romantic School. At the head of this school stand the brothers August William and Frederic Schlegel. Jena, where these two brothers, together with many kindred spirits, were wont to come and go, was the central point from which the new æsthetic dogma radiated. I advisedly say dogma, for this school began with a criticism of the art productions of the past, and with recipes for the art works of the future. In both of these fields the Schlegelian school has rendered good service to æsthetic criticism. In criticising the art works of the past, either their defects and imperfections were set forth, or their merits and beauties illustrated. In their polemics, in their exposure of artistic shortcomings and imperfections, the Schlegels were entirely imitators of Lessing; they seized upon his great battle-sword, but the arm of August William Schlegel was far too feeble, and the sight of his brother Frederic too much obscured by mystic clouds; the former could not strike so strong, nor the latter so sure and telling a blow as Lessing. In reproductive criticism, however, where the beauties of a work of art were to be brought out clearly; where a delicate perception of individualities was required; and where these were to be made intelligible, the Schlegels are far superior to Lessing. But what shall I say concerning their recipes for producing masterpieces? Here the Schlegels reveal the same impotency that we seem to discover in Lessing. The latter also, strong as he is in negation, is equally weak in affirmation; seldom can he lay down any fundamental principle, and even more rarely, a correct one. He lacks the firm foundation of a philosophy, or a synthetic system. In this respect the Schlegels are still more woefully lacking. Many fables are rife concerning the influence of Fichtean idealism and Schelling's philosophy of nature upon the romantic school, and it is even asserted that the latter is entirely the result of the former. I can, however, at the most discover the traces of only a few stray thoughts of Fichte and Schelling, but by no means the impress of a system of philosophy. It is true that Schelling, who at that time was delivering lectures at Jena, had personally a great influence upon the romantic school. Schelling is also somewhat of a poet, a fact not generally known in France, and it is said that he is still in doubt whether he shall not publish his entire philosophical works in poetical, yes, even in metrical form. This doubt is characteristic of the man.

But if the Schlegels could give no definite, reliable theory for the masterpieces which they bespoke of the poets of their school, they atoned for these shortcomings by commending as models the best works of art of the past, and by making them accessible to their disciples. These were chiefly the Christian-Catholic productions of the middle ages. The translation of Shakespeare, who stands at the frontier of this art and with Protestant clearness smiles over into our modern era, was solely intended for polemical purposes, the present discussion of which space forbids. It was undertaken by A. W. Schlegel at a time when the enthusiasm for the middle ages had not yet reached its most extravagant height. Later, when this did occur, Calderon was translated and ranked far above Shakespeare. For the works of Calderon bear most distinctly the impress of the poetry of the middle ages—particularly of the two principal epochs of knight-errantry and monasticism. The pious comedies of the Castilian priest-poet, whose poetical flowers had been besprinkled with holy water and canonical perfumes, with all their pious *grandezza*, with all their sacerdotal splendour, with all their sanctimonious balderdash, were now set up as models, and Germany swarmed with fantastically-pious, insanely-profound poems, over which it was the fashion to work one's self into a mystic ecstasy of admiration, as in *The Devotion to the Cross*, or to fight in honour of the Madonna, as in *The Constant Prince*. Zacharias Werner carried the nonsense as far as it might be safely done without being imprisoned by the authorities in a lunatic asylum.

Our poetry, said the Schlegels, is superannuated; our muse is an old and wrinkled hag; our Cupid is no fair youth, but a shrunken, grey-haired dwarf. Our emotions are withered; our imagination is dried up: we must re-invigorate ourselves. We must seek again the choked-up springs of the naïve, simple poetry of the middle ages, where bubbles the elixir of youth. When the parched, thirsty multitude heard this, they did not long delay. They were eager to be again young and blooming, and, hastening to those miraculous waters, quaffed and gulped with intemperate greediness. But the same fate befell them as happened to the aged waiting-maid who noticed that her mistress possessed a magic elixir which restored youth. During her lady's absence she took from the toilet drawer the small flagon which contained the elixir, but, instead of drinking only a few drops, she took a long deep draught, so that through the power of the rejuvenating beverage she became not only young again, but even a puny, puling babe. In sooth, so was it with our excellent Ludwig Tieck, one of the best poets of this school; he drank so deeply of the mediæval folk tales and ballads that he became almost as a child again, and dropped into that childlike lisping which it cost Madame de Staël so much painstaking to admire. She confesses that she found it rather strange to have one of the characters in a drama make his *début* with a monologue, which begins with the words:—"I am the brave Bonifacius, and I come to tell you," etc.

By his romance, *Sternbald's Wanderungen*, and through his publication of the *Herzensergies sungen eines Kunstliebenden Klosterbruders*, written by a certain Wackenroder, Ludwig Tieck sought to set up the naïve, crude beginnings of art as models. The piety and childishness of these works, which are revealed in their technical awkwardness, were recommended for imitation. Raphael was to be ignored entirely; his teacher, Perugino, fared almost as badly, although rated somewhat higher, for it was claimed that he showed some traces of those beauties which were to be found in their full bloom in the immortal masterpieces of Fra Giovanno Angelico da Fiesole, and were so devoutly admired. If the reader wishes to form an idea of the taste of the art-enthusiasts of that period, let him go to the Louvre, where the best pictures of those masters, who were then worshipped without bounds, are still on exhibition; and if the reader wishes to form an idea of the great mass of poets who at that time, in all possible varieties of verse, imitated the poetry of the middle ages, let him visit the lunatic asylum at Charenton.

I believe, however, that those pictures in the first salon of the Louvre are still too graceful to give the observer a correct idea of the art ideals of that period. The pictures of the old Italian school must be imagined translated into the old German, for the works of the old German painters were considered more artless and childlike, and therefore more worthy of imitation than the old Italian. It was claimed that we Germans, with our *Gemüth*, a word for which the French language has no equivalent, have been able to form a more profound conception of Christianity than other nations, and Frederic Schlegel, and his friend, Joseph Görres, rummaged among the ancient Rhine cities for the remains of old German pictures and statuary, which were superstitiously worshipped as holy relics.

I have just likened the German Parnassus of that period to Charenton. Even that, however, is too mild a comparison. A French madness falls far short of a German lunacy in violence, for in the latter, as Polonius would say, there is method. With a pedantry without its equal, with an intense conscientiousness, with a profundity of which a superficial French fool can form no conception, this German folly was pursued.

The political condition of Germany was particularly favourable to those Christian old German tendencies. "Need teaches prayer," says the proverb; and truly never was the need greater in Germany. Hence the masses were more than ever inclined to prayer, to religion, to Christianity. No people is more loyally attached to its rulers than are the Germans. And more even than the sorrowful condition to which the country was reduced through war and foreign rule did the mournful spectacle of their vanquished princes, creeping at the feet of Napoleon, afflict and grieve the Germans. The whole nation resembled those faithful old servants in once great but now reduced families, who feel more keenly than even their masters all the humiliations to which the latter are exposed, and who in secret weep most bitterly when the family silver is to be sold, and who clandestinely contribute their pitiful savings, so that patrician wax candles and not plebeian tallow dips shall grace the family table—just as we see it so touchingly depicted in the old plays. The universal sadness found consolation in religion, and there ensued a pious resignation to the will of God, from whom alone help could come. And, in fact, against Napoleon none could help but God Himself. No reliance could be placed on the earthly legions; hence all eyes were religiously turned to Heaven.

We would have submitted to Napoleon quietly enough, but our princes, while they hoped for deliverance through Heaven, were at the same time not unfriendly to the thought, that the united strength of their subjects might be very useful in effecting their purpose. Hence they sought to awaken in the German people a sense of homogeneity, and even the most exalted personages now spoke of a German nationality, of a common German fatherland, of a union of the Christian-Germanic races, of the unity of Germany. We were commanded to be patriotic, and straightway we became patriots,—for we always obey when our princes command.

But it must not be supposed that the word "patriotism" means the same in Germany as in France. The patriotism of the French consists in this: the heart warms; through this warmth it expands; it enlarges so as to encompass, with its all-embracing love, not only the nearest and dearest, but all France, all civilisation. The patriotism of the Germans, on the contrary, consists in narrowing and contracting the heart, just as leather contracts in the cold; in hating foreigners; in ceasing to be European and cosmopolitan, and in adopting a narrow-minded and exclusive Germanism. We beheld this ideal empire of churlishness organised into a system by Herr Jahn; with it began the crusade of the vulgar, the coarse, the great unwashed—against the grandest and holiest idea ever brought forth in Germany, the idea of humanitarianism; the idea of the universal brotherhood of mankind, of cosmopolitanism—an idea to which our great minds, Lessing, Herder, Schiller, Goethe, Jean Paul, and all people of culture in Germany, have ever paid homage.

With the events that speedily followed you are only too familiar. After God, the snow, and the Cossacks had destroyed the best portion of Napoleon's forces, we Germans received the command from those highest in authority to free ourselves from the foreign yoke, and we straightway flamed with manly wrath at the bondage too long endured; and we let ourselves be excited to enthusiasm by the fine melodies, but bad verses, of Köerner's ballads, and we fought until we won our freedom—for we always do what our princes command.

61

At a period when the crusade against Napoleon was forming, a school which was inimical to everything French, and which exalted everything in art and life that was Teutonic, could not help achieving great popularity. The Romantic School at that time went hand in hand with the machinations of the government and the secret societies, and A. W. Schlegel conspired against Racine with the same aim that Minister Stein plotted against Napoleon. This school of literature floated with the stream of the times; that is to say, with the stream that flowed backwards to its source. When finally German patriotism and nationality were victorious, the popular Teutonic-Christian-romantic school, "the new-German-religious-patriotic art-school," triumphed also. Napoleon, the great classic, who was as classic as Alexander or Cæsar, was overthrown, and August William and Frederic Schlegel, the petty romanticists, who were as romantic as Tom Thumb and Puss in Boots, strutted about as victors.

But the reaction which always follows excess was in this case not long in coming. As the spiritualism of Christianity was a reaction against the brutal rule of imperial Roman materialism; as the revival of the love for Grecian art and science was a reaction against the extravagances of Christian spiritualism; as the romanticism of the middle ages may also be considered as a reaction against the vapid apings of antique classic art; so also do we now behold a reaction against the re-introduction of that catholic, feudal mode of thought, of that knight-errantry and priestdom, which were being inculcated through literature and the pictorial arts, under bewildering circumstances. For when the artists of the middle ages were recommended as models, and were so highly praised and admired, the only explanation of their superiority that could be given was that these men believed in that which they depicted, and that, therefore, with their artless conceptions they could accomplish more than the later sceptical artists, notwithstanding that the latter excelled in technical skill. In short, it was claimed that faith worked wonders, and, in truth, how else could the transcendent merits of a Fra Angelico da Fiesole or the poems of Brother Ottfried be explained? Hence the artists who were honest in their devotion to art, and who sought to imitate the pious distortions of those miraculous pictures, the sacred uncouthness of those marvel-abounding poems, and the inexplicable mysticisms of those olden works—these artists determined to wander to the same hippocrene whence the old masters had derived their supernatural inspiration. They made a pilgrimage to Rome, where the vicegerent of Christ was to re-invigorate consumptive German art with asses' milk. In brief, they betook themselves to the lap of the Roman-Catholic-Apostolic Church, where alone, according to their doctrine, salvation was to be secured. Many of the adherents of the romantic school—for instance, Joseph Görres and Clemens Brentano—were Catholics by birth, and required no formal ceremony to mark their re-adhesion to the Catholic faith; they merely renounced their former free-thinking views. Others, however, such as Frederic Schlegel, Ludwig Tieck, Novalis, Werner, Schütz, Carové, Adam Müller, etc., were born and bred Protestants, and their conversion to Catholicism required a public ceremony. The above list of names includes only authors; the number of painters, who in swarms simultaneously abjured Protestantism and reason, was much larger.

When it was seen how these young people made obeisance, as it were, to the Roman Catholic Church, and pressed their way into ancient prisons of the mind, from which their fathers had so valiantly liberated themselves, much misgiving was felt in Germany. But when it was discovered that this propaganda was the work of priests and aristocrats, who had conspired against the religious and political liberties of Europe; when it was seen that it was Jesuitism itself which was seeking, with the dulcet tones of Romanticism, to lure the youth of Germany to their ruin, after the manner of the mythical rat-catcher of Hamelin; when all this became known, there was great excitement and indignation in Germany among the friends of Protestantism and intellectual freedom.

I have mentioned intellectual freedom and Protestantism together; although, in Germany, I profess the Protestant religion, yet I trust no one will accuse me of a prejudice in its favour. It is entirely without partiality that I have named Protestantism and free-thought together, for in Germany they really stand on a friendly footing towards one another. At all events they are akin, and that as mother and daughter. Even if the Protestant Church may be charged with a certain odious narrow-mindedness, yet to its immortal honour be it said, that by allowing the right of free investigation in the Christian religion, and by liberating the minds of men from the yoke of authority, it made it possible for free-thought to strike root in Germany, and for science to develop an independent existence. Although German philosophy now proudly takes its stand by the side of the Protestant Church; yes, even assumes an air of superiority; yet it is only the daughter of the latter, and as such owes her filial respect and consideration; and when threatened by Jesuitism, the common foe of them both, the bonds of kindred demanded that they should combine for mutual defence. All the friends of intellectual freedom and the Protestant Church, sceptics as well as orthodox, simultaneously arose against the restoration of Catholicism, and, as a matter of course, the Liberals, who were not specially concerned either for the welfare of the Protestant Church or of philosophy, but for the interests of civil liberty, also joined the ranks of this opposition. In Germany, however, the Liberals had always, up to the present time, been students both of philosophy and theology, and the idea of liberty for which they fought was always the same, whether the subject under discussion was exclusively political, philosophical, or theological. This is most clearly manifest in the life of the man, who, at the very outset of the romantic school in Germany, undermined its foundation, and contributed the most to its overthrow. I refer to Johann Heinrich Voss.

This writer is altogether unknown in France, and yet there are few to whom the German people are more indebted for their intellectual development. After Lessing, he is probably the greatest citizen in German literature. He certainly was a great man, and deserves more than a mere passing mention.

The biography of this man is that of nearly all German authors of the old school. He was the son of poor parents, and was born at Mecklenberg in 1751. He studied theology, but did not pursue it as a career. When, however, he became acquainted with poetry and Greek, he devoted himself zealously to both. In order not to starve he took to teaching, and became schoolmaster at Otterndorf, in

Hadeln. He translated the ancients, and lived to the age of seventy-five, poor, frugal, and industrious. He enjoyed an excellent reputation among the poets of the old school, but the poets of the new romantic school were continually plucking at his laurels, and they scoffed not a little at the honest, old-fashioned Voss, who, however, went on in his straight-forward way, picturing the life on the lower Elbe, sometimes even writing in the Platt-Deutsch dialect. He selected no mediæval knights or madonnas as the heroes and heroines of his works, but chose for his theme the life of a simple Protestant parson and his virtuous family. Voss was so thoroughly wholesome, so bourgeois, so natural; while they, the new troubadours, were so morbid and somnambulistic, so high-flown and aristocratic, and altogether so unnatural. To Frederic Schlegel, the intoxicated poet of the dissolute, romantic Lucinde, the staid and sober Voss, with his "chaste Louise" and his "aged and venerable parson of Grunau," must have been very obnoxious. August Wilhelm Schlegel, who never was so sincere as his brother in his glorification of profligacy and of Catholicism, harmonised much better with old Voss, and between the two there existed only the rivalry of translators, a rivalry which has been very beneficial for German literature. Even before the rise of the new school, Voss had translated Homer; now, with an unprecedented industry, he translated the other heathen poets of antiquity, while August Wilhelm Schlegel translated the Christian poets of the romantic-Catholic period. Secret polemical motives inspired them both. Voss aimed to advance classic poetry and modes of thought through his translations, while A. W. Schlegel sought, through good translations, to make the Christian-romantic poets accessible to the public for imitation and culture. In sooth, this antagonism manifested itself even in the forms of speech used by the two translators. While Schlegel became ever more fastidious and finical in his style, Voss grew more brusque and rugged. The language in the latter's later translations is as rough as a file, and at times almost unpronounceable. If one is liable to slip on the smooth, highly-polished, mahogany-like surface of Schlegel's poems, there is equal danger of stumbling over Voss's versified blocks of granite. In a spirit of rivalry, Voss finally attempted a translation of Shakespeare, a work which Schlegel had accomplished so successfully in his earlier years. In this undertaking Voss fared very badly, and his publisher still worse; the translation was a total failure. If Schlegel's translation, perhaps, reads too smoothly; if his verses sometimes give the impression of whipped cream, and leave the reader in doubt whether it is to be eaten or be drunk;—Voss's, on the other hand, is as hard as stone, and reading his verses aloud makes one fear a dislocation of the jaw-bone. But that which especially distinguished Voss was the energy with which he battled against all difficulties; he not only wrestled with the German language, but also with that aristocratic Jesuitic monster, which at that period raised its unsightly head from amidst the dark forest depths of German literature: and Voss dealt the monster a telling blow.

Herr Wolfgang Menzel, a German author, who is known as one of the bitterest opponents of Voss, dubs him "a Saxon boor." Notwithstanding the unfriendly sense in which this epithet is applied, it is nevertheless very fitting. In truth, Voss is "a Saxon boor," just as Luther was one: he lacks all that is chivalrous, courteous, and gracious; he was every inch one of that rude, rough, sturdy race, to whom Christianity could be preached only by fire and sword, and who only submitted to that religion after losing three battles, but who in their customs and ways still retain much of the old Norse pagan doggedness, and in their material and intellectual combats show themselves as valiant and as stubborn as their ancient gods. When I contemplate Johann Heinrich Voss in his polemics and in his whole manner, I seem to see before me the ancient one-eyed Odin himself, who has left Asgard and has become a school-teacher in the province of Hadeln, and there teaches Latin declination and the Christian catechism to the little flaxen-haired Holsteiners; in his leisure hours he translates the Greek poets into German, and borrows from Thor his great hammer to beat the verses into shape; but after a while, becoming tired of the tedious work, he takes the hammer and cracks poor Fritz Stolberg on the head.

That was a famous affair. Frederick, Count of Stolberg, was a poet of the old school, and was remarkably popular in Germany, not, perhaps, so much on account of his poetic talents as for his title of count, which at that time counted for more in German literature than it does now. Fritz Stolberg, however, was a liberal man and had a noble heart, and he was a friend of those less patrician youths, who in Göttingen were seeking to found a poetic school. I recommend French literary men to read the preface to the poems of Hölty, in which Johann Heinrich Voss describes the idyllic life of the band of poets of which he and Fritz Stolberg were members. Time passed, and these two only were left of all that galaxy of youthful poets. When Fritz Stolberg, with great *éclat*, joined the Catholic Church, abjuring reason and the love of freedom, becoming a promoter of intellectual darkness, and by his aristocratic example drawing many weaklings after him—then Johann Heinrich Voss, the venerable man of three-score and ten, publicly entered the lists against the friend of his youth, and wrote the little book, *Wie Ward Fritz Stolberg ein Unfreier?* In it he analysed Stolberg's whole life, and showed how the aristocratic tendency in the nature of his old comrade had always existed, and that after the events of the French Revolution that tendency had steadily become more pronounced; that Stolberg had secretly joined an association of the nobility, which had for its purpose to counteract the French ideas of liberty; that these nobles entered into a league with the Jesuits; that they sought, through the re-establishment of Catholicism, to advance also the interests of the nobility: he exposed in general the ways and means by which the reactionists were seeking to bring about the restoration of the Christian-Catholic-feudal middle ages, and the destruction of Protestant intellectual freedom and the political rights of the commonalty. Once, ere the era of revolutions, good fellowship existed between German democracy and German aristocracy; the former hoped for nothing, the latter feared nothing; but now as grey-beards, they faced each other, and fought a duel for life or death.

That portion of the German public which did not comprehend the significance and terrible necessity of this struggle blamed poor Voss for the ruthless revelation of confidential relations and private affairs, which, however, taken as a whole, conclusively proved the correctness of his charges. Then certain so-called æsthetic souls, far too exalted and refined for such petty gossip, raised an outcry, and accused poor Voss of being a scandal-monger. Other good citizens, who feared that the curtain might be drawn from them, and their own miserable shortcomings be exposed, waxed indignant over the violation of the established rules of literary polemics, which strictly forbid all personalities and disclosures of private affairs. It so happened that Fritz Stolberg died soon after, and his death was attributed to grief; and when, immediately after his death, his *Liebesbüchlein* was published, in which he assumes the true Jesuitic tone, and speaks of his poor deluded friend in terms of pious Christian forgiveness—then the tears of German compassion fell thick and fast, and the German Michel[10] assumed his most lugubrious expression, and all this flood of sentimentality was turned into wrath against poor Voss; and most of the abuse heaped upon him came from the very ones for whose intellectual and material welfare he had battled.

When one gets soundly thrashed in Germany one can always count on the pity and tears of the multitude. In this respect the Germans resemble those old crones who never miss an opportunity of witnessing an execution, and who eagerly press to the front of the curious spectators, setting up a bitter lamentation at sight of the poor wretch, and even taking his part. The snivelling old women who attend literary executions, and put on such grief-stricken airs, would nevertheless be very much disappointed if the poor sinner was suddenly to receive a pardon, and they be sent trudging homeward without beholding the anticipated flogging. Their worst fury would then be directed against the one who had balked their expectation.

Meanwhile Voss's polemical writings exerted a powerful influence upon the masses, and turned the current of public opinion against that predilection for mediævalism which had been all the fashion. His writings aroused Germany; many declared for Voss personally; a greater portion supported his cause alone. The controversy waxed fiercer and fiercer; attacks and rejoinders followed in quick succession, and the last days of the old man were embittered by these quarrels. He had to deal with the most dangerous opponents, the priesthood, who attacked him under the most-varied guises. Not only the Crypto-Catholic, but also the Pietists, the Quietists, the Lutheran Mystics; in brief, all the supernaturalistic sects of the Protestant church, no matter how decidedly they differed from one another in their creeds, yet they all agreed in their great hatred of Johann Heinrich Voss, the rationalist. This name is in Germany applied to those who hold that the claims of reason should not be put aside in matters of religion, in opposition to the supernaturalists, who to a greater or less degree discard reason in religion. The latter, in their furious hate of the poor rationalists, resemble the inmates of a lunatic asylum, who, although they will not believe in each other's hallucinations, yet in a measure tolerate one another. But with all the fiercer hate do they turn against the man whom they consider their common enemy, who is no other than the physician who seeks to restore their reason.

While the romantic school was severely damaged in public opinion by the discovery of its Catholic tendencies, about the same time it received an utterly crushing blow in its own temple, and that, too, from one of those gods whom itself had enshrined there. For it was Wolfgang Goethe who descended from his pedestal to pronounce the doom of the Schlegels, the same high-priests who had offered him so much incense. That voice annihilated the whole pack of hobgoblins; the spectres of the middle ages fled; the owls crept again into their obscure castle-ruins, and the ravens fluttered back to their old church-steeples. Frederic Schlegel went to Vienna, where he attended mass daily and ate broiled fowl; A. W. Schlegel withdrew into the pagoda of Brahma.

Frankly confessed, Goethe at that time played a very ambiguous rôle, and cannot be unconditionally praised. It is true, the Schlegels never were sincere with him; perhaps they built him an altar, and offered him incense, and taught the multitude to kneel before him, only because, in their warfare against the old school, they needed a living poet to set up as a model, and found none more suited for their purpose than Goethe; and, perhaps, also, because they expected some literary favours from him. Moreover, he was at such an easy distance from them. The road from Jena to Weimar leads through an avenue of fine plum trees, and the luscious fruit is very acceptable to the wayfarer when parched with the summer heat. The Schlegels often travelled this road, and in Weimar they had many an interview with Herr Geheimrath von Goethe, who was always a finished diplomat. He listened quietly to what the Schlegels had to say, smiled approvingly, occasionally dined them, showed them various favours, etc. They also approached Schiller, but the latter was an honest, straight-forward man, and would have nothing to do with them. The correspondence between Schiller and Goethe, which was published three years ago, throws considerable light on the relations between these two poets and the Schlegels. Goethe, haughtily and contemptuously, mocks at them; Schiller is angry at their impertinent scandal-mongering, and at their passion for notoriety, and he calls them "puppies."

But although Goethe assumed such haughty airs towards them, it is nevertheless true that he was indebted to the Schlegels for the greater portion of his fame, for it was they who introduced and promoted the study of his writings. The contemptuous and insulting manner with which he eventually cast them off has a very strong flavour of ingratitude. Perhaps Goethe, with his clear insight, was vexed that the Schlegels should seek to use him as an instrument to accomplish their projects. Perhaps those projects threatened to compromise him as the minister of a Protestant state. Perhaps it was the ancient pagan godlike wrath that awoke in him at sight of the mouldy Catholic follies. For as Voss resembled the stalwart one-eyed Odin, so did Goethe, in form and figure, resemble great Jupiter. The former was compelled to pound long and vigorously with his Thor's hammer; the latter needed but angrily to shake his majestic head, with its ambrosial locks, and the Schlegels trembled and crept out of sight. A public statement of Goethe's opposition to the romantic school appeared in his journal, *Kunst und Alterthum*, and bore the title, *Concerning the Christian-Patriotic-New-German School of Art*. With this article Goethe made his eighteenth brumaire in German literature, for by chasing the Schlegels so summarily out of the temple, and attaching to himself so many of their young and zealous disciples, and being hailed with acclamations by the public, to whom the Schlegelian directory had long been obnoxious, he established his autocratic sovereignty in German literature. From that hour nothing more was heard of the Schlegels. Only now and then their names were mentioned, just as one sometimes casually speaks of Barras or of Gohier. Neither romantic nor classic poetry was henceforth spoken of; everywhere it was nothing but Goethe. It is true that several other poets arose in the meantime, who, in power and imagination, were but little inferior to Goethe. But out of courtesy they acknowledged him as their chief; they paid homage to him, they kissed his hand, they knelt before him. These grandees of Parnassus differed from the common multitude in being permitted to wear their laurel-wreaths in Goethe's presence. Sometimes they even attacked him; but they were always vexed when one of the lesser ones ventured to assail him. No matter how angry aristocrats are with their sovereign, they are always displeased when plebeians also dare to revolt. And, in truth, the aristocrats of intellect had, during the last twenty years, very good reasons to be irritated against Goethe. As I myself unreservedly remarked at the time, not without bitterness, "Goethe resembled Louis XI. of France, who abased the powerful nobility and exalted the *tiers état.*"

That was despicable. Goethe feared every writer of independence and originality, but glorified and praised all the petty authorlings. He carried this so far, that to be praised by Goethe came at last to be considered a brevet of mediocrity.

Later I shall speak of the new poets who grew up during the Goethean imperialism. They constitute a forest of young trees, whose true magnitude has become perceptible only since the fall of that century-old oak by whose branches they had been so completely overtopped and overshadowed. As already stated, there was not lacking a bitter and zealous opposition against Goethe, that giant oak. Men of the most diverse opinions were banded together in this opposition. The orthodox were vexed that in the trunk of this great tree there was no niche provided for the statuettes of the saints, but that, on the contrary, even the nude dryads of heathendom were permitted to carry on their witchery beneath it. The pietists would gladly have imitated Saint Boniface, and with consecrated axe have felled this magic oak. The liberals, on the other hand, were indignant that they could not use it as a liberty tree and as a barricade. But, in truth, the tree was too lofty to have a red cap placed on its top, or a carmagnole danced beneath it. But the public at large honoured it just because it was so stately and independent; because it filled the whole world with its delicious fragrance; because its branches towered majestically to the heavens, so that the stars seemed to be merely the golden fruit of the great and wonderful tree.

It is true, the opposition against Goethe began with the appearance of the so-called pseudo *Wanderjahre*, which was published by Gottfried Basse of Quedlinburg, under the title of *Wilhelm Meister's Wanderjahre*, in 1821; that is, soon after the downfall of the Schlegels. Goethe had announced a sequel to his Wilhelm *Meister's Lehrjahre*, under this title, and very strangely it appeared simultaneously with its literary double, in which not only was Goethe's style imitated, but the hero of Goethe's original novel was represented as the leading personage. This parody evinced much talent, and still greater tact, for as the author managed to maintain his anonymity for a considerable period, baffling all endeavours to discover his personality, public interest was artificially stimulated. Finally it transpired that the author was a hitherto unknown village parson, by the name of Pustkuchen, which translated into French would be *omelette soufflée*, a name which aptly describes the very essence of his book. It was nothing else than the old, stale, sour dough of the pietists, æsthetically kneaded over. In this book it was cast up to Goethe, as a reproach, that his poems had no moral aim; that he could create no lofty characters, but only low, vulgar creatures; that Schiller, on the contrary, had produced the most ideal and exalted conceptions, and that therefore the latter was a greater poet.

That Schiller was a greater poet than Goethe was the special point which Pustkuchen's book sought to establish, and for which it was written. It became the fashion to institute comparisons between the writings of the two poets, and the public divided into partisan camps. The admirers of Schiller enthusiastically praised the purity and nobility of a Max Piccolomini, of a Thekla, of Posa, and other of Schiller's dramatic heroes; on the other hand, they stigmatised Goethe's Philine, Käthchen, Clärchen, and the like pretty creatures, as immoral jades. Goethe's adherents would smilingly admit that neither Goethe's heroes nor his heroines could be called moral, but they claimed that the promotion of morality in nowise came within the province of art. In art, asserted they, as in the universe itself, there is no ulterior purpose; it is only man who introduces the conceptions of end and means. Art, like the universe, said they, exists for itself alone. Although the opinions of mankind concerning the universe are continually changing, the universe itself remains ever the same; so also must art remain uninfluenced by the temporary views of mankind. Art must be kept especially independent of systems of morality, for these change on earth as often as a new religion arises, and supersedes an older faith. In fact, as after the lapse of a number of centuries a new religion always makes its appearance, influences the customs, and thus makes itself felt as a new system of morality, so in every period the art works of the past would be branded as heretical and immoral, were they to be judged by the temporary standard of morality. We have, in truth, lived to see good Christians, who condemn the flesh as of Satan, experience a feeling of anger at sight of the Greek mythological statues. Chaste monks have put an apron on the antique Venus; the ridiculous custom of bestowing a fig leaf on nude figures has continued even up to the present. A pious Quaker went so far as to sacrifice his whole fortune in buying up and burning Giulo Romano's most beautiful mythological paintings; truly he deserves for his pains to reach heaven, and there to be flogged daily. A religion which should recognise God in matter only, and should regard the flesh only as divine, would, when it had impressed itself upon the customs of men, give rise to a system of morality, according to which those works of art which glorify the flesh would be alone deemed worthy of praise; and on the contrary, those Christian art works which depict the nothingness of the flesh would be considered as immoral. The works of art which are accepted as moral in one land would be considered immoral in

69

another country, where a different religion had generated different customs. Thus, our pictorial arts awaken the disgust of a strict Mahometan, while much that in the harems of the Orient is regarded as quite innocent would be an abomination in the eyes of Christians. In India the occupation of a Bayadere is not regarded as dishonourable; hence, the drama of "Vasantasena," the heroine of which is a courtesan, is there not at all considered immoral. If, however, the Théâtre Français ventured to produce this play, the whole pit would raise the cry of "immorality"—the same pit that witnesses with delight plays whose plots are amorous intrigues, and whose heroines are young widows who remarry at the end of the play, instead of having themselves burned to death on their deceased husband's funeral pyre, as required by Hindoo morality.

Starting with this idea, the Goetheans viewed art as a separate, independent world, which they would rank so high, that all the changing and changeable doings of mankind, their religions and systems of morality, should surge far below it. I cannot unconditionally endorse this view; but the Goetheans were led so far astray by it as to proclaim art in and of itself as the highest good. Thus they were induced to hold themselves aloof from the claims of the world of reality, which, after all, is entitled to precedence.

Schiller united himself to the world of reality much more decidedly than did Goethe; and he deserves praise for this. The living spirit of the times thrilled through Frederic Schiller; it wrestled with him; it vanquished him; he followed it to battle; he bore its banner, and, lo! it was the same banner under which the conflict was being enthusiastically waged across the Rhine, and for which we are always ready to shed our heart's best blood. Schiller wrote for the grand ideas of the Revolution; he razed the bastilles of the intellect; he helped to erect the temple of freedom, that colossal temple which shelters all nations like a single congregation of brothers: in brief, he was a cosmopolitan. He began his career with that hate of the past which we behold in *The Robbers*. In this work he resembles a diminutive Titan who has run away from school, got tipsy with schnapps, and throws stones at Jupiter's windows. He ended with that love for the future which already in his *Don Carlos* blossoms forth like a field of flowers. Schiller is himself that Marquis Posa who is simultaneously prophet and soldier, and battles for that which he foretells. Under that Spanish cloak throbs the noblest heart that ever loved and suffered in Germany.

The poet is, on a small scale, but the imitator of the Creator, and also resembles God in creating his characters after his own image. If, therefore, Carl Moor and the Marquis Posa are wholly Schiller himself, so in like manner does Goethe resemble his Werther, his Wilhelm Meister, and his Faust, in whom the different phases of his intellect can be studied. While Schiller devotes himself to the history of the race, and becomes an enthusiast for the social progress of mankind, Goethe, on the other hand, applies himself to the study of the individual, to nature and to art. The physical sciences must of necessity have finally become a leading branch of study with Goethe, the pantheist, and in his poems, as well as in his scientific works, he gave us the result of his researches. His indifferentism was to a certain extent the result of his pantheistic views.

Alas! we must confess that pantheism has often led men into indifferentism. They reasoned thus: if everything is God; if everything is divine, then it is indifferent whether man occupies himself with clouds or ancient gems; with folk-songs or the anatomy of apes; with real human beings or play-actors. But that is just the mistake. Everything is not God, but God is everything. He does not manifest himself equally in all things, but He shows himself in different degrees according to the various matters. Everything bears within itself an impulse to strive after a higher degree of divinity, and that is the great law of progress throughout all nature. The recognition of this law, which has been most profoundly revealed by the disciples of St. Simon, now makes pantheism a cosmic, universal theory, which not only does not lead to indifferentism, but, on the contrary, induces the most self-sacrificing endeavours. No, God does not manifest himself in all things equally, as Wolfgang Goethe believed, who through such a belief became an indifferentist, and, instead of devoting himself to the highest interests of humanity, occupied himself with art, anatomy, theories of colour, botanical studies, and observations of the clouds. No, God is manifest in some things to a greater degree than in others. He lives in motion, in action, in time. His holy breath is wafted through the pages of history, which is God's true book of record. Frederic Schiller felt this, and became an historian, a "prophet of the past," and wrote the *Revolt of the Netherlands*, the *Thirty Years' War*, the *Maid of Orleans*, and *William Tell*.

It is true Goethe also depicted a few of the great struggles of freedom, but he portrayed them as an artist. Christian zeal was odious to him, and he angrily turned from it; and the enthusiasm for philosophy, which is characteristic of our epoch, he either could not understand or purposely avoided understanding, for fear of ruffling his customary tranquillity of mind; so he treated all enthusiasm objectively and historically; as a datum, as a subject to be written about. In his hands the living spirit became dead matter, and he invested it with a lovely and pleasing form. He became thus the greatest artist of our literature, and all that he wrote was a finished work of art.

The example of the master misled the disciples, and there arose in Germany that literary epoch which I once designated as the "art period," and which, as I then showed, had a most disastrous influence on the political development of the German people. At the same time, I by no means deny the intrinsic worth of the Goethean masterpieces. They adorn our beloved fatherland just as beautiful statues embellish a garden; but they are only statues after all. One may fall in love with them, but they are barren. Goethe's poems do not, like Schiller's, beget deeds. Deeds are the offspring of words; but Goethe's pretty words are childless. That is the curse of all that which has originated in mere art. The statue which Pygmalion wrought was a beautiful woman, and even the sculptor himself fell in love with her. His kisses warmed her into life, but, so far as we know, she never bore children. I believe a similar idea has been suggested by Charles Nodier, and this thought came into my mind while wandering through the Louvre, as my glance alighted on the statues of the ancient gods. There they stood, with their white, expressionless eyes, a mysterious melancholy in their stony smiles.

71

Perhaps they are haunted by sad memories of Egypt, that land of the dead from which they came; or perhaps it is a mournful longing for the life from which other divinities have expelled them, or a grieving over their immortality of death. They seem to be awaiting the word that shall liberate them from their cold, motionless rigidity and bring them back to life. How strange that these antique statues should remind me of the Goethean creations, which are likewise so perfect, so beautiful, so motionless, and which also seem oppressed with a dumb grieving that their rigidity and coldness separate them from our present warm, restless life—that they cannot speak and rejoice with us, and that they are not human beings, but unhappy mixtures of divinity and stone.

These few hints will explain the publicly-expressed opposition of the various parties in Germany to Goethe. The orthodox were highly incensed against the great heathen, as Goethe was generally called in Germany; they feared his influence upon the people, whom he indoctrinated with his manner of viewing the world through merry verses, even through the simplest and most unpretentious ballads. They saw in him the most dangerous foe of the Cross, which, as he expressed himself, was as odious to him as vermin, garlic, and tobacco; at least, that is about the purport of the Xenie which Goethe dared to publish in Germany, the very country where vermin, garlic, tobacco, and the Cross form a holy alliance, and are supreme over all. But it was not this that displeased us, the party of action. As previously stated, we found fault with Goethe for the barrenness of his writings; for the engrossing devotion to art, which through him was diffused over Germany; for his influence in creating among the German youth an apathy which was a hindrance to the political regeneration of our fatherland. Hence the indifferentist and pantheist was assailed from the most diverse sides. To use an illustration from French parliamentary life, the extreme right and the extreme left formed an alliance against him. While the cassocked priests brandished the crucifix over him, furious *sans-culottes* simultaneously assaulted him with the pike.

Wolfgang Menzel, who had carried on the war against Goethe with a display of talent worthy of a better cause, evinced in his polemics that he was not merely a one-sided spiritualistic Christian, or a discontented patriot; he rather based a portion of his attacks on the latest remark of Frederic Schlegel, who, after his fall, from the recesses of his Catholic cathedral, gave utterance to his woe concerning Goethe; Goethe, "whose poetry lacked a central point." Menzel went still further, and showed that Goethe was not a man of genius, but only of talent; Schiller, however, was a genius, etc. This was some time before the July Revolution; Menzel was at that time a great admirer of the middle ages, of mediæval art as well as of institutions; he was incessantly attacking Johann Heinrich Voss, and praising Joseph Görres with an enthusiasm hitherto unheard of. These facts prove that Menzel was sincere in his hatred of Goethe, and that he did not write against him merely to make himself conspicuous, as many thought. Although I, myself, was at that time an opponent of Goethe, yet I was displeased at the harshness with which Menzel criticised him, and I complained of this want of respect. I said, Goethe is nevertheless the king of our literature, and in applying the knife of criticism to such a one, it always behoves us to show a proper courtesy, just as the executioner who was to behead Charles I., before performing the duties of his office, knelt before the king and begged his royal forgiveness.

Among the opponents of Goethe was the famous Hofrath Müllner, and his only remaining friend, Professor Schütz. There were several others of less celebrity— Herr Spann, for instance, who had been imprisoned for a long time on account of political offences—belonged to the public adversaries of Goethe. In confidence, dear reader, it was a very motley crowd. The ostensible reasons I have sufficiently indicated, but it is more difficult to guess what special motive influenced each individual to give publicity to his anti-Goethean sentiments. I know the secret motives of only one of these persons, and as that one is myself, I will frankly confess that I was envious of Goethe. To my credit I must say that I assailed in Goethe only the man, never the poet. Unlike those critics who, with their finely-polished glasses, claim to have also detected spots upon the moon, I could never discern blemishes in Goethe's works. What these sharp-sighted people consider spots are blooming forests, silvery streams, lofty mountains, and smiling valleys.

Nothing is more foolish than to depreciate Goethe in order thereby to exalt Schiller, whom it was always customary to praise in order to disparage Goethe. Do such critics really not know that those highly-extolled, highly-idealised figures, those sacred pictures of virtue and morality which Schiller produced, were much easier to construct than those frail, worldly beings of whom Goethe gives us a glimpse in his works? Do they not know that mediocre painters generally select sacred subjects, which they daub in life-size on the canvas? But it requires a great master to paint with lifelike fidelity and technical perfection a Spanish beggar-boy scratching himself, or a Netherlandish peasant having a tooth extracted, or some hideous old woman such as we see in Dutch cabinet pictures. In art it is much easier to picture large tragic subjects than those which are small and droll. The Egyptian sorcerers could imitate Moses in many of his tragic feats: they could make serpents, and blood, and frogs; but when Moses created vermin, which would seemingly be less difficult to copy, then they confessed their impotence, and said, "It is the finger of God." Rail as you will at the coarseness of certain portions of Faust, at the scenes on the Brocken and in Auerbach's cellar, inveigh against the licentiousness in *Wilhelm Meister*, it is nevertheless more than you can do; it is the finger of Goethe! But I hear you say, with disgust, "We do not wish to create such things. We are no sorcerers; we are good Christians." I know quite well that you are no sorcerers.

Goethe's greatest merit consists in the perfection of all his works. Here are no portions that are strong while others are weak; here no one part is painted in detail while another is merely sketched; here is no confusion, nor any of the customary padding, nor any undue partiality for certain special characters. Goethe treats every person that appears in his romances and dramas as if he or she were the leading character. So it is with Homer, so with Shakespeare. In the works of all great poets there are, in fact, no minor characters at all; every character in its place is the chief personage. Such poets are absolute monarchs, and resemble the Emperor Paul of Russia, who, when the French ambassador remarked that a man of importance in his empire was interested in a certain matter, sharply interrupted the speaker with the memorable words—"In my empire there is no man of importance except he to whom I may happen to be speaking; and he is of importance only so long as I address him." An absolute poet, who also holds power by the grace of God, in like manner views that person in his intellectual realm as the most important who at that particular moment is speaking through his pen. From this art-despotism arises that wonderful perfection of the most trivial and unimportant figures which we find in the works of Homer, Shakespeare, and Goethe.

If I have spoken rather harshly of Goethe's adversaries, I should have cause to criticise his defenders still more severely, for most of the latter, in their zeal, have been guilty of even greater follies. At the head of those who have made themselves ridiculous in this respect is one by the name of Eckermann, a writer not generally lacking in talent. In the campaign against Pustkuchen, Carl Immermann, who is now our greatest dramatic poet, won his spurs as a critic by publishing an excellent *brochure*. Berlin chiefly distinguished itself on this occasion. Goethe's leading champion, at all times, was Varnhagen von Ense, a man whose heart is filled with thoughts grand as the universe, and who expresses them in words as precious and as dainty as cut jewels. He is the noble-minded man in whose judgment Goethe ever placed the most reliance. Perhaps it may be well to mention here that Wilhem von Humboldt once wrote an excellent book concerning Goethe. During the last ten years every Leipsic Fair has brought to light a large number of works on Goethe. Herr Schubart's studies of Goethe are among the marvels of fine criticism. Herr Häring, whose *nom de plume* is Willibald Alexis, has written for various periodicals clever and valuable articles on Goethe. Herr Zimmermann, professor at Hamburg, has, in his oral lectures, given some most excellent criticisms of Goethe; in his writings on dramaturgy we find similar thoughts, more briefly expressed, perhaps, but more profound. At various German universities there were courses of lectures on Goethe, and of all his works the public chiefly devoted itself to the study of *Faust*. It was the theme of endless dissertations and commentaries, and became the secular Bible of the Germans.

I would be no true German if I wrote of *Faust* without giving expression to some explanatory thoughts concerning it, for from the greatest thinker down to the most insignificant penny-a-liner, from philosophers down to professors of philosophy, every one tries his wit on this book. It is, in fact, as wide in its compass as the Bible; like the latter, it embraces heaven and earth, mankind and its exegesis. The subject matter of *Faust* is the chief reason of its popularity, and its selection from among the many folk-legends is a proof of Goethe's profound judgment and genius, which ever seized on that which was nearest and best. I may assume that the story of *Faust* is familiar to my readers, for the book has recently become celebrated in France also; but I know not if the original legend itself is known here. I know not if at your annual rustic fairs there is hawked for sale a little book of grey, fleecy paper, badly printed, with rude woodcuts, containing a circumstantial account of how the arch-sorcerer, Johannes Faustus, a learned scholar who had studied all the sciences, finally threw away his books and made a compact with the devil, by which he was enabled to enjoy all the material pleasures of the earth, but in return for which his soul was to be given up to the powers of hell. During the middle ages the populace attributed all extraordinary intellectual powers to a compact with the devil, and Albertus Magnus, Raimond Lullus, Theophrastus Paracelsus, Agrippa von Nettesheim, and Roger Bacon in England, were held to be magicians, sorcerers, and conjurers. But the ballads and romances tell much stranger stories concerning Doctor Faustus, who is reputed to have demanded from the devil not only a knowledge of the profoundest secrets of nature, but also the most realistic physical pleasures. This is the self-same Faust who invented printing,[11] and who lived at a time when people began to inveigh against the strictness of church authority, and to make independent researches. With Faust the mediæval epoch of faith ends, and the modern era of critical, scientific investigation begins. It is, in fact, of the greatest significance that Faust should have lived, according to popular tradition, at the very beginning of the Reformation, and that he himself should have invented printing, the art which gave science the victory over faith; an art, however, which has also robbed us of the catholic peace of mind, and plunged us into doubts and revolutions, and had finally delivered us into the power of Satan. But no! knowledge, science, the comprehension of nature through reason, eventually gives us the enjoyments of which faith, that is, Catholic Christianity, has so long defrauded us; we now recognise the truth that mankind is destined to an earthly, as well as to a heavenly equality. The political brotherhood which philosophy inculcates is more beneficial to us than the purely spiritual brotherhood, for which we are indebted to Christianity. The thought becomes transformed into words, the words become deeds, and we may yet be happy during our life on this earth. If in addition to this, we also attain after death that heavenly felicity which Christianity promises so assuredly, so much the better.

The German people had, for a long time, felt a profound presentiment of this, for the Germans themselves are that learned Doctor Faust; they themselves are that spiritualist, who, having at last comprehended the inadequateness of the spiritual life alone, reinstates the flesh in its rights. But still biassed by the symbolism of Catholic poetry, in which God is pictured as the representative of the spirit, and the devil as that of the flesh, the rehabilitation of the flesh was characterised as an apostasy from God, and a compact with the devil.

But some time must yet elapse ere the deeply-significant prophecy of that poem will be fulfilled as regards the German people, and the spirit itself, comprehending the usurpation of spiritualism, become the champion of the rights of the flesh. That will be the Revolution, the great daughter of the Reformation.

Less known in France than *Faust* is Goethe's *West-Ostlichen Divan*, a later work with which Madame de Staël was unacquainted, and which demands especial notice. It reveals the peculiar thoughts and feelings of the Orient in graceful ballads and pithy proverbs, which exhale an atmosphere of fragrance and passion, like a harem of love-sick odalisques, with the dark eyes of gazelles, and amorous white arms. The reader is filled with a mixed sensation of shuddering and desire, like lucky Caspar Debureau, when he stood at the top of a ladder in Constantinople, and beheld *de haut en bas* what the Commander of the Faithful is wont to see only *de bas en haut*. At times a feeling steals o'er the reader as if he lay comfortably stretched upon a Persian carpet, smoking a long Turkish pipe, filled with the yellow tobacco of Turkestan, while a negress slave gently waves over him a variegated fan of peacock feathers, and a handsome boy serves a cup of Mocha coffee—the sweetest and most blissful sense of life and its pleasures has Goethe expressed in these verses—in verses so dainty, so felicitous, so airy, so ethereal, that one is lost in astonishment that such things are possible in the German language. In addition to all this, the book contains the most beautiful prose descriptions and explanations of the customs and manners of the Orient, the patriarchal life of the Arabs; and withal Goethe is as easy, merry, and harmless as a child, and yet as full of wisdom as a greybeard. Goethe's prose in this work is as translucent as the green sea, when, on a bright, calm summer afternoon, we can look far down into the depths below, and catch glimpses of ancient drowned cities, and all their fabulous splendours. Then, at times, that prose is as magical and as mysterious as the firmament, when the darkness of twilight has lifted, and the grand Goethean thoughts appear, pure and golden, like the stars. The charm of this book is indescribable; it is a salaam sent by the Occident to the Orient, and many a quaint and curious flower is gathered there; passionate red roses, snowdrops white as a maiden's bosom, comical dandelions, purple digitalis like long human fingers, contorted crocuses, and peeping slyly forth, in the midst, modest German violets. The meaning of this salaam is that the Occident, grown weary of its frigid, meagre spiritualism, seeks again to refresh itself amid the wholesome physical pleasures of the Orient. After Goethe had expressed in *Faust* his aversion to abstract spiritualism, and his desire for realistic enjoyments, in writing the *West-Ostlichen Divan* he threw himself with his whole soul, as it were, into the arms of sensualism.

Hence it is of the utmost significance that this work appeared soon after *Faust*. It was the last phase of Goethe's genius, and his example was of the greatest influence upon literature. The Orient was now the theme of our lyric poets. It may be worthy of mention, that while Goethe so rapturously celebrated Persia and Arabia in his verses, he expressed the most decided aversion to India. The bizarre and confused characteristics of that country were repugnant to him, and perhaps this dislike originated in the suspicion that some Catholic stratagem was at the bottom of the Sanscrit studies of the Schlegels and their friends. These men regarded Hindostan as the cradle of Catholicism; they claimed to have discovered there the model of the Catholic hierarchy, the doctrine of the trinity, of the incarnation, of penance, of atonement, of the maceration of the flesh, and all their other favourite crotchets. Goethe's antipathy towards India nettled these people not a little, and A. W. Schlegel, with transparent malice, called him "a heathen converted to Mahometanism."

Amongst the most noteworthy writings on Goethe which have appeared this year is a posthumous work by Johannes Falk, entitled *Goethe aus Persönlichen Umgange Dargestellt*. With the exception of a detailed treatise on *Faust*, which, of course, must not be omitted, the author of this book has given us most excellent sketches of Goethe; he has depicted him in all the walks of life, naturally, impartially, with all his virtues and all his failings. In this book we behold Goethe in his relations to his mother, whose temperament was so wonderfully reflected in that of her son; we see him as the naturalist, watching a caterpillar developing into a butterfly; we see the great Herder expostulating with him against the indifferentism with which he let the development of humanity itself pass before him, unregarded; we behold him at the court of the Grand Duke of Weimar, seated among the blonde court dames, making merry improvisations, like Apollo guarding the flocks of King Admetus; again we see him, with the haughtiness of a Dalai-Lama, refusing to recognise Kotzebue; then we see the latter giving a public celebration in honour of Schiller, in order thereby to depreciate Goethe; we see him in all things, wise, handsome, amiable, a blessed and inspiring figure, like the eternal gods.

In fact, that harmony of personal appearance with genius, which we demand in eminent men, existed in its fullest degree in Goethe. His outward appearance was as impressive as the thoughts that live in his writings. His figure was symmetrical and majestic, and in that noble form Grecian art might be studied as in an ancient statue. That stately form was never bent in Christian humility; the features of that noble countenance were never distorted with Christian self-reproach; those eyes were never downcast with Christian remorse, nor turned devoutly and tremulously towards heaven. No, his eyes had a godlike steadfastness, for it is in general the distinctive mark of a god, that his look is unmoved. Hence when Agni, Varuna, Yama, and Indra assume the form of Nala at Damayanti's wedding, the latter recognises her lover by the twitching of his eyes, for, as I have said, the eyes of a god are always steadfast and unmoved.

Napoleon's eyes possessed this peculiarity, and hence I am convinced that he also was a god. Goethe's eyes, even at an advanced age, remained just as godlike as in his youth, and although time could whiten, it could not bow that noble head. He always bore himself proudly and majestically, and when he spoke he seemed to grow statelier still, and when he stretched out his hand it seemed as though he could prescribe to the stars the paths they should traverse. It is said that a cold, egotistic twitching might be observed around the corners of his mouth. But this trait is also peculiar to the eternal gods, and especially to the father of gods, great Jupiter, to whom I have already likened Goethe. When I visited him at Weimar I involuntarily glanced around to see if I might not behold at his side the eagle with the thunderbolt in its beak. I was about to address him in Greek, but, as I noticed that he understood German, I told him in the latter language that the plums along the roadside from Jena to Weimar were excellent. Many a long winter's night I had pondered on the exalted and profound remarks I should make to Goethe if I should ever see him. And now that I did at last see him face to face, I told him that the plums of Saxony were delicious. And Goethe smiled.

He smiled with the same lips with which he had once kissed the beautiful Leda, Europa, Danaë, Semele, and many another princess or ordinary nymph.

Les Dieux s'en vont. Goethe is dead. He died on March 22nd, last year, that memorable year in which the world lost its greatest celebrities. It is as if death had become suddenly aristocratic, and sought to designate particularly the great ones of this earth by sending them contemporaneously to the grave. Perhaps death wished to found a *pairie* in the shadowy realms of Hades, in which case its *fournée* were well chosen. Or, perhaps, on the contrary, death sought during the past year to favour democracy by destroying these great celebrities, and their authority over the minds of men, and thus to bring about an intellectual equality. Was it out of respect or from irreverence that death spared the crowned heads during the past year? In a fit of abstraction death did raise his scythe over the King of Spain, but he recollected himself in time, and spared his life. During the past twelve months not a single king has died. *Les Dieux s'en vont*—but the kings are still with us.

. . . .

Schelling's influence on the romantic school was chiefly of a personal nature, but in addition to this, by the philosophy of nature which came into vogue through him, the poets have elevated themselves to much more profound conceptions of nature. One portion let themselves be absorbed with all their human emotions into nature; others remembered a few magic formulas, with which to conjure out of nature something that possessed human form and speech. The former were the genuine mystics, and resembled in many respects the devotees of India, who dissolve in nature, and at last begin to feel as if they and nature were one. The latter were rather sorcerers, who by their own will summoned forth even hostile spirits; they resembled those Arabian magicians, who, at their caprice, could endow stones with life, and turn living beings into stone. Novalis belonged to the first class, Hoffman to the latter. Novalis saw marvels in everything, and charming marvels they were. He listened to the language of the plants, he knew the secret of every young rose, finally he identified himself with all nature, and when autumn came and the leaves began to fall, then he died. Hoffman, on the contrary, saw spectres in everything; they nodded to him from every Chinese tea-pot, and from under each Berlin periwig. He was a sorcerer who transformed human beings into beasts, and beasts into human beings, even into royal Prussian court-counsellors. He would raise the dead from their graves, but life itself turned away from him, as from some gloomy spectre. He realised this; he felt that he himself had become a ghost. All nature was to him an imperfect mirror, in which he saw, distorted in a thousand ways, the cast of his own dead face; and his works are naught else than a horrible shriek of terror in twenty volumes.

Hoffman does not belong to the romantic school. He did not come into contact with the Schlegels, and was in no way affected by their tendencies. I only mention him in contrast to Novalis, who was peculiarly a poet of that school. Novalis is less known here than Hoffman, who has been introduced to the French public by Loeve-Veimars in a very attractive form, and thus has acquired a great reputation in France. In Germany, Hoffman is by no means *en vogue*, but he was so formerly. In their time his works were much read, but only by persons whose nerves were either too strong or too weak to be affected by less violent accords. The minds that were really intellectual, and the natures that were truly poetical, would have nothing to do with him. Such as these much preferred Novalis. But frankly confessed, Hoffman was a much greater poet than Novalis, for the latter with his idealistic pictures ever floats in the blue skies; while Hoffman, notwithstanding all his grotesque bogies, still clings fast to earthly realities. Just as the giant Anteus remained strong and invincible so long as his feet rested on mother earth, and lost his strength the moment Hercules held him aloft; so also the poet is strong and mighty as long as he does not forsake the *terra firma* of reality, but becomes powerless as soon as he attempts to float enraptured in the blue ether.

The great resemblance between these two poets lies in the fact that their poetry was really a disease. It has been said that it does not come within the province of the critic, but of the physician, to pass judgment on their writings. The rosy glow in Novalis's poems is not the hue of health, but the hectic flush of consumption; and the brilliant light in Hoffman's fantastic conceptions is not the flame of genius, but of fever.

But have we a right thus to criticise—we, who are ourselves not blest with robust health? and especially now, when all literature appears like one vast hospital? or is poetry, perhaps, a disease of humanity, as the pearl is the morbid matter of the diseased oyster?

Novalis was born May 2nd, 1772. His real name was Hardenberg. He loved a young lady who was afflicted with consumption, and died of that dread disease. This sad experience left its impress upon all his writings. His life was but a dreamy, lingering death, and he also died of consumption in 1801, before he had completed his twenty-ninth year, or his romance. This romance, in its present shape, is only the fragment of a great allegorical poem, which, like the divine comedy of Dante, was to embrace all earthly and celestial matters. Heinrich von Ofterdingen, the celebrated poet, is the hero of this romance. We see him as a youth in Eisenach, the pretty little village which lies at the foot of the ancient Wartburg, which has been the scene of some of the greatest, as well as some of the most stupid, deeds; for here Luther translated his Bible, and here, also, a few silly Teuto-maniacs burned Kamptz's *Gendarmerie-Codex*. At this burg was held the famous tournament of minstrelsy, at which, among other poets, Heinrich von Ofterdingen met Klingsohr of Hungary in the perilous duel of poetry, an account of which has been handed down to us in the Manessa collection. The head of the vanquished was to be forfeited to the executioner, and the Landgraf of Thuringia was the judge. Wartburg, the scene of his later glory, towers ominously over the hero's cradle, and we behold him, in the beginning of Novalis's romance, under the paternal roof at Eisenach. "The parents are abed and asleep, the old clock on the wall keeps up its monotonous ticking, the wind howls and the windows rattle; ever and anon the room is lit up by fitful glimpses of the moon.

"The youth lay tossing restlessly on his couch, thinking of the stranger and his narratives. 'It is not the treasures that have awakened within me such an unspeakable longing,' said he to himself; 'far from me is all avarice; but I yearn to behold the blue flower. It is always in my thoughts, and of nought else can I think or muse. I never felt so strangely before. It is as if until now I had been dreaming, or as if in my sleep I had passed into another world; for in the world in which I formerly dwelt, who would there have concerned themselves about flowers? And so strange a passion for a flower, I never heard of there.'"

These are the opening words of *Heinrich von Ofterdingen*, and the whole romance is full of the fragrance and the radiance of the blue flower. It is remarkable and significant that the most fabulous personages in this book seem as well known to us, as though in earlier times we had lived in friendly, confidential intercourse with them. Old memories awaken, Sophia's features are so familiar, and memory brings back long avenues of beech trees, the scene of so many promenades and tender caresses. But all this lies dimly back of us, like some half-forgotten dream.

The muse of Novalis was a fair and slender maiden, with earnest blue eyes, golden hyacinthine tresses, smiling lips, and a small mole on the left side of the chin, for I imagine his muse to be the self-same maid through whom I first became acquainted with his works, as I saw the red morocco-bound, gilt-edged volume, containing *Heinrich von Ofterdingen*, in her dainty fingers. She always dressed in blue, and her name was Sophia. She lived a few stations from Göttingen with her sister, the postmistress—a merry, buxom, ruddy-cheeked dame, whose full bust, surmounted with stiff white lace, resembled a fortress. This fortress, however, was impregnable; the good dame was a very Gibraltar of virtue. She was an industrious, practical housewife, and yet her only pleasure consisted in reading Hoffman's romances. Hoffman was just the writer who could agitate her coarse-grained nature and awaken pleasant emotions. But her pale, delicate sister was disagreeably affected at the mere sight of one of Hoffman's books, and if she accidentally laid hands on one, she shrank from the touch. She was as delicate as a sensitive plant, and her words were so fragrant and melodious, that, taken together, they were poetry. I have written down some of her sayings, and they are poems wholly after the manner of Novalis, only more tuneful and ethereal. One of them, which she recited to me as I bade her farewell ere setting out on my travels to Italy, is an especial favourite of mine. The time is autumn; the scene, a garden wherein there had been an illumination, and we hear the conversation between the last glimmering taper, the last rose, and a wild swan. The morning mists approach, the solitary light flickers and dies out, the rose leaves fall, and the swan unfolds its white wings and flies away to the south.

For Hanover abounds with wild swans that seek the warm south in autumn, and return again in summer. They probably spend the winter in Africa, for in the breast of a dead swan an arrow was once found, which Professor Blumenbach recognised as of African origin. The poor bird, with the arrow in its breast, had returned to its northern nest to die. But many a swan, when pierced by such an arrow, may not have the strength for such a journey, and is left helpless in the burning deserts, or with wearied pinions is perched on some Egyptian pyramid, gazing with longing eyes towards the north, towards the cool summer home in Hanover.

Late in the autumn of 1828, as I returned from the south, also with a burning arrow in my heart, my route led through the vicinity of Göttingen, and I stopped over at the dwelling-place of my old friend, the postmistress, in order to change horses. A long time had elapsed since I last saw her, and a woeful change had taken place in the good dame. Her buxom form still resembled a fortress,—but a ruined and dismantled fortress. The bastions were razed, no sentinels were on guard, and her heart, the citadel, was broken. The postillion, Pieper, informed me that she had even lost her relish for Hoffman's novels, but, as a substitute, she indulged all the more freely in brandy at bedtime. The latter is a much simpler plan, for the brandy is always at hand, whereas the novels must be procured at the Deurlich circulating library at Göttingen, at some hours' distance. Postillion Pieper was quite diminutive, and looked as sour as if the contraction in his size was the result of drinking vinegar. When I asked the fellow concerning the postmistress's sister, he answered, "She will soon die; she is already an angel," How good a being must she have been to draw from such a churlish person the remark, "She is an angel." While saying this, he was driving off the fluttering, cackling poultry, by kicking at them with his high top-boots. The house, once so white and cheerful, had changed for the worse, like its mistress; its colour was now a sickly yellow, and the walls were wrinkled with fissures. In the court-yard lay broken vehicles, and a postillion's scarlet mantle, soaking wet, was hanging on a post to dry. Mademoiselle Sophia stood by the window, reading, and when I approached her, I found it was a gilt-edged volume, bound in red morocco; it was Novalis's *Heinrich von Ofterdingen*. She had read and re-read this book, until its pages had inoculated her with consumption, and now she looked like a luminous shadow. But her beauty was now so ethereal, that the sight of it touched me most painfully. I took both of her pale, thin hands in mine, and looked steadily into her blue eyes, and then I asked, "Mademoiselle Sophia, how are you?" "I am well," she answered, "and I shall soon be still better!" Then she pointed out of the window to a little hillock, in the new churchyard, not far from the house. On this barren mound stood a small, thin, solitary poplar, almost leafless, and it swayed to and fro in the autumn winds, not like a living plant, but like the ghost of a tree.

Mademoiselle Sophia now lies under that poplar, and the gilt-edged, red morocco volume, Novalis's *Heinrich von Ofterdingen*, which she left me as a souvenir, lies on the desk before me as I write. I have used it in the composition of this chapter.

. . . .

Jean Paul Richter anticipated the Young Germany school in its most marked tendency. The latter, however, occupied with practical questions, avoided the abstract intricacies, the abrupt mannerisms, and the unenjoyable style of Jean

81

Paul Richter. No Frenchman with a clear, well-regulated mind can form a conception of that peculiar style. Jean Paul's style is a structure consisting entirely of very small compartments, which are sometimes so narrow that when one thought encounters another, their heads collide and bruise each other. From the ceiling are suspended hooks, on which Jean Paul hangs all sorts of ideas, and the walls are full of secret drawers, in which he conceals emotions. No German author is so rich as Jean Paul in ideas and in emotions; but he never permits them to ripen; and, notwithstanding his wealth of mind and heart, he excites more astonishment than pleasure. Thoughts and sentiments which would grow into colossal trees, if permitted to strike root properly and develop all their branches, blossoms, and leaves—these he uproots while they are still insignificant shrubs, mere sprouts even; and whole intellectual forests are thus served up to us as an ordinary dish. Now, although curious, this is decidedly unpalatable fare, for not every stomach can digest such a mess of young oaks, cedars, palms, and banana trees. Jean Paul is a great poet and philosopher; but no one can be more inartistic than he in his modes of thought and work, In his romances he has brought to light some truly poetical creations, but all his offspring carry with them a long umbilical cord in which they become entangled and choke.

Instead of thought he gives us his thinking itself. We see the material activity of his brain; he gives us, as it were, more brain than thought, and meanwhile the flashes of his wit skip about, like the fleas of his heated imagination. He is the merriest, and, at the same time, the most sentimental of authors. In fact, sentimentality always finally overcomes him, and his laughter abruptly turns into tears. He sometimes disguises himself as a gross, beggarly fellow; but then, like stage princes, he suddenly unbuttons the coarse overcoat and reveals the glittering insignia of his rank.

In this respect Jean Paul resembles Laurence Sterne, with whom he has been often compared. The author of *Tristram Shandy*, when apparently sunk in the most vulgar trivialities, possesses the art of rising by sudden transitions to the sublime, reminding us that he is of princely rank and the countryman of Shakespeare. Jean Paul, like Laurence Sterne, reveals in his writings his own personality, and lays bare his own human frailties; but yet with a certain awkward bashfulness, especially in sexual matters. Laurence Sterne parades before the public entirely unrobed, quite naked; but Jean Paul has only holes in his trousers. A few critics erroneously believe that Jean Paul possessed more true feeling than Sterne, because the latter, whenever the subject under treatment reaches a tragic elevation, suddenly assumes a merry, jesting tone. Jean Paul, on the contrary, if the subject verges in the least towards the serious, gradually becomes lachrymose, and composedly lets his tears trickle. Sterne probably felt more deeply than Jean Paul, for he is a greater poet. Laurence Sterne, like Shakespeare, was fostered by the muses on Parnassus. After the manner of women, they early spoiled him with their caresses. He was the special pet of the pale Goddess of Tragedy. Once, in a paroxysm of fierce tenderness, she kissed him so passionately, with such fervour, with so ardent a pressure of her lips, that his young heart began to bleed, and at once understood all earthly sorrows, and was filled with a boundless compassion. Poor young poet-heart! But the younger sister, the rosy Goddess of Mirth, sprang quickly to his side, took the suffering lad into her arms, and sought to cheer him with song and merriment. She gave him as playthings the mask of comedy and the jingling bells, and pressed a soothing kiss upon his lips; and with that kiss she imbued him with all her levity, all her frolicsome mirth, all her sportive wit.

And since then Sterne's heart and Sterne's lips have drifted into a strange contradiction. Sometimes, when his soul is most deeply agitated with tragic emotion, and he seeks to give utterance to the profound sorrows of his bleeding heart, then, to his own astonishment, the merriest, most mirth-provoking words will flutter from his lips.

. . . .

The Baron de la Motte-Fouqué was formerly a major in the Prussian military service, and is one of the most conspicuous of those poet-heroes, or hero-poets, whose lyre and sword won renown during the so-called war of liberation.

His laurels are of the genuine kind. He is a true poet, and the inspiration of poetry is on his brow. Few authors receive such universal homage as did our good Fouqué. Now his readers consist only of the patrons of the circulating libraries. But that public is still large enough, and Fouqué may boast that he was the only one of the romantic school who was also received with favour by the lower classes. At the time when at the aesthetic tea-gatherings in Berlin it was the fashion to sneer at the fallen knight, in a little Hartz village I became acquainted with a lovely maiden, who spoke of Fouqué with a charming enthusiasm, and blushingly confessed that she would gladly give a year of her life if she might but once kiss the author of "Undine"—and this maiden had the prettiest lips that I have ever seen.

"Undine" is indeed a charming poem. This poem is itself a kiss! The genius of poetry kissed the sleeping spring, and as it opened its laughing eyes all the roses exhaled their sweetest perfumes, and all the nightingales sang; and the fragrance of the roses and the songs of the nightingales, all this did our good Fouqué clothe in words, and called it "Undine."

I know not if this novel has been translated into French. It is the story of a lovely water-fairy who has no soul, and who only acquires one by falling in love with an earthly knight. But, alas! with this soul she also learns human sorrows. Her knightly spouse becomes faithless, and she kisses him dead. For in this book death also is only a kiss.

This "Undine" may be regarded as the muse of Fouqué's poetry. Although she is indescribably beautiful, although she suffers as we do, and earthly sorrows weigh full heavily upon her, she is yet no real human being. But our age turns away from all fairy-pictures, no matter how beautiful. It demands the figures of actual life; and least of all will it tolerate water-fays who fall in love with noble knights. This reactionary tendency, this continual praise of the nobility, this

83

incessant glorification of the feudal system, this everlasting knight-errantry balderdash, became at length distasteful to the educated portion of the German middle classes, and they turned their backs on the minstrel who sang so out of time. In fact, this everlasting sing-song of armours, battle-steeds, high-born maidens, honest guild-masters, dwarfs, squires, castles, chapels, minnesingers, faith, and whatever else that rubbish of the middle ages may be called, wearied us; and as the ingenuous hidalgo Friedrich de la Motte-Fouqué became more and more immersed in his books of chivalry, and, wrapped up in the reveries of the past, he ceased to understand the present, and then even his best friends were compelled to turn away from him with dubious head-shakings.

His later writings are unenjoyable. The faults of his earlier works are repeated, only more glaringly. His knights are combinations of iron and sentimentality; they have neither flesh nor common-sense. His heroines are mere semblances of women; they are dolls, whose golden tresses daintily curl over features that are as pretty and as expressionless as flowers. Like the works of Walter Scott, so also do Fouqué's romances of chivalry remind us of the fantastic tapestries known as gobelins, whose rich texture and brilliant colours are more pleasing to our eyes than edifying to our souls. We behold knightly pageantry, shepherds engaged in festive sports, hand to hand combats, and ancient customs, charmingly intermingled. It is all very pretty and picturesque, but shallow, brilliant superficiality. Among the imitators of Fouqué, as among the imitators of Walter Scott, this mannerism of portraying—not the inner nature of men and things, but merely the outward garb and appearance—was carried to still greater extremes. This shallow art and frivolous style is still in vogue in Germany, as well as in England and France. Even if the portrayal no longer attempts to glorify the age of chivalry, but is directed to our modern affairs, it is still the same mannerism, which grasps not the essential points of phenomena, but merely the superficial and the accidental. In lieu of a knowledge of mankind, our recent novelists evince a profound acquaintance with clothes; they perhaps justify themselves by the old saying: "The tailor makes the man." How different from the older, especially the English, novelists! Richardson gives us the anatomy of the emotions. Goldsmith treats of the affections of his heroes pragmatically. The author of *Tristram Shandy* reveals to us the profoundest depths of the human soul; he opens, as it were, a crevice of the soul; permits us to take one glance into its abysses, into its paradise and into its filthiest recesses; then quickly lets the curtain fall over it. We have had a front view of that marvellous theatre, the soul; the arrangements of lights and the perspective have not failed in their effects, and while we imagined that we were gazing upon the infinite, our own hearts have been exalted with a sense of infinity and poetry. Fielding at once takes us behind the scenes, and there shows us all the emotions covered with deceitful rouge; the gross motives that underlie the most generous deeds; the colophony that is afterwards to blaze aloft into enthusiasm; the bass drum, while on it repose the drumsticks, which are destined to sound the furious thunder of passion. In short, he shows us the whole interior machinery by which theatrical effects are produced; he exposes the colossal deceit by which men assume an appearance far different from the reality, and through which the truth and gladness of life are lost. But what need to cite the English as an example, since our own Goethe has given us in his *Wilhelm Meister* the best model of a novel?

Fouqué's romances are a legion in number; he is one of the most prolific of authors. *The Magic Ring* and *Thiodolph the Icelander* merit a specially favourable mention. His metrical dramas, which were not intended for the stage, contain great beauties. *Sigurd the Serpent-slayer* is a bold work, in which the ancient Scandinavian mythology is mirrored with all its gigantesque and magical characteristics. Sigurd, the chief personage of the drama, is a colossal creation. He is as strong as the rocky crags of Norway, and as fierce as the sea that beats around their base. He has as much courage as a hundred lions, and as much sense as two asses.

Herr Ludwig Uhland is the true lyric poet. He was born in Tübingen in 1787, and is now an advocate at Stuttgard. This author has written a volume of poems, two tragedies, and two treatises on Walther von der Vogelweide, and on the French troubadours. The latter are two small historical researches, and give evidence of a diligent study of the middle ages. The tragedies are entitled *Louis the Bavarian*, and *Duke Ernest of Suabia*. I have not read the former, nor is it considered the better of the two. The latter, however, contains many beauties, and pleases by its noble and exalted sentiments. It is fragrant with the sweet breath of poetry, such as we fail to find in the pieces that reap so much applause on the stage at the present day. German fidelity is the theme of the drama, and we see it here strong as an oak, defying all storms. German love blossoms, scarcely visible, in the far distance, but its violet-perfume appeals the more touchingly to our hearts. This drama, or rather this poem, contains passages which are among the most precious pearls of our literature; notwithstanding which, the theatre-going public received, or rather rejected, the piece with indifference. I will not censure the good people of the pit too severely for that. These people have certain needs, which they demand that the poet shall gratify. The poet's productions must not merely express the sympathies of his own heart, but must accord with the desires of the audience. The latter resembles the hungry Bedouin in the desert, who thinks he has found a sack of peas, and opens it eagerly, but, alas! they are only pearls.

. . . .

...Twenty years ago I was a lad, and what overflowing enthusiasm would I then have lavished upon Uhland! At that time I could better appreciate his merits than now; we were then more akin in modes of thought and feeling. But so much has happened since then! What then seemed to me so grand: all that chivalry and Catholicism; those cavaliers that hack and hew at each other in knightly tournaments; those gentle squires and virtuous dames of high degree; the Norseland heroes and minnesingers; the monks and nuns; ancestral tombs thrilling with prophetic powers; colourless passion, dignified by the high-sounding title of renunciation, and set to the accompaniment of tolling bells; a ceaseless whining of the Miserere; how distasteful all that has become to me since then! But once, it was, oh! so different. How often have I sat on the ruins of the old castle at Düsseldorf on the Rhine, declaiming the loveliest of all Uhland's poems:—

A wandering shepherd, young and fair,
Beneath the royal castle strayed;
And when the princess saw him there,
Love's longing thrilled the maid.

And then with accents sweet, she said,
"Oh! would that I might come to thee!
How white the lambkins there; how red
The flowerets on the lea."

The youth made answer from below,
"If thou would'st but come down to me!
How rosy red thy cheeks do glow,
How white those arms I see."

And every morn, with silent pain,
He drove his flock the castle by,
And gazed aloft, until again
His love appeared on high.

"Oh, welcome! welcome! princess sweet!"
His joyous tones rang bright and clear.
Then softly she in turn did greet,
"Kind thanks, my shepherd dear."

Cold winter fled, spring came again,
The flowerets blossomed far and near.
The shepherd sought his love;—in vain!
No more did she appear.

"Oh, welcome! welcome! princess fair!"
His words were mournful now, and drear.
A spirit voice rang through the air,
"Farewell, my shepherd dear."

And as I sat on the ruins of the old castle and recited this poem, at times I heard the water-fays of the Rhine mockingly, and with comic pathos, take up my refrain, and from amidst the sighing and the moaning of the river that ran below I could hear in faint tones——

"A spirit voice ring through the air,
'Farewell, my shepherd dear.'"

But I would not let myself be disturbed by the bantering of the mermaids, even when at some of the most beautiful passages in Uhland's poems they tittered ironically. At that time I modestly ascribed the tittering to myself, particularly when the twilight was sinking into darkness, and I raised my voice somewhat to overcome the mysterious feeling of awe with which the old castle ruins inspired me, for there was a legend that the ruins were haunted by a headless woman. At times I seemed to hear the rustling of her silken gown, and my heart beat quickly;—that was the time, and that the place, to be an enthusiast over the poems of Ludwig Uhland.

I hold the same volume again in my hands, but twenty years have flown since then, and I have seen much and learned much. I no longer believe in headless human beings, and the old ghost story has no longer power to move me. The house wherein I sit and read is situated on the Boulevard Montmartre; the fiercest turmoil of the day breaks in tumultuous billows around this spot, and loud and shrill are heard the voices of the modern epoch. First, a burst of laughter; then a heavy rumbling; next, drums beating quick time; and then, like a flash, the national guards dash by in quick march; and every one speaks French. And is this the place to read Uhland's poems? Thrice have I again declaimed the concluding lines of the same poem, but I do not feel the keen, unspeakable pain that once thrilled me when the little princess died, and the handsome shepherd lad so pathetically calls to her, "Oh, welcome! welcome! princess fair!"

"A spirit voice rang through the air,
'Farewell, my shepherd dear.'"

Perhaps my lack of enthusiasm for this class of poems also partly arises from my experience that the most painful love is not that which fails to win possession of the object of its affections, or loses her through death. In truth, it is more painful to fold the loved one in our arms, and yet have her worry us with her contrariness, and her silly caprices, until night and day are rendered unendurable, and we are finally forced to close our heart against her who is most precious, and send the dear plague of a woman off in a post chaise—

"Farewell, oh! princess fair!"

Verily, more grievous than the loss through death is the loss through life; for instance, when the loved one in the spirit of mischievous coquetry turns away from us; when she insists upon going to a masked ball, to which no respectable person dare escort her; and when there, with jaunty dress and roguish curls, takes the arm of the first scamp that comes along, and leaves you all alone.

"Farewell, my shepherd dear!"

Perhaps Herr Uhland himself fared no better than ourselves. Perhaps his temperament has changed since then. With a few exceptions, he has produced no new poems in twenty years. I cannot believe that this beautiful poet soul was so stingily endowed by Nature, and had but one spring-time. No, I explain Uhland's silence as the result of the contradiction between the tendencies of his muse and his political position. The elegiac poet, in whose ballads and romances the praises of the Catholic-feudal past were sung so beautifully; the Ossian of the middle ages has since then become a member of the assembly of notables in

87

Wurtemburg, a zealous champion of popular rights, and a bold advocate of the equality of all citizens, and of freedom of opinion. Herr Uhland has proved the absolute sincerity of his democratic and Protestant convictions by the great personal sacrifices that he has made in their behalf. In his earlier days he fairly earned the poet's laurels, and now he has also won the bays of civic virtue. But just because he was so honest in his sympathy for the modern epoch, he could no longer sing the olden songs of the olden time with the former fervour. His Pegasus was a knightly steed that gladly trotted back to the past, but obstinately refused to budge when urged forward into modern life; and so our worthy Uhland smilingly dismounted, quietly unsaddled the unruly steed, and led it back to the stable. There it remains to this very day; like its colleague, the famous war-horse Bayard, it possesses all possible virtues, and only one fault; it is dead.

It will not have escaped keener eyes than mine, that the stately war-horse, decked with its brilliant coat of arms and proudly-waving plumes, was never rightly suited to its *bourgeois* rider, who, instead of boots with golden spurs, wore shoes with silk stockings; and who, instead of helm, wore the hat of a Tübingen professor. Some claim to have discovered that Herr Ludwig Uhland never was wholly in sympathy with his theme; that in his writings, the naïve, rude, powerful tones of the middle ages are not reproduced with idealised fidelity, but rather they are dissolved into a sickly, sentimental melancholy. It is claimed that Uhland has taken up into his temperament the strong, coarse strains of the heroic legends and folk-songs, and boiled them down, as it were, to make them palatable to our modern public. And in truth, when we closely observe the women in Uhland's poems, we find that they are only beautiful shadows, embodied moonshine; milk flows in their veins, and sweet tears in their eyes; that is, tears which lack salt. If we compare Uhland's knights with the knights in the old ballads, it seems to us as if the former were composed of suits of leaden armour, which were entirely filled with flowers, instead of flesh and bones. Hence Uhland's knights are more pleasing to delicate nostrils than the old stalwarts, who wore heavy iron trousers, and were huge eaters, and still greater drinkers.

But that is no reason for finding fault with Herr Uhland; he did not seek to give an exact copy of the German past; perhaps he only wished to please us with a fanciful reflection, and so he mirrored a flattering picture by the crepuscular lights of his genius. This perhaps lends an especial charm to his poems, and wins for them the admiration and affection of many gentle and worthy persons. The pictures of the past cast some of their magic glamour over us, even in the feeblest conjuration. Even the men who have warmly espoused the cause of modernism always retain a secret sympathy for the heritages of the olden time. Those ghostly voices of the past, no matter how faint their re-echo, marvellously stir our souls. Hence it is to be readily understood that the ballads and romances of our worthy Uhland not only received the most cordial applause from the patriots of 1813, from pious youths and sentimental maidens, but also from more powerful and more modern minds.

RELIGION AND PHILOSOPHY IN GERMANY.

[A considerable portion of this, which is one of Heine's most important works, marked by luminous exposition and bold and brilliant ideas, is here presented. It was published in French, under the title *De l'Allemagne depuis Luther*, in the *Revue des Deux Mondes* for 1834, and shortly afterwards it appeared in German, terribly mutilated by the censor, like nearly everything that Heine wrote. It was written at the suggestion of Prosper Enfantin, and dedicated to him, as at that time, in Heine's opinion, the foremost champion of human progress. The translation here given is Mr. Fleishman's; it has been revised and brought closer to the original.]

Preface To Second Edition (1852).

...THE book which lies before you is a fragment, and shall remain a fragment. To be candid, I would prefer to leave the book wholly unprinted; for since its first publication my views concerning many subjects, particularly those which relate to religious questions, have undergone a marked change, and much that I then asserted is now in opposition to my better convictions. But the arrow belongs not to the archer when once it has left the bow, and the word no longer belongs to the speaker when once it has passed his lips, especially when it has been multiplied by the press.... At that time I was yet well and hearty; I was in the zenith of my prime, and as arrogant as Nebuchadnezzar before his downfall.

Alas! a few years later, a physical and spiritual change occurred. How often since then have I mused over the history of that Babylonian king who thought himself a god, but who was miserably hurled from the summit of his self-conceit, and compelled to crawl on the earth like a beast, and to eat grass (probably it was only salad). This legend is contained in the grand and magnificent book of Daniel; and I recommend all godless self-worshippers to lay it devoutly to heart. There are, in fact, in the Bible many other beautiful and wonderful narrations, well deserving their consideration; for instance, the story of the forbidden fruit in Paradise, and the serpent which already six thousand years before Hegel's birth promulgated the whole Hegelian philosophy. This footless blue-stocking demonstrates very sagaciously how the absolute consists in the identity of being and knowing; how man becomes God through knowledge, or, what amounts to the same thing, how God arrives at the consciousness of himself through man. To be sure, this formula is not so clear as in the original words: "If ye eat of the tree of knowledge, ye shall be as gods, knowing good and evil." Dame Eve understood of the whole demonstration only this—that the fruit was forbidden; and because it was forbidden she ate of it. But no sooner had she eaten of the tempting apple than she lost her innocence, her naïve guilelessness, and discovered that she was far too scantily dressed for a person of her quality, the mother of so many future kings and emperors, and she asked for a dress—truly, only a dress of fig-leaves, because at that time there were as yet no Lyons silk fabrics in existence, and because there were in Paradise no dressmakers or milliners—oh, Paradise!

Strange, that as soon as a woman arrives at self-consciousness her first thought is of a new dress!

...Officious, pious Christian souls seem very anxious to know how my conversion was brought about, and seem desirous that I should impose upon them an account of some wonderful miracle. With true Christian importunity they inquire if I did not, like Saul, behold a light when on the way to Damascus; or if, like Balaam, the son of Beor, I was not riding a restive ass, which suddenly opened its mouth and discoursed like a human being. No, ye credulous souls, I never journeyed to Damascus. Even the name would be unknown to me if I had not read the "Song of Songs," wherein King Solomon compares the nose of his beloved to a tower looking towards Damascus. Nor have I ever seen an ass—that is, no four-footed one—that spoke like a human being; whereas I have met human beings in plenty that every time they opened their mouths spoke like asses. In fact, it was neither a vision, nor a seraphic ecstasy, nor a voice from heaven, nor a remarkable dream, nor any miraculous apparition, that brought me to the path of salvation. I owe my enlightenment simply to the reading of a book! one book! yes, it is a plain old book, as modest as nature, and as simple; a book that appears as work-day-like and as unpretentious as the sun that warms, as the bread that nourishes us; a book that looks on us as kindly and benignly as an old grandmother, who, with her dear tremulous lips, and spectacles on nose, reads in it daily: this book is briefly called *the* book—the Bible. With good reason it is also called the Holy Scriptures: he that has lost his God can find Him again in this book, and towards him who has never known Him it wafts the breath of the divine word. The Jews, who are connoisseurs of precious things, well knew what they were about when, at the burning of the second temple, they left in the lurch the gold and silver sacrificial vessels, the candlesticks and lamps, and even the richly-jewelled breast-plate of the high-priest, to rescue only the Bible....

——

...DISTINGUISHED German philosophers who may accidentally cast a glance over these pages will superciliously shrug their shoulders at the meagreness and incompleteness of all that which I here offer. But they will be kind enough to bear in mind that the little which I say is expressed clearly and intelligibly, whereas their own works, although very profound, unfathomably profound—very deep, stupendously deep—are in the same degree unintelligible. Of what benefit to the people is the grain locked away in the granaries to which they have no key? The masses are famishing for knowledge, and will thank me for the portion of intellectual bread, small though it be, which I honestly share with them. I believe it is not lack of ability that holds back the majority of German scholars from discussing religion and philosophy in proper language. I believe it is a fear of the results of their own studies, which they dare not communicate to the masses. I do not share this fear, for I am not a learned scholar; I, myself, am of the people. I am not one of the seven hundred wise men of Germany. I stand with the great masses at the portals of their wisdom. And if a truth slips through, and if this truth falls in my way, then I write it with pretty letters on paper, and give it to the compositor, who sets it in leaden type and gives it to the printer; the latter prints it, and then it belongs to the whole world.

The religion of Germany is Christianity. Therefore I shall have to relate what Christianity is, how it became Roman Catholicism, how out of this sprang Protestantism, and out of the latter German philosophy. Inasmuch as I am about to speak of religion, I beg beforehand of all pious souls not to be uneasy. Fear naught, ye pious ones! No profane witticisms shall offend your ears. It is true that these are yet necessary in Germany, where, at this juncture, it is important to neutralise ecclesiastical power. For there we are now in the same situation that you in France were before the Revolution, when Christianity was yet in the closest union with the old *régime*. The latter could not be overthrown so long as the former maintained its sway over the masses. Voltaire's keen ridicule was needed ere Samson could let his axe descend. But neither the ridicule nor the axe proved anything; they only effected something. Voltaire could only wound the body of Christianity. All his jests gathered from the annals of the Church, all his witticisms against the doctrines and public worship of the Church, against the Bible, this holiest book of humanity, against the Virgin Mary, that loveliest flower of poesy, the whole encylclopædia of philosophical shafts which he launched against the clergy and priesthood, wounded only the outward, mortal body of Christianity, not its inner being, not its profound spirit, nor its eternal soul.

For Christianity is an idea, and as such is indestructible and immortal, like every idea. But what is this idea?

Just because this idea has not yet been clearly comprehended, and because the essential has been mistaken for the fundamental, there is as yet no history of the Church. Two antagonistic factions write the history of the Church, and contradict each other incessantly. But the one as little as the other will ever distinctly state what that idea really is which is the underlying principle of Christianity, of its symbolism, of its dogma, of its public worship, and which strives to reveal itself throughout its whole history, and has manifested itself in the actual life of Christian nations.

...How this idea was historically evolved, and disclosed itself in the world of phenomena, may be discovered as early as the first centuries after the birth of Christ, if we study impartially the history of the Manicheans and the Gnostics. Although the first were branded as heretics, and the latter defamed, and both anathematised by the Church, yet their influence on the doctrines of the Church was lasting. Out of their symbolism Catholic art was developed, and their modes of thought penetrated the whole life of Christendom. The First Cause of the Manicheans does not differ much from that of the Gnostics. The doctrine of the two principles, the good and the evil, constantly opposing each other, is common to both. The Manicheans derived this doctrine from the ancient Persian religion, in which Ormuz, the light, is at enmity with Ahriman, the darkness. The others, the real Gnostics, believed in the pre-existence of the good principle, and accounted for the rise of the evil through emanation, through the generation of Æons, which, the farther they are removed from their origin, the more vicious and evil do they become.

...This Gnostic theory of the universe originated in ancient India, and brought with it the doctrine of the incarnation of God, of the mortification of the flesh, of spiritual introspection and self-absorption. It gave birth to the ascetic, contemplative, monkish life, which is the most logical outgrowth of the Christian principle. This principle has become entangled among the dogmas of the Church, and has been able to express itself but very obscurely in the public worship. But everywhere we find the doctrine of the two principles prominent; the wicked Satan is always contrasted with the good Christ. Christ represents the spiritual world, Satan the material; to the former belong our souls, to the latter our bodies. Accordingly, the whole visible world, which constitutes nature, is originally evil, and Satan, the prince of darkness, through it seeks to lure us to ruin. Therefore it behoves us to renounce all the sensuous joys of life, to torture the body, which is Satan's portion, in order that the soul may the more majestically soar aloft to the bright heavens, to the radiant kingdom of Christ.

This theory of the universe, which is the true fundamental idea of Christianity, spread itself with incredible rapidity, like a contagious disease, over the whole Roman empire. These sufferings, at times strung to fever-pitch, then again relaxing into exhaustion, lasted all through the middle ages; and we moderns still feel in our limbs those convulsions and that debility. And if among us, here and there, there be one who is already convalescent, he cannot flee from the universal hospital, and feels himself unhappy as the only healthy person among invalids.

When once mankind shall have recovered its perfect life, when peace shall be again restored between body and soul, and they shall again interpenetrate each other with their original harmony, then it will be scarcely possible to comprehend the factitious feud which Christianity has instigated between them. Happier and more perfect generations, begot in free and voluntary embraces, blossoming forth in a religion of joy, will then smile sadly at their poor ancestors, who held themselves gloomily aloof from all the pleasures of this beautiful world, and through the deadening of all warm and cheerful sensuousness almost paled into cold spectres. Yes, I say it confidently, our descendants will be more beautiful, more happy, than we; for I have faith in progress; mankind is destined to be happy, and I have a more favourable opinion of the Divinity than those pious souls who imagine that He created mankind only to suffer. Already here on earth, through the blessings of free political and industrial institutions, would I seek to found that millennium which, according to the belief of the pious, is not to be until the day of judgment. The one is perhaps as visionary a hope as the other, and possibly there will be no resurrection of humanity, either in the politico-moral or in the apostolic-Catholic sense. Perhaps mankind *is* doomed to eternal misery; the masses *are* perhaps condemned to be for ever trodden under foot by despots, to be plundered by their accomplices, and to be jeered at by their lackeys. Alas! in that case we must seek to maintain Christianity, even if we recognise it to be an error. Barefoot, and clad in monkish cowls, we must traverse Europe, preaching the vanity of all earthly good, and inculcating resignation. We must hold up the consoling crucifix before scourged and derided humanity, and promise, after death, all the seven heavens above.

...The final fate of Christianity is dependent upon our need of it. This religion has for eighteen centuries been a blessing to suffering humanity; it was providential, divine, holy. All that it has benefited civilisation, by taming the strong and strengthening the weak, by uniting the nations through like emotions and a like language, by all that its panegyrists extol—all these are insignificant in comparison with that great consolation which in itself is bestowed upon mankind. Eternal praise is due to that symbol of a suffering God, the Saviour with the crown of thorns, the Christ crucified, whose blood was a soothing balsam dripping into humanity's wounds. The poet, in particular, will reverently recognise the solemn grandeur of that symbol. The whole system of allegory, as expressed in the life and art of the middle ages, will in all times excite the admiration of poets. What colossal consistency in *the* Christian art!—that is, in architecture! How harmoniously those Gothic cathedrals are adapted to the religious services of the Church, and how the fundamental idea of the Church itself is revealed in them! Everything towers upward; everything transubstantiates itself; the stone blossoms into branches and foliage and becomes a tree; the fruits of the vine and of the wheat-stalk become blood and flesh; man becomes God, and God becomes a pure, abstract spirit. The Christian life during the middle ages is for the poet a rich, inexhaustible store-house of precious materials. Only through Christianity could, in this world, such varied phases arise—contrasts so striking, sorrows so diverse, beauties so strange, that one is inclined to believe that they never did exist in reality, and that all was but a colossal fever-dream, a delirious fantasy of an insane God. Nature herself appeared in those times fantastically disguised; but notwithstanding that man, occupied with abstract metaphysical speculations, turned peevishly away from her, yet at times she awoke him with a voice so solemnly sweet, so deliciously terrible, so enchanting, that he involuntarily listened and smiled, then shrank back with terror, and sickened even unto death. The story of the nightingale of Basle here comes to my mind, and, as it is probably unknown to you, I will relate it.

In May 1433, at the time of the Ecumenical Council, a party of ecclesiastics, prelates, learned scholars, and monks of every shades took a walk in a grove near Basle, wrangling over theological disputations, drawing hair-splitting distinctions, or arguing concerning annates, expectatives, and reservations, debating whether Thomas of Aquinas was a greater philosopher than Bonaventura, and what not! But suddenly, in the midst of their abstract and dogmatical discussions, they paused, transfixed, before a blooming linden-tree, on which sat a nightingale, trilling and trolling the sweetest and tenderest strains. The learned men were ravished with delight. The glowing melodies of spring penetrated to their scholastic, musty, bookworm hearts, their souls awoke from the mouldy, wintry sleep, they looked at one another in astonished ecstasy. But finally one of them made the sagacious remark that such things could not come of good, that the nightingale might be a devil, and that this devil might be seeking through its sweet music to decoy them from their pious conversations and to lure them to voluptuousness and similar pleasant sins; and then he began to exorcise, probably with the usual formula—"Adjuro te per cum, qui venturus est, judicare vivos et mortuos," etc. It is said that at this conjuration the bird replied, "Yes, I am an evil spirit!" and flew away, laughing. But those who heard its song sickened that very night, and soon after died.

This legend needs no commentary. It bears distinctly the horrible impress of a time when all that was sweet and lovely was denounced as diabolical. Even the nightingale was slandered, and it was customary to make the sign of the cross when she sang. The true Christian, like an abstract spectre, walked timorously, with closed senses, amidst the loveliness of nature.

...As regards the good principle, the same conception prevailed over all the Christian countries of Europe. The Roman Catholic Church took care of that, and whoever deviated from the prescribed faith was a heretic. But in relation to the evil principle and the empire of Satan, different views were held in different countries, and the Germanic North had quite different conceptions from the Latin South. This was caused by the fact that the Christian priesthood did not reject the previously existing national gods as baseless fantasies of the brain, but conceded to them an actual existence; asserting, however, that all these gods were nothing but male and female devils, who, through the victory of Christ, had lost their power over mankind, and now sought through wiles and stratagems to lure them to sin. All Olympus was now transformed into an airy hell; and if a poet of the middle ages sang of Grecian mythology ever so beautifully, the pious Christian would persist in seeing therein only devils and hobgoblins. The gloomy fanaticism of the monks alighted with special severity on poor Venus: she was considered a daughter of Beelzebub, and the good knight Tannhäuser tells her to her face—

"O Venus, lovely wife of mine,
You are but a she-devil!"

Tannhäuser had been enticed by her into that wondrous mountain-cavern called the Venusburg, where, according to tradition, dwelt the beautiful goddess with her nymphs and her paramours, beguiling the hours with the most wanton carousings and dancing. Even poor Diana was not spared, and, notwithstanding her previous reputation for chastity, similar scandals were fastened on her good name. It is said that she, together with her nymphs, indulged in nightly rides through the forest; hence the legend of a strange midnight chase, by wild and furious hunters. This legend reveals clearly the then pervading Gnostic theory of the degeneration of the former divinities. In this transformation of the ancient national religion the underlying principle of Christianity is most fully manifested. The national religion of Europe in the North, even more than in the South, was pantheism. All the mysteries and symbols of that religion were founded on and had reference to a worship of nature; each of the elements was regarded as the embodiment of some mysterious being, and as such was revered and worshipped; in every tree dwelt a divinity, and all nature swarmed with gods and goddesses. Christianity exactly reversed this, and in place of gods it substituted devils and demons. The cheerful figures of Grecian mythology, beautified as they were by art, had taken root in the South along with Roman civilisation, and were not so easily to be displaced by the hideous, weird, and satanic divinities of the German North. The latter seemed to have been fashioned without any particular artistic design, and even before the advent of Christianity they were as sombre and as gloomy as the North itself. Hence there could not arise in France so frightful a devil-dom as among us in Germany, and even the witchcraft and sorcery of the former assumed a cheerful guise. How lovely, fair, and picturesque are the popular superstitions of France as compared with the bloody, hazy, and misshapen monsters which loom gloomily and savagely from out the mists of German legendary lore!

Those German poets of the middle ages who chose such themes as had originated, or been first treated, in Brittany and Normandy, thereby invested their poems with somewhat of the cheerfulness of the French temperament. But the old Northern sombreness, of whose gloom we can now scarcely form any idea, exercised full sway over such of our literature as was distinctly national, and over such popular traditions as have been orally transmitted. The superstitions of the two countries offer as striking a contrast as that which exists between a Frenchman and a German. The supernatural beings that figure in old French *fabliaux* and legends are bright and cheerful creations, and remarkable for a cleanliness which is noticeably lacking in our filthy rabble of German hobgoblins. French fairies and sprites are as distinguishable from German spectres as a spruce and daintily-gloved dandy, jauntily promenading the Boulevard Coblence, is different from a burly German porter, carrying a heavy load upon his shoulders. A French nixen, such as a Melusina, is to a German elf as a princess to a washerwoman. The fay Morgana would stand aghast at sight of a German witch, her body naked and besmeared with ointment, riding on a broom-stick to the Brocken. The Brocken is no merry Avalon, but a rendezvous for all that is weird and hideous. On the very summit of the mountain sits Satan, in the shape of a black goat. The infamous sisterhood form a circle around him and dance, and sing, "Donderemus! Donderemus!" Mingled in the infernal din are heard the bleating of the goat and the shouting of the demoniac crew. If, during the dance, a witch happens to drop a shoe, it is an evil omen, and portends that she will be burned at the stake ere the year ends. But all the terror which such a portent inspires is forgotten amid the wild and maddening Berlioz-like music of the witches' sabbath—and when in the morning the poor witch awakens from her delirium, she finds herself lying, stark naked and tired, by the glimmering embers of her hearth.

The most complete account of witches we find in the learned Dr. Nicolai Remigius's *Demonology*. This sagacious man had the best opportunity to learn the tricks of witches, as he officiated at their trials, and during his time, in Lotharingia alone, eight hundred women were burned at the stake, after trial and conviction. The trial was generally as follows:—Their hands and feet were tied together, and then they were thrown into the water. If they went under and were drowned, it was a proof that they were innocent, but if they floated on the surface, they were recognised as guilty and burned. Such was the logic of those times.... When the learned Dr. Remigius had completed his great work on witchcraft, he deemed himself so great a master of his subject as to be able to work magic, and, conscientious man that he was, did not fail to accuse himself before the courts; in consequence of which accusation he was burned as a sorcerer.

...I must confess that Luther did not understand the real nature of Satan. Whatever evil may be said of the devil, it cannot be denied that he is a spiritualist. Still less did Luther understand the real nature of Catholicism. He did not comprehend that the fundamental idea of Christianity, the deadening of the senses, was too antagonistic to human nature to be ever entirely practicable in life; he did not comprehend that Catholicism was a concordat between God and the devil—that is to say, between the spirit and the senses, in which the absolute reign of the spirit was promulgated in theory, but in which the senses were nevertheless practically reinstated in the enjoyment of their rights. Hence a wise system of concessions allowed by the Church to the senses, always, however, under formalities which cast a slur on every act of the senses, and maintained the sham usurpation of the spirit. You might yield to the tender impulses of your heart and embrace a pretty girl, but you must confess that it was a flagrant sin, and for this sin you must make atonement. That this atonement might be made with money was as beneficial to humanity as useful to the Church. The Church imposed fines, so to say, for every indulgence of the flesh; hence there arose taxes on all sorts of sins, and there were pious colporteurs who, in the name of the Roman Catholic Church, hawked for sale through the land absolutions for every taxed sin. Such a one was that Tetzel against whom Luther first entered the field.

...Leo X., the keen Florentine, the pupil of Politian, the friend of Raphael, the Greek philosopher with the triple crown, bestowed by the Conclave, probably because he suffered from a disease, nowise due to Christian abstinence, which was then very dangerous, Leo of Medici, how he must have smiled at the poor, chaste, simple-minded monk who imagined that the evangelic gospels were the chart of Christianity, and that this chart must be a truth! Perhaps he never comprehended what Luther was aiming at, for at that time he was busily occupied with the building of St. Peter's Cathedral, the cost of which was defrayed by the money derived from these sales of absolutions, so that sin actually furnished the means wherewith to build this church, which became thereby, as it were, a monument to the lusts of the flesh, like that pyramid which an Egyptian girl built with the money she had earned by prostitution. Of this house of God it perhaps might be said more truly than of Cologne Cathedral, that it was built by the devil. This triumph of spiritualism, compelling sensualism itself to build its most beautiful temple—this reaping from the multitude, by concessions made to the flesh, the means wherewith to beautify spiritualism, was not understood in the German North. For there, more easily than under the burning skies of Italy, was it possible to practice a Christianity that should make the fewest concessions to the senses. We Northerners are cold-blooded, and

96

needed not so many price-lists of absolution for sins of the flesh as the fatherly Leo sent us. The climate makes the exercise of Christian virtues easier for us; and when, on the 31st of October 1517, Luther nailed to the door of St Augustine's Church his thesis against indulgences, the city moat of Wittenberg was, perhaps, already frozen over with ice thick enough for skating, which is a chilly pleasure, and therefore no sin.

...In Germany the battle against Catholicism was nothing else than a war begun by spiritualism when it perceived that it only reigned nominally and *de jure*; whereas sensualism, through conventional subterfuges, exercised the real sovereignty and ruled *de facto*. When this was perceived, the hawkers of indulgences were chased off, the pretty concubines of the priests were exchanged for plain but honest wedded wives, the charming Madonna pictures were demolished, and there reigned in certain localities a puritanism inimical to every gratification of the senses. In France, on the contrary, during the seventeenth and the eighteenth centuries, the war was begun by sensualism against Catholicism, when it saw that while it, sensualism, reigned *de facto*, yet every exercise of its sovereignty was restrained in the most aggravating manner by spiritualism, and stigmatised as illegitimate. While in Germany the battle was fought with chaste earnestness, in France it was waged with licentious witticisms, and while there theological disputations were in vogue, here many satires were the fashion.

...Truly, Jansenism had much more cause than Jesuitism to feel aggrieved at the delineation of Tartuffe, and Molière would be as obnoxious to the Methodists of to-day as to the Catholic devotees of his own time. It is just because of this that Molière is so great, for, like Aristophanes and Cervantes, he levelled his *persiflage* not only at temporary follies, but also against that which is ever ridiculous—the inherent frailties of mankind. Voltaire, who always attacked only the temporary and the unessential, is in this respect inferior to Molière.

...Then why my aversion to spiritualism? Is it something so evil? By no means. Attar of roses is a precious article, and a small vial of it is refreshing, when one is doomed to pass one's days in the closely-locked apartments of the harem. But yet we would not have all the roses of life crushed and bruised in order to gain a few drops of the attar of roses, be they ever so consoling. We are like the nightingales, that delight in the rose itself, and derive as delicious a pleasure from the sight of the blushing, blooming flower as from its invisible fragrance.

...But there was one man at the Diet of Worms who, I am convinced, thought not of himself, but only of the sacred interests which he was there to champion. That man was Martin Luther, the poor monk whom Providence had selected to shatter the world-controlling power of the Roman Catholic Church, against which the mightiest emperors and most intrepid scholars had striven in vain. But Providence knows well on whose shoulders to impose its tasks; here not only intellectual but also physical strength was required. It needed a body steeled from youth through chastity and monkish discipline to bear the labour and vexations of such an office.

...Luther was not only the greatest, but also the most thoroughly German hero of our history. In his character are combined, on the grandest scale, all the virtues and all the faults of the Germans, so that, in his own person, he was the representative of that wonderful Germany. For he possessed qualities which we seldom find united, and which we usually even consider to be irreconcilably antagonistic. He was simultaneously a dreamy mystic and a practical man of action. His thoughts possessed not only wings, but also hands; he could speak and could act. He was not only the tongue, but also the sword of his time. He was both a cold, scholastic word-caviller, and an enthusiastic, God-inspired prophet. When, during the day, he had wearily toiled over his dogmatic distinctions and definitions, then in the evening he took his lute, looked up to the stars, and melted into melody and devotion. The same man who could scold like a fish-wife could be as gentle as a tender maiden. At times he was as fierce as the storm that uproots oaks; and then again he was mild as the zephyr caressing the violets. He was filled with a reverential awe of God. He was full of the spirit of self-sacrifice for the honour of the Holy Ghost; he could sink his whole personality in the most abstract spirituality, and yet he could well appreciate the good things of this earth, and from his mouth blossomed forth the famous saying —

"Who loves not wine, women, and song,
Will be a fool all his life long."

He was a complete man—I would say an absolute man, in whom spirit and matter were not antagonistic. To call him a spiritualist would, therefore, be as erroneous as to call him a sensualist. How shall I describe him? He had in him something aboriginal, incomprehensible, miraculous.

...All praise to Luther! Eternal honour to the blessed man to whom we owe the salvation of our most precious possessions, and whose benefactions we still enjoy. It ill becomes us to complain of the narrowness of his views. The dwarf, standing on the shoulders of the giant, particularly if he puts on spectacles, can, it is true, see farther than the giant himself; but for noble thoughts and exalted sentiments a giant heart is necessary. It were still more unseemly of us to pass a harsh judgment on his faults, for those very faults have benefited us more than the virtues of thousands of other men. The refinement of Erasmus, the mildness of Melanchthon, could never have brought us so far as the godlike brutality of Brother Martin.

...From the day on which Luther denied the authority of the Pope, and publicly declared in the Diet "that his teachings must be controverted through the words of the Bible itself, or with sensible reasons," there begins a new era in Germany. The fetters with which Saint Boniface had chained the German Church to Rome are broken. This Church, which has hitherto formed an integral part of the great hierarchy, now splits into religious democracies. The character of the religion itself is essentially changed: the Hindoo-Gnostic element disappears from it, and the Judaic-theistic element again becomes prominent. We behold the rise of evangelical Christianity. By recognising and legitimising the most importunate claims of the senses, religion becomes once more a reality. The priest becomes man, takes to himself a wife, and begets children, as God desires.

...If in Germany we lost through Protestantism, along with the ancient miracles, much other poetry, we gained manifold compensations. Men became nobler and more virtuous. Protestantism was very successful in effecting that purity of morals and that strictness in the fulfilment of duty which is generally called morality. In certain communities, indeed, Protestantism assumed a tendency which in the end became quite identical with morality, and the gospels remained as a beautiful parable only. Particularly in the lives of the ecclesiastics is a pleasing change now noticeable. With celibacy disappeared also monkish obscenities and vices. Among the Protestant clergy are frequently to be found the noblest and most virtuous of men, such as would have won respect from even the ancient Stoics. One must have wandered on foot, as a poor student, through Northern Germany, in order to learn how much virtue—and in order to give virtue a complimentary adjective, how much evangelical virtue—is to be found in an unpretentious-looking parsonage. How often of a winter's evening have I found there a hospitable welcome,—I, a stranger, who brought with me no other recommendation save that I was hungry and tired! When I had partaken of a hearty meal, and, after a good night's rest, was ready in the morning to continue my journey, then came the old pastor, in his dressing-gown, and gave me a blessing on the way,—and it never brought me misfortune; and his good-hearted, gossipy wife placed several slices of bread-and-butter in my pocket, which I found not less refreshing; and silent in the distance stood the pastor's pretty daughters, with blushing cheeks and violet eyes, whose modest fire in the mere recollection warmed my heart for many a whole winter's day.

...How strange! We Germans are the strongest and wisest of nations; our royal races furnish princes for all the thrones of Europe; our Rothschilds rule all the exchanges of the world; our learned men are pre-eminent in all the sciences; we invented gunpowder and printing;—and yet if one of us fires a pistol he must pay a fine of three thalers; and if we wish to insert in a newspaper, "My dear wife has given birth to a little daughter, beautiful as Liberty," then the censor grasps his red pencil and strikes out the word "Liberty."

...I have said that we gained freedom of thought through Luther. But he gave us not only freedom of movement, but also the means of movement; to the spirit he gave a body; to the thought he gave words. He created the German language.

This he did by his translation of the Bible.

In fact, the divine author of that book seems to have known, as well as we others, that the choice of a translator is by no means a matter of indifference; and so He himself selected His translator, and bestowed on him the wonderful gift to translate from a language which was dead and already buried, into another language that as yet did not exist.

...The knowledge of the Hebrew language had entirely disappeared from the Christian world. Only the Jews, who kept themselves hidden here and there in stray corners of the world, yet preserved the traditions of this language. Like a ghost keeping watch over a treasure which had been confided to it during life, so in its dark and gloomy ghettos sat this murdered nation, this spectre-people, guarding the Hebrew Bible.

...Luther's Bible is an enduring spring of rejuvenation for our language. All the expressions and phrases contained therein are German, and are still in use by writers. As this book is in the hands of even the poorest people, they require no special learned education in order to be able to express themselves in literary forms. When our political revolution breaks out, this circumstance will have remarkable results. Liberty will everywhere be gifted with the power of speech, and her speech will be biblical.

...More noteworthy and of more importance than his prose writings are Luther's poems, the songs which in battle and in trouble blossomed forth from his heart. Sometimes they resemble a floweret that grows on a rocky crag, then again a ray of moonlight trembling over a restless sea. Luther loved music, and even wrote a treatise on the art; hence his songs are particularly melodious. In this respect he merits the name, Swan of Eisleben. But he is nothing less than a wild swan in those songs wherein he stimulates the courage of his followers and inflames himself to the fiercest rage of battle. A true battle-song was that martial strain with which he and his companions marched into Worms. The old cathedral trembled at those unwonted tones, and the ravens, in their dark nests in the steeple, startled with affright. That song, the Marseillaise of the Reformation, preserves to this day its inspiriting power.

...The expressions "classic" and "romantic" refer only to the spirit and the manner of the treatment. The treatment is classic when the form of that which is portrayed is quite identical with the idea of the portrayer, as is the case with the art-works of the Greeks, in which, owing to this identity, the greatest harmony is found to exist between the idea and its form. The treatment is romantic when the form does not reveal the idea through this identity, but lets this idea be surmised parabolically. (I use the word "parabolically" here in preference to "symbolically.") The Greek mythology had an array of god-figures, each of which, in addition to the identity of form and idea, was also susceptible of a symbolic meaning. But in this Greek religion only the figures of the gods were clearly defined; all else, their lives and deeds, was left to the arbitrary treatment of the poet's fancy. In the Christian religion, on the contrary, there are no such clearly-defined figures, but stated facts—certain definite holy events and deeds, into which the poetical faculty of man could place a parabolic signification. It is said that Homer invented the Greek gods and goddesses. That is not true. They existed previously in clearly-defined outlines; but he invented their histories. The artists of the middle ages, on the other hand, never ventured the least addition to the historical part of their religion. The fall of man, the incarnation, the baptism, the crucifixion, and the like, were matters of fact, which were not to be intermeddled with, and which it was not permissible to remould in the least, but to which poetry might attach a symbolic meaning. All the arts during the middle ages were treated in this parabolic spirit, and this treatment is romantic. Hence

100

we find in the poetry of the middle ages a mystic universality; the forms are all so shadowy, what they do is so vaguely indicated, all therein is as if seen through a hazy twilight intermittently illumined by the moon. The idea is merely hinted at in the form, as in a riddle; and we dimly see a vague, indefinite figure, which is the peculiarity of spiritual literature. There is not, as among the Greeks, a harmony, clear as the sun, between form and meaning, but occasionally the meaning overtops the given form, and the latter strives desperately to reach the former, and then we behold bizarre, fantastic sublimity; then, again, the form has overgrown itself, and is out of all proportion to the meaning. A silly, pitiful thought trails itself along in some colossal form, and we witness a grotesque farce: misshapenness is nearly always the result.

The universal characteristic of that literature was that in all its productions it manifested the same firm, unshaken faith which in that period reigned over worldly as well as spiritual matters. All the opinions of that time were based on authorities. The poet journeyed along the abysses of doubt as free from apprehension as a mule, and there prevailed in the literature of that period a dauntless composure and blissful self-confidence such as became impossible in after-times, when the influence of the Papacy, the chief of those authorities, was shattered, and with it all the others were overthrown. Hence the poems of the middle ages have all the same characteristics, as if composed not by single individuals, but by the whole people *en masse*: they are objective, epic, naïve.

In the literature that blossomed into life with Luther we find quite opposite tendencies.

Its material, its subject, is the conflict between the interests and views of the Reformation and the old order of things. To the new spirit of the times, that hodge-podge religion which arose from the two elements already referred to— Germanic nationality and the Hindoo-Gnostic Christendom—was altogether repugnant. The latter was considered heathen idol-worship, which was to be replaced by the true religion of the Judaic-theistic Gospel. A new order of things is established; the spirit makes discoveries which demand the well-being of matter. Through industrial progress and the dissemination of philosophical theories, spiritualism becomes discredited in popular opinion. The *tiers-état* begins to rise; the Revolution already rumbles in the hearts and brains of men, and what the era feels, thinks, needs, and wills is openly spoken; and that is the stuff of which modern literature is made. At the same time the treatment is no longer romantic, but classic.

...The universal characteristic of modern literature consists in this, that now individuality and scepticism predominate. Authorities are overthrown; reason is now man's sole lamp, and conscience his only staff in the dark mazes of life. Man now stands alone, face to face with his Creator, and chants his songs to Him. Hence this literary epoch opens with hymns. And even later, when it becomes secular, the most intimate self-consciousness, the feeling of personality, rules throughout. Poetry is no longer objective, epic, and naïve, but subjective, lyric, and reflective.

...The God of the pantheists differs from the God of the theists in so far that the former is in the world itself, while the latter is external to, or, in other words, is over the world. The God of the theists rules the world from above as a quite distinct establishment. Only in regard to the manner of that rule do the theists differ among themselves. The Hebrews picture God as a thunder-hurling tyrant; the Christians regard him as a loving father; the disciples of Rousseau and the whole Genevese school portray him as a skilful artist, who has made the whole world somewhat in the same manner as their papas manufacture watches; and as art-connoisseurs, they admire the work and praise the Maker above.

...From the moment that religion seeks assistance from philosophy her downfall is unavoidable. She strives to defend herself, and always talks herself deeper into ruin. Religion, like all other absolutisms, may not justify herself. Prometheus is bound to the rock by a silent power. Æschylus represents the personification of brute force as not speaking a single word. It must be dumb.

...Moses Mendelssohn was the reformer of the German Israelites, his companions in faith. He overthrew the prestige of Talmudism, and founded a pure Mosaism. This man, whom his contemporaries called the German Socrates, and whose nobleness of soul and intellectual powers they so admired, was the son of a poor sexton of the synagogue at Dessau. Besides this curse of birth, Providence made him a hunchback, in order to teach the rabble in a very striking manner that men are to be judged not by outward appearance but by inner worth. As Luther overthrew the Papacy, so Mendelssohn overthrew the Talmud; and that, too, by a similar process. He discarded tradition, declared the Bible to be the well-spring of religion, and translated the most important parts of it. By so doing he destroyed Jewish Catholicism, for such is the Talmud. It is a Gothic dome which, although overladen with fanciful, childish ornamentation, yet amazes us by the immensity of its heaven-aspiring proportions.

...No German can pronounce the name of Lessing without a responsive echo in his breast. Since Luther, Germany has produced no greater and better man than Gotthold Ephraim Lessing. These two are our pride and joy. In the troubles of the present we look back at their consoling figures, and they answer with a look full of bright promise. The third man will come who will perfect what Luther began and what Lessing carried on—the third Liberator.

Like Luther, Lessing's achievements consisted not only in effecting something definite, but in agitating the German people to its depths, and in awakening through his criticism and polemics a wholesome intellectual activity. He was the vivifying critic of his time, and his whole life was a polemic. His critical insight made itself felt throughout the widest range of thought and feeling—in religion, in science, and in art. His polemics vanquished every opponent, and grew stronger with every victory. Lessing, as he himself confessed, needed conflict for the full development of his powers. He resembled that fabulous Norman who inherited the skill, knowledge, and strength of those whom he slew in single combat, and in this manner became finally endowed with all possible excellencies and perfections. It is easily conceivable that such a contentious champion should stir up not a little commotion in Germany,—in that quiet Germany which was then even more sabbatically quiet than now. The majority were stupefied at his literary audacity. But this was of the greatest assistance to him, for *oser*! is the secret of success in literature, as it is in revolutions,—and in love. All trembled before the sword of Lessing. No head was safe from him. Yes, many heads he struck off from mere wantonness, and was moreover so spiteful as to lift them up from the ground and show to the public that they were hollow inside. Those whom his sword could not reach he slew with the arrows of his wit. His friends admired the pretty feathers of those arrows; his enemies felt their barbs in their hearts. Lessing's wit does not resemble that *enjouement*, that *gaîté*, those lively *saillies*, which are so well known here in France. His wit was no petty French greyhound, chasing its own shadow: it was rather a great German tom-cat, who plays with the mouse before he throttles it.

Yes, polemics were our Lessing's delight, and so he never reflected long whether an opponent was worthy of him,—thus through his controversies he has saved many a name from well-merited oblivion. Around many a pitiful authorling he has spun a web of the wittiest sarcasm, the most charming humour; and thus they are preserved for all time in Lessing's works, like insects caught in a piece of amber. In slaying his enemies he made them immortal. Who of us would have ever heard of that Klotz on whom Lessing wasted so much wit and scorn? The huge rocks which he hurled at, and with which he crushed, that poor antiquarian, are now the latter's indestructible monument.

It is noteworthy that this wittiest man of all Germany was also the most honourable. There is nothing equal to his love of truth. Lessing made not the least concession to falsehood, even if thereby, after the manner of the worldly-wise, he could advance the victory of truth itself. He could do everything for truth, except lie for it. Whoever thinks, he once said, to bring Truth to man, masked and rouged, may well be her pander, but he has never been her lover.

...It is heart-rending to read in his biography how fate denied this man every joy, and how it did not even vouchsafe to him to rest with his family from his daily struggles. Once only fortune seemed to smile on him; she gave him a loved wife, a child—but this happiness was like the rays of the sun gilding the wings of a swift-flying bird: it vanished as quickly. His wife died in consequence of her confinement, the child soon after birth. Concerning the latter, he wrote to a friend the horribly-witty words, "My joy was brief. And I lost him so unwillingly, that son! For he was so wise, so wise! Do not think that the few hours of my fatherhood have already made a doting parent of me. I know what I say. Was it not wisdom that he had to be reluctantly dragged into the world with iron tongs, and that he so soon discovered his folly? Was it not wisdom that he seized the first opportunity to leave it? For once I have sought to be happy like other men; but I have made a miserable failure of it."

...Lessing was the prophet who from the New Testament pointed towards the Third Testament. I have called him the successor of Luther; and it is in this character that I have to speak of him here. Of his influence on German art I shall speak hereafter. On this he effected a wholesome reform, not only through his criticism, but also through his example; and this latter phase of his activity is generally made the most prominent, and is the most discussed. But, viewed from our present standpoint, his philosophical and theological battles are to us more important than all his dramas, or his dramaturgy. His dramas, however, like all his writings, have a social import, and *Nathan the Wise* is in reality not only a good play, but also a philosophical, theological treatise in support of the doctrine of a pure theism. For Lessing, art was a tribune, and when he was thrust from the pulpit or the professor's chair he sprang on to the stage, speaking out more boldly, and gaining a more numerous audience.

I say that Lessing continued the work of Luther. After Luther had freed us from the yoke of tradition and had exalted the Bible as the only well-spring of Christianity, there ensued a rigid word-service, and the letter of the Bible ruled just as tyrannically as once did tradition. Lessing contributed the most to the emancipation from the tyranny of the letter.

Lessing died in Brunswick, in the year 1781, misunderstood, hated, and denounced. In the same year there was published at Königsberg the *Critique of Pure Reason*, by Immanuel Kant. With this book there begins in Germany an intellectual revolution, which offers the most wonderful analogies to the material revolution in France, and which to the profound thinker must appear equally important. It develops the same phases, and between the two there exists a very remarkable parallelism. On both sides of the Rhine we behold the same rupture with the past: it is loudly proclaimed that all reverence for tradition is at an end. As in France no privilege, so in Germany no thought is tolerated without proving its right to exist: nothing is taken for granted. And as in France fell the monarchy, the keystone of the old social system, so in Germany fell theism, the keystone of the intellectual *ancien régime*.

. . . .

It is horrible when the bodies which we have created ask of us a soul. But it is still more horrible, more terrible, more uncanny, to create a soul, which craves a body and pursues us with that demand. The idea which we have thought is such a soul, and it allows us no peace until we have given it a body, until we have brought it into actual being. The thought seems to become deed; the word, flesh. And, strange! man, like the God of the Bible, needs but to speak his thought, and the world shapes itself accordingly: light dawns, or darkness descends; the waters separate themselves from the dry land, and even wild beasts appear. The universe is but the signature of the word.

Mark this, ye haughty men of action. Ye are naught but the unconscious servants of the men of thought, who, oftentimes in the humblest obscurity, have marked out your tasks for you with the utmost exactitude. Maximilian Robespierre was only the hand of Jean Jacques Rousseau—the bloody hand that from the womb of time drew forth the body whose soul Rousseau had created. Did the restless anxiety that embittered the life of Jean Jacques arise from a foreboding that his thoughts would require such a midwife to bring them into the world?

Old Fontenelle was perhaps in the right when he declared, "If I carried all the ideas of this world in my closed hand, I should take good heed not to open it." For my part, I think differently. If I held all the ideas of the world in my hand, I might perhaps implore you to hew off my hand at once, but in no case would I long keep it closed. I am not adapted to be a jailor of thoughts. By Heaven! I would set them free. Even if they assumed the most threatening shapes and swept through all lands like a band of mad Bacchantes; even if with their thyrsus staffs they should strike down our most innocent flowers; even if they should break into our hospitals and chase the sick old world from its bed! It would certainly grieve me sadly, and I myself should come to harm. For, alas! I too belong to that sick old world; and the poet says rightly that scoffing at our own crutches does not enable us to walk any the better. I am the most sick among you all, and the most to be pitied, for I know what health is. But you know it not, you enviable ones. You can die without noticing it yourselves. Yes, many of you have already been dead for these many years, and you think that now only does the true life begin. When I contradict such madness, then they become enraged against me, and rail at me, and, horrible! the corpses spring on me and reproach me; and more even than their revilings does their mouldy odour oppress me. Avaunt, ye spectres! I am speaking of one whose very name possesses an exorcising power: I speak of Immanuel Kant.

It is said that the spirits of darkness tremble with affright when they behold the sword of an executioner. How, then, must they stand aghast when confronted with Kant's *Critique of Pure Reason*! This book is the sword with which, in Germany, theism was decapitated.

To be candid, you French are tame and moderate compared with us Germans. At the most, you have slain a king; and he had already lost his head before he was beheaded. And withal you must drum so much, and shout, and stamp, so that the whole world was shaken by the tumult. It is really awarding Maximilian Robespierre too much honour to compare him with Immanuel Kant. Maximilian Robespierre, the great citizen of the Rue Saint Honoré, did truly have an attack of destructive fury when the monarchy was concerned, and he writhed terribly enough in his regicidal epilepsy; but as soon as the Supreme Being was mentioned, he wiped the white foam from his mouth and the blood from his hands, put on his blue Sunday coat with the bright buttons, and attached a bouquet of flowers to his broad coat-lapel.

The life-history of Immanuel Kant is difficult to write, for he had neither a life nor a history. He lived a mechanical, orderly, almost abstract, bachelor life, in a quiet little side-street of Königsberg, an old city near the north-east boundary of Germany. I believe that the great clock of the cathedral did not perform its daily work more dispassionately, more regularly, than its countryman, Immanuel Kant. Rising, coffee-drinking, writing, collegiate lectures, dining, walking—each had its set time. And when Immanuel Kant, in his grey coat, cane in hand, appeared at the door of his house, and strolled towards the small linden avenue, which is still called "the philosopher's walk," the neighbours knew it was exactly half-past four. Eight times he promenaded up and down, during all seasons; and when the weather was gloomy, or the grey clouds threatened rain, his old servant Lampe was seen plodding anxiously after, with a large umbrella under his arm, like a symbol of Providence.

What a strange contrast between the outer life of the man and his destructive, world-convulsing thoughts! Had the citizens of Königsberg surmised the whole significance of these thoughts, they would have felt a more profound awe in the presence of this man than in that of an executioner, who merely slays human beings. But the good people saw in him nothing but a professor of philosophy; and when at the fixed hour he sauntered by, they nodded a friendly greeting, and regulated their watches.

But if Immanuel Kant, that arch-destroyer in the realms of thought, far surpassed Maximilian Robespierre in terrorism, yet he had certain points of resemblance to the latter that invite a comparison of the two men. In both we find the same inflexible, rigid, prosaic integrity. Then we find in both the same instinct of distrust,—only that the one exercises it against ideas, and names it a critique, while the other applies it to men, and calls it republican virtue. In both, however, the narrow-minded shopkeeper type is markedly manifest. Nature had intended them to weigh out sugar and coffee, but fate willed it otherwise, and into the scales of one it laid a king, into those of the other, a God. And they both weighed correctly.

...Pantheism had already in Fichte's time interpenetrated German art; even the Catholic Romanticists unconsciously followed this current, and Goethe expressed it most unmistakably. This he already does in *Werther*. In *Faust* he seeks to establish an affinity between man and nature by a bold, direct, mystic method, and conjures the secret forces of nature through the magic formula of the powers of hell. But this Goethean pantheism is most clearly and most charmingly disclosed in his short ballads. The early philosophy of Spinoza has shed its mathematical shell, and now flutters about us as Goethean poetry. Hence the wrath of our pietists, and of orthodoxy in general, against the Goethean ballads. With their pious bear-paws they clumsily strike at this butterfly, which is so daintily ethereal, so light of wing, that it always flits out of reach. These Goethean ballads have a tantalising charm that is indescribable. The harmonious verses captivate the heart like the tenderness of a loving maiden; the words embrace you while the thought kisses you.

...This giant was minister in a lilliputian German state, in which he could never move at ease. It was said of Phidias's Jupiter seated in Olympus, that were he ever to stand erect the sudden uprising would rend asunder the vaulted roof. This was exactly Goethe's situation at Weimar; had he suddenly lifted himself up from his peaceful, sitting posture, he would have shattered the gabled canopy of state, or, more probably, he would have bruised his own head. But the German Jupiter remained quietly seated, and composedly accepted homage and incense.

...When it was seen that such saddening follies were budding out of philosophy and ripening into a baleful maturity—when it was observed that the German youth were generally absorbed in metaphysical abstractions, thereby neglecting the most important questions of the time and unfitting themselves for practical life,—it was quite natural that patriots and lovers of liberty should be led to conceive a justifiable dislike to philosophy; and a few went so far as to condemn it utterly and entirely, as idle, useless, chimerical theorising.

We shall not be so foolish as to attempt seriously to refute these malcontents. German philosophy is a matter of great weight and importance, and concerns the whole human race. Only our most remote descendants will be able to decide whether we deserve blame or praise for completing first our philosophy and afterwards our revolution. To me it seems that a methodical people, such as we Germans are, must necessarily have commenced with the Reformation, could only after that proceed to occupy ourselves with philosophy, and not until the completion of the latter could we pass on to the political revolution. This order I find quite sensible. The heads which philosophy has used for thinking, the revolution can afterwards, for its purposes, cut off. But philosophy would never have been able to use the heads which had been decapitated by the revolution, if the latter had preceded.

...Christianity—and this is its fairest service—has to a certain degree moderated that brutal lust of battle, such as we find it among the ancient Germanic races, who fought, not to destroy, not yet to conquer, but merely from a fierce, demoniac love of battle itself; but it could not altogether eradicate it. And when once that restraining talisman, the cross, is broken, then the smouldering ferocity of those ancient warriors will again blaze up; then will again be heard the deadly clang of that frantic Berserkir wrath, of which the Norse poets say and sing so much. The talisman is rotten with decay, and the day will surely come when it will crumble and fall. Then the ancient stone gods will arise from out the ashes of dismantled ruins, and rub the dust of a thousand years from their eyes; and finally Thor, with his colossal hammer, will leap up, and with it shatter into fragments the Gothic Cathedrals.

And when ye hear the rumbling and the crumbling, take heed, ye neighbours of France, and meddle not with what we do in Germany. It might bring harm on you. Take heed not to kindle the fire; take heed not to quench it. Ye might easily burn your fingers in the flame. Smile not at my advice as the counsel of a visionary warning you against Kantians, Fichteans, and natural philosophers. Scoff not at the dreamer who expects in the material world a revolution similar to that which has already taken place in the domains of thought. The thought goes before the deed, as the lightning precedes the thunder. German thunder is certainly German, and is rather awkward, and it comes rolling along tardily; but come it surely will, and when ye once hear a crash the like of which in the world's history was never heard before, then know that the German thunderbolt has reached its mark. At this crash the eagles will fall dead in mid air, and the lions in Afric's most distant deserts will cower and sneak into their royal dens. A drama will be enacted in Germany in comparison with which the French Revolution will appear a harmless idyl. To be sure, matters are at present rather quiet, and if occasionally this one or the other rants and gesticulates somewhat violently, do not believe that these are the real actors. These are only little puppies, that run around in the empty arena, barking and snarling at one another, until the hour shall arrive when appear the gladiators, who are to battle unto death.

And that hour *will* come. As on the raised benches of an amphitheatre the nations will group themselves around Germany to behold the great tournament. I advise you, ye French, keep very quiet then: on your souls take heed that ye applaud not. We might easily misunderstand you, and in our blunt manner roughly quiet and rebuke you, for if in our former servile condition we could sometimes overcome you, much more easily can we do so in the wantonness and delirious intoxication of freedom. Ye yourselves know what one can do in such a condition—and ye are no longer in that condition. Beware! I mean well with you, therefore I tell you the bitter truth. You have more to fear from emancipated Germany than from the whole Holy Alliance, with all its Croats and Cossacks. For, in the first place, you are not loved in Germany,—which is almost incomprehensible, for you are so very amiable, and during your sojourn in Germany took much pains to please at least the better and lovelier half of the Germans. But even if that half should love you, it is just the half that does not bear arms, and whose friendship would therefore avail you but little.

What they really have against you, I could never make out. Once in a beer-cellar at Göttingen, a young Teuton said that revenge must be had on the French for Conrad von Stauffen, whom they beheaded at Naples. You have surely long since forgotten that. But we forget nothing. You see that if we should once be inclined to quarrel with you, good reasons will not be wanting. At all events, I advise you to be on your guard. Let what will happen in Germany, whether the Crown Prince of Prussia or Dr. Wirth hold sway, be always armed, remain quietly at your post, musket in hand. I mean well with you; and I almost stood aghast when I learned lately that your ministry propose to disarm France.

As, notwithstanding your present Romanticism, you are inborn classics, you know Olympus. Among the naked gods and goddesses who there make themselves merry with nectar and ambrosia, you behold one goddess who, although surrounded with mirth and sport, yet wears always a coat of mail, and keeps helm on head and spear in hand.

It is the goddess of wisdom.

FLORENTINE NIGHTS.

[Heine wrote the fragment entitled *Florentine Nights* in 1835, and published it two years later in the third volume of the *Salon*. It is a series of brilliant pictures united by a very slight thread of connection. There is unquestionably an additional element of autobiographical interest; Maximilian's visits to Potsdam and London correspond to Heine's, and throughout this various record of impressions we frequently hear Heine's own voice. The translation here given has not been previously published.]

108

FIRST NIGHT.

IN the ante-room Maximilian found the doctor just as he was drawing on his black gloves. "I am greatly pressed for time," the latter hurriedly said to him. "Signora Maria has not slept during the whole night; she has only just now fallen into a light slumber. I need not caution you not to wake her by any noise; and when she wakes on no account must she be allowed to talk. She must lie still, and not disturb herself; mental excitement will not be salutary. Tell her all kinds of odd stories, so that she must listen quietly."

"Be assured, doctor," replied Maximilian, with a melancholy smile. "I have educated myself for a long time in chattering, and will not let her talk. I will narrate abundance of fantastic nonsense, as much as you require. But how long can she live?"

"I am greatly pressed for time," answered the doctor, and slipped away.

Black Deborah, quick of hearing as she was, had already recognised the stranger's footstep, and softly opened the door. At a sign from him she left as softly, and Maximilian found himself alone with his friend. A single lamp dimly lighted the chamber. This cast now and then half timid, half inquisitive gleams upon the countenance of the sick lady, clothed entirely in white muslin, who lay stretched on a green sofa in calm sleep.

Silent, and with folded arms, Maximilian stood a little while before the sleeping figure, and gazed on the beautiful limbs which the light garments revealed rather than covered; and every time that the lamp threw a ray of light over the pale countenance, his heart quivered. "For God's sake!" he said softly, "what is that? What memories are awaking in me? Yes, now I know. This white form on the green ground, yes, now...."

At this moment the invalid awoke, and gazing out, as it were, from the depths of a dream, the tender dark-blue eyes rested upon him, asking, entreating.... "What were you thinking of, just now, Maximilian?" she said, in that awful, gentle voice so often found in consumptives, and wherein we seem to recognise the lisping of children, the twittering of birds, and the gurgle of the dying. "What were you thinking of, just then, Maximilian?" she repeated again, and started up so hastily that the long curls, like roused snakes, fell in ringlets around her head.

"For God's sake!" exclaimed Maximilian, as he gently pressed her back on to the sofa, "lie still, do not talk; I will tell you all I think, I feel, yes, what I myself do not know!

"In fact," he pursued, "I scarcely know what I was thinking and feeling just now. Dim visions of childhood were passing through my mind. I was thinking of my mother's castle, of the deserted garden there, of the beautiful marble statue that lay in the grass.... I said, 'my mother's *castle*,' but pray do not imagine anything grand and magnificent. To this name I have indeed accustomed myself; my father always laid a special emphasis on the words, 'the castle,' and accompanied them always with a singular smile. The meaning of that smile I understood later, when, a boy of some twelve years, I travelled with my mother to the castle. It was my first journey. We spent the whole day in passing through a thick forest; I shall never forget its gloomy horror; and only towards evening did we stop before a long cross-bar which separated us from a large meadow. Here we waited nearly half-an-hour before the boy came out of the wretched hut near by, removed the barrier, and admitted us. I say 'the boy,' because old Martha always called her forty years' old nephew 'the lad.' To receive his gracious mistress worthily, he had assumed the livery of his late uncle; and it was in consequence of its requiring a little previous dusting that he had kept us waiting so long. Had he had time, he would have also put on stockings; the long red legs, however, did not form a very marked contrast with the glaring scarlet coat. Whether there were any trousers underneath I am unable to say. Our servant, John, who had likewise often heard of 'the castle,' put on a very amazed grimace as the boy led us to the little ruined building in which his master had lived. He was, however, altogether at a loss when my mother ordered him to bring in the beds. How could he guess that at the 'castle' no beds were to be found, and my mother's order that he should bring bedding for us he had either not heard or considered as superfluous trouble.

"The little house, only one storey high, which in its best days contained, at the most, five habitable rooms, was a lamentable picture of transitoriness. Broken furniture, torn carpets, not one window-frame left entire, the floor pulled up here and there, everywhere the hated traces of the wantonest military possession. 'The soldiers quartered with us have always amused themselves,' said the boy, with a silly smile. My mother signed that we should all leave her alone, and while the boy and John were busying themselves, I went out to see the garden. This also offered the most disconsolate picture of ruin. The great trees were partly destroyed, partly broken down, and parasites were scornfully spreading over the fallen trunks. Here and there by the grown-up box-bushes the old paths might be recognised. Here and there also stood statues, for the most part wanting heads, or at all events noses. I remember a Diana whose lower half the dark ivy grew round in a most amusing way, as I also remember a Goddess of Plenty, out of whose cornucopia mere ill-odorous weeds were blooming. Only one statue had been spared from the malice of men and of time; it had, indeed, been thrown from off its pedestal into the high grass; but there it lay, free from mutilation, the marble goddess with pure lovely features and the noble deep-cleft bosom, which seemed, as it glowed out of the grass, like a Greek revelation. I almost started when I saw it; this form inspired me with a singular feeling, and bashfulness kept me from lingering long near so sweet a sight.

"When I returned to my mother, she was standing at the window, lost in thought, her head resting on her right arm, and the tears were flowing over her cheeks. I had never seen her weep so before. She embraced me with passionate tenderness, and asked my forgiveness, because, owing to John's negligence, I should have no regular bed. 'Old Martha,' she said, 'is very ill, dear child, and cannot give up her bed to you; but John will arrange the cushions out of the coach, so that you will be able to sleep upon them, and he can also give you his cloak for a covering. I shall sleep on the straw; this was my dear father's bed-room; it was much better here once. Leave me alone!' And the tears came still more impetuously.

"Whether it was owing to my unaccustomed place of rest or to my disturbed heart, I could not sleep. The moonlight streamed in through the broken window-panes, and seemed to allure me out into the bright summer night. I might lie on the right or the left side, close my eyes or impatiently open them again—I could still think of nothing but the lovely marble statue I had seen lying in the grass. I could not understand the shyness which had come over me at the sight of it; I was vexed at this childish feeling, and 'To-morrow,' I said softly to myself, 'to-morrow I will kiss you, you lovely marble face, kiss you just on that pretty corner of your mouth where the lips melt into such a sweet dimple!' An impatience I had never before felt was stirring through all my limbs; I could no longer rule the strange impulse, and I sprang up at last with audacious vivacity, exclaiming, 'And why should I not kiss you to-night, you dear image?' Quietly, so that mother might not hear my steps, I left the house; with the less difficulty, since the entrance was furnished with an escutcheon indeed, but no longer with a door, and hastily worked my way through the abundant growth of the neglected garden. There was no sound; everything was resting silent and solemn in the still moonlight. The shadows of the trees seemed to be nailed on the earth. In the green grass lay the beautiful goddess, likewise motionless, yet no stony death, but only a quiet sleep, seemed to hold her lovely limbs fettered; and as I came near, I almost feared lest the least noise should awake her out of her slumber. I held my breath, as I leant over to gaze on the beautiful features; a shuddering pain thrust me back, but a boyish wantonness drew me again towards her; my heart was beating wildly, and at last I kissed the lovely goddess with such passion and tenderness and despair as I have never in this life kissed with again. And I have never been able to forget the fearful and sweet sensation which flowed through my soul as the blissful cool of those marble lips touched my mouth.... And so you see, Maria, that as I was just now standing before you, and saw you lying in your white muslin garments on the green sofa, your appearance suggested to me the white marble form in the green grass. Had you slept any longer my lips would not have been able to resist——"

"Max! Max!" she cried from the depth of her soul. "Horrible! You know that a kiss from your mouth——"

"Oh, be silent only; I know you think that something horrible. Do not look at me so imploringly. I do not misunderstand your feelings, although their causes are hidden from me. I have never dared to press my mouth on your lips."

But Maria would not let him finish speaking; she seized his hand, covered it with passionate kisses, and then said, smiling—"Please tell me more of your love affairs. How long did you adore the marble beauty that you kissed in your mother's castle garden?"

"We went away the next day," Maximilian answered, "and I have never seen the lovely statue again. It occupied my heart, however, for nearly three years. A wonderful passion for marble statues has since then developed in my soul, and

111

this very day I have felt its transporting power. I was coming out of the Laurentian, the library of the Medici, and I wandered, I know not how, into the chapel where that most magnificent of Italian families built for itself a resting-place of jewels, and is quietly sleeping. For a whole hour I was absorbed in gazing on the marble figure of a woman, whose powerful body witnesses to the cunning strength of Michael Angelo, while yet the whole form is pervaded by an ethereal sweetness which we are not accustomed to seek in that master. The whole dream-world, with its silent blisses, lives in that marble; a tender repose dwells in the lovely limbs, a soothing moonlight seems to course through the veins. It is the Night of Michael Angelo Buonarotti. O, how willingly would I sleep the eternal sleep in the arms of that Night!

"Painted women forms," Maximilian pursued, after a pause, "have never so powerfully interested me as statues. Only once was I in love with a painting. It was a wondrously lovely Madonna that I learnt to know at a church in Cologne. I was at that time a very zealous church-goer, and my heart was absorbed in the mysticism of the Catholic religion. I would then have willingly fought like a Spanish knight, at the peril of my life, for the immaculate conception of Mary, the Queen of Angels, the fairest lady of Heaven and earth! I was interested in all the members of the holy family at that time, and I took my hat off in an especially friendly manner whenever I passed near a picture of the holy Joseph. This disposition did not last long, however, and I deserted the Mother of God almost without any explanations, having become acquainted, in a gallery of antiquities, with a Grecian nymph, who for a long time held me enchained in marble fetters."

"And you only loved sculptured or painted women?" said Maria, smiling.

"No, I have also loved dead women," answered Maximilian, over whose face an expression of seriousness had spread. He failed to perceive Maria start and shrink at these words, and quietly proceeded—

"Yes, it is very strange that I once fell in love with a girl after she had been seven years dead. When I became acquainted with little Very I liked her extremely. For three days I occupied myself with this young person, and experienced the greatest pleasure in all that she said and did, and in every expression of her charming wayward being, without being betrayed withal into any over-tender emotion. And so I was not too deeply grieved when a few months later I heard that a fever that had seized her suddenly resulted in death. I forgot her entirely, and I am convinced that from one year's end to another's I had not one thought of her. Seven years passed away, and I found myself at Potsdam, to enjoy the beautiful summer in undisturbed solitude. My society was confined to the statues in the garden of Sansouci. It happened there one day that I recollected certain features, and a singular, lovely way of speaking and moving, without being able to remember to whom they belonged. Nothing is more annoying than such a drifting into old memories, and I was therefore joyfully surprised when, after some days, I recollected little Very, and discovered that it was her dear, forgotten form that had hovered before me so restlessly. Yes, I rejoiced at this discovery like one who unexpectedly meets his most intimate friend; the pale hues gradually grew bright, and at last her sweet little person seemed to stand bodily before me, smiling, pouting, witty, and prettier than ever. From that time forth the sweet vision never left me, it filled my whole soul; wherever I went or stood, that went and stood at my side, spoke with me, laughed with me, always gentle, and yet never over-tender. I was, however, more and more fascinated with this vision, which daily gained more and more reality for me. It is easy to raise ghosts, but it is difficult to send them back again to their dark night; they look at us then so imploringly, our own hearts lend them such powerful intercession. I could not tear myself free, and fell in love with little Very after she had been seven years dead. I lived thus at Potsdam for six months, quite buried in this love. I guarded myself more carefully than ever from any contact with the outer world, and if anyone in the street came at all near me, I experienced the most miserable oppression. I cherished a deep horror of every occurrence, such as, perhaps, the night-wandering spirits of the dead experience; for these, it is said, are terrified when they meet a living man, as much as a living man is terrified when he meets a spectre. By chance a traveller came at that time to Potsdam whom I could not escape—namely, my brother. His appearance and his accounts of the latest news woke me as from a deep dream, and I suddenly felt, with a shudder, in what a frightful solitude I had been so long living. In this condition I had not once noted the change of the seasons, and I now gazed with wonder on the trees, long since leafless, decked in their autumn mellowness. I immediately left Potsdam and little Very, and in another town, where important business was awaiting me, and by means of difficult circumstances and relations, I was soon again plunged into crude reality.

"The living women," Maximilian pursued, while a sorrowful smile played on his upper lip, "the living women with whom I then came into unavoidable contact, how they tormented me, tenderly tormented me with their pouting, jealousy, and constant sighs. At how many balls must I trot round with them, in how much gossip must I mix myself! What restless vanity, what delight in lying, what kissing treachery, what envenomed flowers! These women spoilt all pleasure and love for me, and I was for some time a misogynist, who damned the whole sex. It went with me almost as with the French officer, who, in the Prussian campaign, only saved himself with the greatest difficulty from the ice-pits at Beresina, and since that retains such an antipathy to everything frozen, that now he thrusts away with disgust the sweetest and most delicious of Tortoni's ices. Yes, the remembrance of the Beresina of love that I passed through then spoilt for me, for a time, even the most charming ladies, women like angels, girls like Vanilla sherbert."

"Pray, do not abuse women," exclaimed Maria. "That is a worn-out commonplace among men. In the end, to be happy, you need women after all."

"Oh," sighed Maximilian, "that is true, certainly. But women, unfortunately, have only one way of making us happy, while they have thirty thousand ways of making us unhappy."

"Dear friend," replied Maria, suppressing a little smile, "I am speaking of the concord of two souls in unison. Have you never experienced this joy? But I see an unaccustomed blush spreading over your cheeks. Tell me, Max."

"It is true, Maria, I feel as confused almost as a boy at confessing to you the happy love with which I was once infinitely blessed. That memory is not yet lost to me, and to its cool shades my soul often flies, when the burning dust and day's heat of life grow almost unbearable. Yet I am not able to give you a just idea of her. She was such an ethereal creature that she only seemed revealed to me in dreams. I think that you, Maria, have no vulgar prejudice against dreams; those nightly visions have, in truth, as much reality as the coarser shapes of day, which we can touch with our hands, and by which we are not seldom besmutched. Yes, it was in a dream that I knew that sweet being who has made me most happy on earth. I can say little of her outward appearance. I am not able to describe the form of her features with precision. It was a face that I had never seen before, and that I have never in my life seen since. So much I remember; it was not white and rosy, but all of one colour—a soft, reddened, pale-yellow, transparent as crystal. The charm of this face was not in firm regularity of beauty, nor in interesting vivacity; its characteristic was, rather, a charming, enrapturing, almost terrible veracity. It was a face full of conscious fire and gracious goodness; it was more a soul than a face, and on that account I have never been able to make her outward form quite present to myself. The eyes were soft as flowers, the lips rather pale, but charmingly arched. She wore a silk dressing-gown of a corn-flour blue colour, and in that consisted her entire clothing; neck and feet were naked, and through the thin delicate garment now and then peeped stealthily the slender tenderness of the limbs. Nor can I make plain the words we said to one another; I only know that we betrothed each other, and that we chatted with one another, gay and familiar and open-hearted, like bridegroom and bride, almost like brother and sister. Often we left off talking, and gazed into each other's eyes; we spent whole eternities so. What waked me I cannot say, but I revelled for a long time in the after-feeling of these love-blisses. I was long, as it were, intoxicated with ineffable delight, the pining depth of my heart was filled with bliss, a hitherto unknown joy seemed poured over all my emotions, and I remained glad and joyful, though I never saw the beloved form in my dreams again. But had I not enjoyed whole eternities in her gaze? and she knew me too well not to be aware that I do not like repetitions."

"Truly," exclaimed Maria, "you are an *homme à bonne fortune*. But, tell me, was Mademoiselle Laurence a marble statue or a painting—was she dead or a dream?"

"Perhaps she was all these together," answered Maximilian, very earnestly.

"I can imagine, dear friend, that this sweetheart was of very doubtful character. And when will you tell me the history?"

"To-morrow. It is too long, and I am tired to-night. I have just come from the opera, and have too much music in my ears."

"You often go to the opera now, and I think, Max, you go there more to see than

114

to hear."

"You are not mistaken, Maria; I go to the opera, indeed, to look at the faces of the beautiful Italian women. In truth, they are beautiful enough outside the theatre, and a connoisseur in faces could easily trace in the ideality of their features the influence which the arts have had on the physique of the Italian people. Nature has taken back from the artists the capital she once lent, and see how delightfully the interest has increased! Nature, who once furnished the artists with their model, now on her side copies the masterpieces which have thus arisen. The sense of the beautiful has permeated the whole people, and as once the flesh on the spirit, so now the spirit works on the flesh. The devotion paid before those fair Madonnas and lovely altar-pieces, which impress themselves on the mind of the bridegroom, while the bride bears a handsome saint in her ardent heart, is not fruitless. From this affinity a race has arisen still fairer than the gracious earth on which it flourishes, and the sunny sky that is as bright around it as a golden frame. The men do not interest me much when they are not painted or sculptured, and I resign to you, Maria, all possible enthusiasm in regard to those handsome, supple Italians, who have such wild-black beards, such bold noble noses, and such soft subtle eyes. They say the Lombards are the most handsome men. I have never made any investigations on the subject, but I have earnestly considered the Lombardy women, and they, I have noted well, are indeed as beautiful as report announces. Even in the middle ages they must have been tolerably beautiful. It is said of Francis I. that the fame of the beauty of the Milanese women was a secret motive which impelled him to the Italian campaign; the chivalrous king was certainly curious whether the kinsfolk of his spiritual muses were really as beautiful as fame reported. Poor rogue! he had to atone dearly for this curiosity at Pavia!

"But how beautiful they are, these Italian women, when music illuminates their countenances! I say 'illuminates,' because the effect of the music, which I marked in the opera, on the faces of the beautiful women altogether resembled those light-and-shade effects which surprise us so when we look at statues by torch-light at night-time. These marble forms reveal to us then, with terrifying truth, their indwelling spirit and their horrible dumb secrets. In the same way the whole life of the fair Italian women becomes known to us when we see them in the opera; the changing melodies wake in their souls a succession of emotions, memories, wishes, scandals, which visibly speak in the movements of their features, in their blushes, in their pallors, and even in their eyes. He who knows how to read them may then see in their faces many very sweet and interesting things—histories as remarkable as Boccaccio's tales, emotions as tender as Petrarch's sonnets, caprices as full of adventure as Ariosto's *ottaverime*, sometimes, too, fearful treachery and sublime wickedness as poetic as Dante's *Inferno*. It is worth while to gaze at the boxes. If the men would only express their enthusiasm meanwhile with less frightful sounds! This mad noise in an Italian theatre often annoys me. But music is the soul of these men, their life, their national business. In other countries, certainly, there are musicians who equal the greatest Italian masters, but there is no other musical nation. Here, in

115

Italy, music is not represented by individuals; it manifests itself in the whole population; music has become a nation. With us in the north it is quite different; there music only becomes a man, and is called Mozart or Meyerbeer; and when, moreover, they would accurately investigate what is the best that this northern music offers us, they find it in Italian sunshine and orange-perfume; and much rather than to our Germany those belong to fair Italy, the home of music. Yes, Italy will always be the home of music, even though her great *maestri* descend early into the grave or become dumb—even though Bellini dies and Rossini keeps silence."

"Indeed," remarked Maria, "Rossini has preserved a very long silence. If I do not mistake, he has been silent for ten years."

"Perhaps that is a joke on his part," answered Maximilian. "He wishes to show that the title, "Swan of Pesaro," which has been conferred upon him, is quite unsuitable. Swans sing at the end of their lives, but Rossini has left off singing in the middle of his life. And I believe that he has done well in that, and shown, even by that, that he is a genius. The artist who has only talent retains to the end of his life the impulse to exercise that talent; ambition stimulates him; he feels that he is constantly perfecting himself, and he is compelled to strive after the highest. But genius has already accomplished the highest; it is content; it contemns the world and small ambition, and goes home to Stratford-on-Avon, like William Shakespeare, or walks about the Boulevard des Italiens at Paris, and laughs and jokes, like Giacomo Rossini. If genius has a not altogether badly constituted body, it lives on in this way for a good while after it has given forth its masterpieces, or, as people express it, after it has fulfilled its mission. It is owing to a prepossession that people say that genius must die early; I think that from the thirtieth to the thirty-fourth year has been indicated as the most dangerous period for genius. How often have I bantered poor Bellini on this subject, and playfully prophesied that, being a genius, and having reached that dangerous age, he must soon die. Singular! in spite of the playful tone, he tormented himself about this prophecy; he called me his *jettatore*, his evil eye, and always made the *jettatore* sign. He so wished to live, he had an almost passionate hatred of death: he would hear nothing of dying; he was frightened of it as a child who is afraid to sleep in the dark.... He was a good, dear child, often rather naughty, but then one only needed to threaten him with an early death, and he would immediately draw in, and entreat, and make with his two raised fingers the *jettatore* sign. Poor Bellini!"

"So you knew him personally? Was he handsome?"

"He was not ugly. You see, we cannot answer affirmatively when anyone asks us such a question about our own sex. He had a tall, slender figure, which moved in an elegant, I might say a coquettish, manner; always *a quatre épingles*; a long, regular face, with a pale rosiness; very fair, almost golden, hair, put into small curls; very high noble brows, a straight nose, pale blue eyes, a beautifully-chiselled mouth, a round chin. His features had something vague and characterless; something like milk, and in this milk-face often mingled, half sweet, half bitter, an expression of sorrow. This expression of sorrow compensated for the want of soul in Bellini's face, but it was a sorrow without depth; it glistened in the eyes without poetry, it played passionless about his lips. The young *Maestro* seemed anxious to make this flat, languid sorrow conspicuous in his whole person. His hair was curled in such a fanciful, melancholy way, his clothes sat so languidly about his frail body, he carried his little Spanish cane in so idyllic a way, that he always reminded me of the affected young shepherds with their be-ribboned sticks, and bright-coloured jackets, and pantaloons that we see in our pastorals. And his gait was so young-lady-like, so elegiac, so ethereal. The whole man looked like a sigh *en escarpins*. He had received much applause among women, but I doubt if he anywhere awakened a strong passion. In himself his appearance had something comically unenjoyable, the reason of which lay in his way of speaking French. Although Bellini had lived many years in France, he spoke the language so badly, that even in England it could scarcely be spoken worse. I ought not to call it 'bad;' bad is here much too good. One must call it awful, a violation, something enough to overturn the world. Yes, when one was in society with him, and he mangled the poor French words like an executioner, and displayed, unmoved, his colossal *coq-à-l'âne*, one thought sometimes that the world must fall in with a crash of thunder. The stillness of the grave reigned on the whole room; a death agony was painted on all faces in chalk or in vermilion; the ladies were uncertain whether to faint or to escape; the gentlemen gazed in alarm at their trousers, to convince themselves that they actually had them on; and what was most horrible, this fright raised at the same time a convulsive desire to laugh, which could hardly be suppressed. So that when one was in Bellini's society, his presence inspired a certain anxiety, which by a horrible charm was at once repellant and attractive. Often his involuntary *calembours* were merely amusing, and in their droll insipidity reminded one of the castle of his fellow-countryman, the Prince of Pallagonia, which Goethe in his *Italian Journey* has described as a museum of uncouth distortions and absurd deformities. As Bellini on such occasions always imagined he had said something quite harmless and earnest, his face and his words formed the maddest contrast. That which displeased me in his face came at such moments specially prominent. What I disliked could not be exactly described as something lacking, and may not have been displeasing to women at all. Bellini's face, like his whole appearance, had that physical freshness, that bloom of flesh, that rosiness which makes a disagreeable impression on me—on me, because I like much more what is death-like and marble. Later on, when I had known him a long time, I felt some liking for Bellini. This arose after I had observed that his character was thoroughly noble and good. His soul was certainly pure and unspotted by any hateful contagion. And he was not wanting in that good-natured, childlike quality which we never miss in men of genius, even if they do not wear it as an outward show.

"Yes, I remember," Maximilian pursued, sinking down on the chair, on the back of which he had been hitherto leaning—"I remember one moment when Bellini appeared in so amiable a light, that I gazed on him with pleasure, and resolved to become more intimately acquainted with him. But, unhappily, it was the last time I should see him in this life. It was one evening after we had been dining together at the house of a great lady who had the smallest foot in Paris. We were very merry, and the sweetest melodies rang out from the piano. I see him still, the good-natured Bellini, as, at last, exhausted with the mad Bellinism that he chattered, he sank into a seat.... It was a very low one, so that Bellini found himself sitting at the foot, as it were, of a beautiful lady, stretched on a sofa opposite, who gazed down on him with a sweet, malicious delight, as he worked off some French expressions to entertain her, and was compelled, as usual, to communicate what he had said in his Sicilian jargon to show that it was no *sottise*, but, on the contrary, the most delicate flattery. I think the fair lady paid little attention to Bellini's conversation. She had taken from his hand the little Spanish cane with which he often used to assist his weak rhetoric, and was making use of it for a calm destruction of the elegant curl-edifice on the young *Maestro's* brows. But this wanton occupation was well repaid by the smile which gave her face an expression which I have seen on no other living human countenance. That face will never leave my memory! It was one of those faces which belong more to the kingdom of poetry than to the crude reality of life, contours which remind one of Da Vinci—that noble oval, with the naïve cheek-dimples and the sentimental pointed chin of the Lombard school. The colouring was more soft and Roman, with the dull gleam of pearls, a distinguished pallor, *morbidezza*. In short, it was one of those faces which can only be found in early Italian portraits, which, perhaps, represent those great ladies with whom the Italian artists of the sixteenth century were in love when they created their masterpieces, of whom the poets of those days thought when they sang themselves immortal, and which kindled German and French heroes with desire when they girded on their swords and started across the Alps in search of great deeds. Yes, it was such a face, and on it played a smile of sweetest, malicious delight and most delicate wantonness, as she, the fair lady, with the point of the little Spanish cane destroyed the blonde curls on the good-natured Bellini's brows. At that moment Bellini seemed to me as if touched by an enchanted wand, as if transformed, and he was at once akin to my heart. His face shone with the reflection of that smile; it was, perhaps, the most joyful moment of his life. I shall never forget it. Fourteen days afterwards I read in the papers that Italy had lost one of her most famous sons!

"Strange! At the same time Paganini's death was announced. About his death I had no doubt, for the old, ash-coloured Paganini always looked like a dying man; but the death of the young, rosy Bellini seemed to me incredible. And yet the news of the death of the first was only a newspaper error; Paganini is safe and sound at Genoa, and Bellini lies in his grave at Paris!"

"Do you like Paganini?" asked Maria. "He is the ornament of his country," answered Maximilian, "and deserves the most distinguished mention in speaking of the musical notabilities of Italy."

"I have never seen him," Maria remarked, "but according to report his outward appearance does not altogether satisfy the sense of beauty. I have seen portraits of him."

118

"Which are all different," broke in Maximilian; "they either make him uglier or handsomer than he is; they do not give his actual appearance. I believe that only one man has succeeded in putting Paganini's true physiognomy on to paper—a deaf painter, Lyser by name, who, in a frenzy full of genius, has, with a few strokes of chalk, so well hit Paganini's head that one is at the same time amused and terrified at the truth of the drawing. 'The devil guided my hand,' the deaf painter said to me, chuckling mysteriously, and nodding his head with good-natured irony in the way he generally accompanied his genial witticisms. This painter was, however, a wonderful old fellow; in spite of his deafness he was enthusiastically fond of music, and he knew how, when near enough to the orchestra, to read the music on the musicians' faces, and to judge the more or less skilful execution by the movements of their fingers; indeed, he wrote critiques on the opera for an excellent journal at Hamburg. And is that peculiarly wonderful? In the visible symbols of the performance the deaf painter could see the sounds. There are men to whom the sounds themselves are invisible symbols in which they hear colours and forms."

"You are one of those men!" exclaimed Maria.

"I am sorry that I no longer possess Lyser's little drawing; it would perhaps have given you an idea of Paganini's outward appearance. Only with black and glaring strokes could those mysterious features be seized, features, which seemed to belong more to the sulphurous kingdom of shades than to the sunny world of life. 'Indeed, the devil guided my hand,' the deaf painter assured me, as we stood before the Alster pavilion at Hamburg on the day when Paganini gave his first concert there. 'Yes, my friend,' he pursued, 'it is true, as everyone believes, that he has sold himself to the devil, body and soul, in order to become the best violinist, to fiddle millions of money, and principally to escape the damnable galley where he had already languished many years. For, you see, my friend, when he was chapel-master at Lucca he fell in love with a princess of the theatre, was jealous of some little *abbate*, was perhaps deceived by the faithless *Amata*, stabbed her in approved Italian fashion, came in the galley to Genoa, and, as I said, sold himself to the devil to escape from it, become the best violin-player, and impose upon us this evening a contribution of two thalers each. But, you see, all good spirits praise God; there in the avenue he comes himself, with his suspicious Famulus!'

"It was indeed Paganini himself, whom I then saw for the first time. He wore a dark grey overcoat, which reached to his feet, and made his figure seem very tall. His long black hair fell in neglected curls on his shoulders, and formed a dark frame round the pale, cadaverous face, on which sorrow, genius, and hell had engraved their indestructible lines. Near him danced along a little pleasing figure, elegantly prosaic—with rosy, wrinkled face, bright grey little coat with steel buttons, distributing greetings on all sides in an insupportably friendly way, leering up, nevertheless, with apprehensive air at the gloomy figure who walked earnest and thoughtful at his side. It reminded one of Retzsch's representation of Faust and Wagner walking before the gates of Leipsic. The deaf painter made comments to me in his mad way, and bade me observe especially the broad,

119

measured walk of Paganini. 'Does it not seem,' said he, 'as if he had the iron cross-pole still between his legs? He has accustomed himself to that walk for ever. See, too, in what a contemptuous, ironical way he sometimes looks at his guide when the latter wearies him with his prosaic questions. But he cannot separate himself from him; a bloody contract binds him to that companion, who is no other than Satan. The ignorant multitude, indeed, believe that this guide is the writer of comedies and anecdotes, Harris from Hanover, whom Paganini has taken with him to manage the financial business of his concerts. But they do not know that the devil has only borrowed Herr George Harris's form, and that meanwhile the poor soul of this poor man is shut up with other rubbish in a trunk at Hanover, until the devil returns its flesh-envelope, while he perhaps will guide his master through the world in a worthier form—namely, as a black poodle.'

"But if Paganini seemed mysterious and strange enough when I saw him walking in bright mid-day under the green trees of the Hamburg Jungfernstieg, how his awful bizarre appearance startled me at the concert in the evening! The Hamburg Opera House was the scene of this concert, and the art-loving public had flocked thither so early, and in such numbers, that I only just succeeded in obtaining a little place in the orchestra. Although it was post-day, I saw in the first row of boxes the whole educated commercial world, a whole Olympus of bankers and other millionaires, the gods of coffee and sugar by the side of their fat goddesses, Junos of Wandrahm and Aphrodites of Dreckwall. A religious silence reigned through the assembly. Every eye was directed towards the stage. Every ear was making ready to listen. My neighbour, an old furrier, took the dirty cotton out of his ears in order to drink in better the costly sounds for which he had paid two thalers. At last a dark figure, which seemed to have arisen from the under-world, appeared upon the stage. It was Paganini in his black costume—the black dress-coat and the black waistcoat of a horrible cut, such as is perhaps prescribed by infernal etiquette at the court of Proserpina; the black trousers anxiously hanging around the thin legs. The long arms appeared to grow still longer, as, holding the violin in one hand and the bow in the other, he almost touched the ground with them while displaying to the public his unprecedented obeisances. In the angular curves of his body there was a horrible woodenness, and also something absurdly animal-like, that during these bows one could not help feeling a strange desire to laugh; but his face, that appeared still more cadaverously pale in the glare of the orchestra lights, had about it something so imploring, so simply humble, that a sorrowful compassion repressed one's desire to laugh. Had he learnt these complimentary bows from an automaton or a dog? Is that the entreating gaze of one sick unto death, or is there lurking behind it the mockery of a crafty miser? Is that a man brought into the arena at the moment of death, like a dying gladiator, to delight the public with his convulsions? Or is it one risen from the dead, a vampire with a violin, who, if not the blood out of our hearts, at any rate sucks the gold out of our pockets?

"Such questions crossed our minds while Paganini was performing his strange bows, but all those thoughts were at once still when the wonderful master placed his violin under his chin and began to play. As for me, you already know my musical second-sight, my gift of seeing at each tone a figure equivalent to the sound, and so Paganini with each stroke of his bow brought visible forms and situations before my eyes; he told me in melodious hieroglyphics all kinds of brilliant tales; he, as it were, made a magic-lantern play its coloured antics before me, he himself being chief actor. At the first stroke of his bow the stage scenery around him had changed; he suddenly stood with his music-desk in a cheerful room, decorated in a gay, irregular way after the Pompadour style; everywhere little mirrors, gilded Cupids, Chinese porcelain, a delightful chaos of ribbons, garlands of flowers, white gloves, torn lace, false pearls, diadems of gold leaf and spangles—such tinsel as one finds in the room of a prima-donna. Paganini's outward appearance had also changed, and certainly most advantageously; he wore short breeches of lily-coloured satin, a white waistcoat embroidered with silver, and a coat of bright blue velvet with gold buttons; the hair in little carefully curled locks bordered his face, which was young and rosy, and gleamed with sweet tenderness as he ogled the pretty little lady who stood near him at the music-desk, while he played the violin.

"Yes, I saw at his side a pretty young creature, in antique costume, the white satin swelled out below the waist, making the figure still more charmingly slender; the high raised hair was powdered and curled, and the pretty round face shone out all the more openly with it glancing eyes, its little rouged cheeks, its little beauty-patches, and the sweet impertinent little nose. In her hand was a roll of white paper, and by the movements of her lips as well as by the coquettish waving to and fro of her little upper lip she seemed to be singing; but none of her trills were audible to me, and only from the violin with which the young Paganini led the lovely child could I discover what she sang, and what he himself during her song felt in his soul. O, what melodies were those! Like the nightingale's notes, when the fragrance of the rose intoxicates her yearning young heart with desire, they floated in the evening twilight. O, what melting, languid delight was that! The sounds kissed each other, then fled away pouting, and then, laughing, clasped each other and became one, and died away in intoxicated harmony. Yes, the sounds carried on their merry game like butterflies, when one, in playful provocation, will escape from another, hide behind a flower, be overtaken at last, and then, wantonly joying with the other, fly away into the golden sunlight. But a spider, a spider can prepare a sudden tragical fate for such enamoured butterflies. Did the young heart anticipate this? A melancholy sighing tone, a foreboding of some slowly approaching misfortune, glided softly through the enrapturing melodies that were streaming from Paganini's violin. His eyes became moist. Adoringly he knelt down before his *Amata*. But, alas! as he bowed down to kiss her feet, he saw under the bed a little *abbate*! I do not know what he had against the poor man, but the Genoese became pale as death, he seized the little fellow with furious hands, gave him sundry boxes on the ear, as well as a considerable number of kicks, flung him outside, drew a stiletto from its sheath, and buried it in the young beauty's breast.

"At this moment, however, a shout of 'Bravo! Bravo!' broke out from all sides. Hamburg's enthusiastic sons and daughters were paying the tribute of their

121

uproarious applause to the great artist, who had just ended the first part of his concert, and was now bowing with even more angles and contortions than before. And on his face the abject humility seemed to me to have become more intense. From his eyes stared a sorrowful anxiety like that of a poor malefactor. 'Divine!' cried my neighbour, the furrier, as he scratched his ears; 'that piece alone was worth two thalers.'

"When Paganini began to play again a gloom came before my eyes. The sounds were not transformed into bright forms and colours; the master's form was clothed in gloomy shades, out of the darkness of which his music moaned in the most piercing tones of lamentation. Only at times, when a little lamp that hung above cast its sorrowful light over him, could I catch a glimpse of his pale countenance, on which the youth was not yet extinguished. His costume was singular, in two colours, yellow and red. Heavy chains weighed upon his feet. Behind him moved a face whose physiognomy indicated a lusty goat-nature. And I saw at times long hairy hands seize assistingly the strings of the violin on which Paganini was playing. They often guided the hand which held the bow, and then a bleating laugh of applause accompanied the melody, which gushed from the violin ever more full of sorrow and anguish. They were melodies which were like the song of the fallen angels who had loved the daughters of earth, and, being exiled from the kingdom of the blessed, sank into the under-world with faces red with shame. They were melodies in whose bottomless shallowness glimmered neither consolation nor hope. When the saints in heaven hear such melodies, the praise of God dies upon their paled lips, and they cover their heads weeping. At times when the *obligato* goat's laugh bleated in among the melodious pangs, I caught a glimpse in the background of a crowd of small women-figures who nodded their odious heads with wicked wantonness. Then a rush of agonising sounds came from the violin, and a fearful groan and a sob, such as was never heard upon earth before, nor will be perhaps heard upon earth again; unless in the valley of Jehoshaphat, when the colossal trumpets of doom shall ring out, and the naked corpses shall crawl forth from the grave to abide their fate. But the agonised violinist suddenly made one stroke of the bow, such a mad despairing stroke, that his chains fell rattling from him, and his mysterious assistant and the other foul mocking forms vanished.

"At this moment my neighbour, the furrier, said, 'A pity, a pity; a string has snapped—that comes from the constant *pizzicato*.'

"Had a string of the violin really snapped? I do not know. I only observed the alteration in the sounds, and Paganini and his surroundings seemed to me again suddenly changed. I could scarcely recognise him in the monk's brown dress, which concealed rather than clothed him. With savage countenance half hid by the cowl, waist girt with a cord, and bare feet, Paganini stood, a solitary defiant figure, on a rocky prominence by the sea, and played his violin. But the sea became red and redder, and the sky grew paler, till at last the surging water looked like bright scarlet blood, and the sky above became of a ghastly, corpse-like pallor, and the stars came out large and threatening; and those stars were black, black as glooming coal. But the tones of the violin grew ever more stormy and defiant, and the eyes of the terrible player sparkled with such a scornful lust of destruction, and his thin lips moved with such a horrible haste, that it seemed as if he murmured some old accursed charms to conjure the storm and loose the evil spirits that lie imprisoned in the abysses of the sea. Often, when he stretched his long thin arm from the broad monk's sleeve, and swept the air with his bow, he seemed like some sorcerer who commands the elements with his magic wand; and then there was a wild wailing from the depth of the sea, and the horrible waves of blood sprang up so fiercely that they almost besprinkled the pale sky and the black stars with their red foam. There was a wailing and a shrieking and a crashing, as if the world was falling into fragments, and ever more stubbornly the monk played his violin. He seemed as if by the power of violent will he wished to break the seven seals wherewith Solomon sealed the iron vessels in which he had shut up the vanquished demons. The wise king sank those vessels in the sea, and I seemed to hear the voices of the imprisoned spirits while Paganini's violin growled its most wrathful bass. But at last I thought I heard the jubilee of deliverance, and out of the red billows of blood emerged the heads of the fettered demons: monsters of legendary horror, crocodiles with bats' wings, snakes with stags' horns, monkeys with shells on their heads, seals with long patriarchal beards, women's faces with breasts in place of cheeks, green camels' heads, hermaphrodites of incomprehensible combination—all staring with cold, crafty eyes, and with long fin-like claws grasping at the fiddling monk. From the latter, however, in the furious zeal of his conjuration, the cowl fell back, and the curly hair, fluttering in the wind, fell round his head in ringlets, like black snakes.

"So maddening was this vision that, to keep my senses, I closed my ears and shut my eyes. When I again looked up the spectre had vanished, and I saw the poor Genoese in his ordinary form, making his ordinary bows, while the public applauded in the most rapturous manner.

"'That is the famous performance upon G,' remarked my neighbour; 'I myself play the violin, and I know what it is to master that instrument.' Fortunately, the pause was not considerable, or else the musical furrier would certainly have engaged me in a long conversation upon art. Paganini again quietly set his violin to his chin, and with the first stroke of his bow the wonderful transformation of melodies again also began. They no longer fashioned themselves so brightly and corporeally. The melody gently developed itself, majestically billowing and swelling like an organ chorale in a cathedral, and everything around, stretching larger and higher, had extended into a colossal space which, not the bodily eye, but only the eye of the spirit could seize. In the midst of this space hovered a shining sphere, upon which, gigantic and sublimely haughty, stood a man who played the violin. Was that sphere the sun? I do not know. But in the man's features I recognised Paganini, only ideally lovely, divinely glorious, with a reconciling smile. His body was in the bloom of powerful manhood, a bright blue garment enclosed his noble limbs, his shoulders were covered by gleaming locks of black hair; and as he stood there, sure and secure, a sublime divinity, and played the violin, it seemed as if the whole creation obeyed his melodies. He was the man-planet about which the universe moved with measured solemnity and ringing out beatific rhythms. Those great lights, which so quietly gleaming swept around, were they the stars of heaven, and that melodious harmony which arose from their movements, was it the song of the spheres, of which poets and seers have reported so many ravishing things? At times, when I endeavoured to gaze out into the misty distance, I thought I saw pure white garments floating around, in which colossal pilgrims passed muffled along with white staves in their hands, and, singular to relate, the golden knob of each staff was even one of those great lights which I had taken for stars. These pilgrims moved in large orbit around the great performer, the golden knobs of their staves shone even brighter at the tones of the violin, and the chorale which resounded from their lips, and which I had taken for the song of the spheres, was only the dying echo of those violin tones. A holy, ineffable ardour dwelt in those sounds, which often trembled, scarce audibly, in mysterious whisper on the water, then swelled out again with a shuddering sweetness, like a bugle's notes heard by moonlight, and then finally poured forth in unrestrained jubilee, as if a thousand bards had struck their harps and raised their voices in a song of victory. These were sounds which the ear never hears, which only the heart can dream when it rests at night on a beloved breast. Perhaps also the heart can grasp them in the bright light of day, when it loses itself with joy in the curves of beauty in a Grecian work of art...."

"Or when one has drunk one too many bottles of champagne!" broke in suddenly a laughing voice, which woke our story-teller as from a dream. Turning round, he saw the doctor, who, under the guidance of black Deborah, had gently entered the room to inform himself of the effect of his medicine on the patient.

"That sleep does not please me," he said, pointing to the sofa.

Maximilian, who, absorbed in the fancies of his own discourse, had not observed that Maria had long since fallen asleep, bit his lip with vexation.

"That sleep," the doctor pursued, "gives to her countenance already the appearance of death. Does it not look like those white masks, those plaster casts, in which we seek to preserve the features of the dead?"

"I should like," Maximilian whispered in his ear, "to have such a cast of our friend's face. Even as a corpse she would be very lovely."

"I do not advise you to do so," answered the doctor. "Such masks spoil the recollection of those we love. We think that in the plaster we have procured something of their life, but it is only death that we have caught. Beautiful regular features get something horribly rigid, mocking, fatal, with which they terrify rather than delight us; but the casts of those faces whose charm was of a more spiritual kind, whose features were less regular than interesting, are absolute caricature; for as soon as the graces of life are extinguished, the real declinations from the line of ideal beauty are no longer compensated by the spiritual charm. A certain enigmatic expression is common to all these casts, which, after long contemplation, send an intolerable chill through our souls; they look as if on the point of going a long journey."

124

"Whither?" asked Maximilian, as the doctor took his arm and led him from the room.

Second Night.

"And why will you torment me with this horrible medicine, since I must die so soon?"

It was Maria who, as Maximilian entered, spoke these words. The doctor was standing before her with a medicine bottle in one hand and in the other a little glass in which a brownish liquor frothed nauseously. "My dear fellow," he exclaimed, turning to the new-comer, "you have just come at the right time; try and persuade Signora to swallow these few drops; I am in a hurry."

"I entreat you, Maria!" whispered Maximilian, in that tender voice which one did not often observe in him, and which seemed to come from so wounded a heart that the patient, singularly touched, took the glass in her hand. Before she put it to her mouth, she said, smiling, "Will you reward me with the story of Laurence?"

"All that you wish shall be done," nodded Maximilian.

The pale lady then drank the contents of the glass, half smiling, half shuddering.

"I am in a hurry," said the doctor, drawing on his black gloves. "Lie down quietly, Signora, and move as little as possible."

Led by black Deborah, who lighted him, he left the room. When the two friends were left alone, they looked at each other for a long time in silence. In the souls of both thoughts were clamorous which each strove to hide from the other. The woman, however, suddenly seized the man's hand and covered it with glowing kisses.

"For God's sake," said Maximilian, "do not agitate yourself so, and lie back quietly on the sofa."

As Maria fulfilled this wish, he covered her feet carefully with a shawl, which he previously touched with his lips. She probably noticed him, for her eyes winked with contentment, like a happy child's.

"Was Mademoiselle Laurence very beautiful?"

"If you will not interrupt me, dear friend, and promise to listen quite silently, I will tell you circumstantially all that you wish to know." Smiling in response to Maria's affirmative glance, Maximilian seated himself on the chair which was beside the sofa, and began his story:—

It is now eight years since I travelled to London to become acquainted with the language and the people. Confound the people and their language too! There they take a dozen monosyllables in their mouths, chew them, gnash them, spit them out again, and they call that speaking! Fortunately, they are by nature tolerably taciturn, and though they always gape at us with open mouths, they spare us long conversations. But woe unto us if we fall into the hands of a son of Albion who has made the great tour and learnt French on the Continent. He will use the opportunity to exercise the achieved language, and overwhelm us with questions on all possible subjects. And scarcely is one question answered before he comes out with another about one's age or home or length of one's stay, and with these incessant inquiries he thinks he is entertaining us in the most delightful manner. One of my friends at Paris was perhaps right when he maintained that the English learn their French conversation at the *Bureaux des Passeports*. Their talk is most useful at table, when they carve their colossal roast beef and inquire which cut you like, overdone or underdone, the inside or the brown outside, fat or lean. This roast beef and this roast mutton are the only good things they have. Heaven preserve every Christian man from their sauces, which consist of one part of flour and two of butter, or when the composition aims at a change, of one part of butter and two of flour. Heaven preserve anyone also from their vegetables, which they bring on the table cooked in water, just as God created them. Still more horrible than the cookery of the English are their toasts and *obligato* speeches, when the table-cloth is taken away and the ladies retire, and instead of them just so many bottles of port wine are brought up; for they think that that is the best way to replace the absence of the fair sex. I say the 'fair' sex, for the English women deserve that name. They are fair, slender creatures. Only the excessive space between the nose and the mouth, which is found in them as frequently as in the men, has often spoiled for me in England the most beautiful faces. This declination from the type of beauty acts upon me still more fatally when I see the English here in Italy, where their sparingly chiselled noses, and the broad space of flesh that stretches from there to the mouth, forms so much the more uncouth contrast with the faces of the Italians, whose features have a more antique regularity, and whose noses, either curved in the Roman way or inclined in the Grecian, degenerate into too great a length. Very correct is the observation of a German traveller that the English, when among the Italians, all look like statues with the points of their noses broken off.

Yes, when one meets the English in a foreign land, the contrast brings out their deficiencies distinctly. They are the gods of *ennui*, who travel through all lands at post haste in shining, lacquered coaches, and leave everywhere a grey, dark cloud of mournfulness behind them. Their curiosity without interest, their dressed-up awkwardness, their insolent timidity, their angular egotism, and their empty joy at all melancholy objects, aid in this impression. In the last three weeks an Englishman has been visible every day on the Piazza del Gran Duca, gazing for an hour at a time at a quack sitting on a horse who draws people's teeth. Perhaps this performance compensates the noble son of Albion for the loss of the executions of his own dear native land. For after boxing and cock-fights, there is no more delightful sight for a Briton than the agony of some poor devil who has stolen a sheep, or imitated somebody's handwriting, and is exhibited for an hour in front of the Old Bailey before he is thrown into eternity. It is no exaggeration to say that forgery and the theft of a sheep in that detestable and barbarous land are punished in the same way as the most awful crimes, as parricide and incest.[12] I, myself, led by a sad chance, saw a man hanged for stealing a sheep, and after that I lost all pleasure in roast mutton; the fat reminded me of the poor culprit's white cap. Near him an Irishman was hanged for forging the signature of a rich banker; I still see poor Paddy's death agony; he could not understand at the assizes why he should be so hardly punished for imitating a signature when he would allow any human being to imitate his own! And these people talk constantly of Christianity, and never miss church on Sunday, and flood the whole world with Bibles.

"I confess to you, Maria, that if I relished nothing in England, men or cookery, the reason lay partly in myself. I brought over a good store of ill-humour with me, and I was seeking amusement among a people who can only kill their *ennui* in the whirlpool of political and mercantile activity. The perfection of machinery, which is applied to everything here, and has superseded so many human functions, has for me something dismal; this artificial life of wheels, bars, cylinders, and a thousand little hooks, pins, and teeth which move almost passionately, fills me with horror. I am annoyed no less by the definiteness, the precision, the strictness, in the life of the English; for just as the machines in England seem to have the perfection of men, so the men seem like machines. Yes, wood, iron, and brass seem to have usurped the human mind there, and to have gone almost mad from fulness of mind, while the mindless man, like a hollow ghost, exercises his ordinary duties in a machine-like fashion; at the appointed moment eats beef-steaks, makes parliamentary speeches, trims his nails, mounts the stage-coach, or hangs himself.

"You can well imagine how my dissatisfaction increased in this country. Nothing, however, equalled the gloomy mood which once came over me as I stood on Waterloo Bridge towards evening and gazed on the water. It seemed to me as if my soul was mirrored there, and was gazing up out of the water at me with all its scars. The most sorrowful stories came to my recollection. I thought of the rose which was always watered with vinegar, and so lost its sweet fragrance and faded early. I thought of the strayed butterfly which a naturalist, who ascended Mount Blanc, saw fluttering amid the ice. I thought of the tame monkey who was so familiar with men, played with them, eat with them, but once at table recognised in the roast meat on the dish her own little monkey baby, quickly seized it, and hastened to the woods, never more to be seen among her human friends. Ah, I felt so sorrowful that the hot tears started from my eyes. My tears fell down into the Thames, and floated on to the great sea which has swallowed so many tears without noticing them.

"At this moment it happened that a singular music awoke me from my gloomy dreams, and looking round, I saw on the bank a crowd of people, who seemed to have formed a circle round some amusing display. I drew nearer, and saw a family of performers, consisting of the following four persons:—

"Firstly, a short, thick-set woman, dressed entirely in black, who had a very little head and a very large, protuberant belly. Upon this belly was hung an immense drum, upon which she drummed away most unmercifully.

"Secondly, a dwarf, who wore an embroidered coat like an old French marquis. He had a large powdered head, but for the rest, had very thin contemptible limbs, and danced to and fro striking the triangle.

"Thirdly, a young girl of about fifteen years, who wore a short close-fitting jacket of blue-striped silk, and broad pantaloons also with blue stripes. She was an ærially-made figure. The face was of Grecian loveliness. A straight nose, sweet lips turned outwards, a dreamy, tender, rounded chin, the colour a sunny yellow, the hair of a gleaming black, wound round the brows. So she stood, slender and serious; yes, ill-humoured, and gazed upon the fourth person of the company, who was just then engaged in his performance.

"This fourth person was a learned dog, a very hopeful poodle, and to the great delight of the English public, he had just put together from some wooden letters before him, the name of the Duke of Wellington, and joined to it a very flattering word—namely, "Hero." Since the dog, as one might conclude from his witty expression, was no English beast, but had, like the other three persons, come from France, the sons of Albion rejoiced that their great general had at least obtained from the French dog that recognition which the other French creatures had so disgracefully denied.

"In fact, this company consisted of French people, and the dwarf, who now announced himself as Monsieur Turlutu, began to bluster in French, and with such vehement gestures, that the poor English opened their mouths and noses still wider than usual. Often, after a long phrase, he crowed like a cock, and these cock-a-doodle-doos, as also the names of many emperors, kings, and princes which he mixed up with his discourse, were probably the only sounds the poor spectators understood. Those emperors, kings, and princes he extolled as his patrons and friends. When only a boy of eight years, so he assured us, he had had an interview with his most sacred majesty Louis XVI., who also, later on, always asked his advice on weighty matters. He escaped the storms of the Revolution, like many others, by flight, and he only returned under the empire to his beloved country to take part in the glory of the great nation. Napoleon, he said, never loved him, whereas His Holiness Pope Pius VII. almost idolised him. The Emperor Alexander gave him bon-bons, and the Princess Wilhelm von Kyritz always placed him on her lap. His Highness Duke Charles of Brunswick often allowed him to ride on his dogs, and his majesty King Ludwig of Bavaria read to him his sublime poems. The Princes of Reuss-Schleiz-Kreuz and of Schwarzburg-Sondershausen loved him as a brother, and always smoked the same pipe with him. Yes, from childhood up, he said, he had lived among sovereigns; the present monarchs, had, as it were, grown up with him; he looked upon them as equals, and he felt deep sorrow every time that one of them passed from the scene of life. After these solemn words he crowed like a cock.

"Monsieur Turlutu was, in fact, one of the most curious dwarfs I ever saw; his wrinkled old face formed such a droll contrast with his scanty, childish, little body, and his whole person again contrasted so comically with his performances. He threw himself into the most sprightly postures, and with thrusts of an inhumanly long rapier he transfixed the air, affirming all the while, on his honour, that no one could parry this *quarte* or that *tierce*; that, on the contrary, his own defence could be broken through by no mortal man, and he challenged anyone to engage with him in the noble art. After the dwarf had carried this performance

128

on for some time, and found no one who would resolve on open conflict with him, he bowed with old French grace, gave thanks for the applause which was bestowed upon him, and took the liberty of announcing to the very honourable public the most extraordinary performance ever displayed upon English ground. 'You see this person,' he exclaimed, after drawing on dirty kid gloves, and leading the young girl of the company with respectful gallantry into the middle of the circle—'this is Mademoiselle Laurence, the only daughter of the honourable Christian lady whom you see there with the drum, and who still wears mourning for the loss of her dearly-beloved husband, the greatest ventriloquist in Europe! Mademoiselle Laurence will now dance! Now, admire the dancing of Mademoiselle Laurence.' After these words, he again crowed like a cock.

"The young girl appeared to care not the least either for these words or the gaze of the spectators; ill-humouredly absorbed in herself, she waited till the dwarf had spread a large carpet at her feet, and under the guidance of the great drum had again begun to play his triangle. It was strange music, a mixture of awkward humming and a delightful tinkling, and I caught a pathetic, foolish, melancholy, bold, bizarre melody of, nevertheless, the most singular simplicity. But I soon forgot the music when the young girl began to dance.

"Dance and dancer powerfully seized my attention. It was not the classical dance which we still see in our great ballets, where, just as in classical tragedy, only sprawling unities and artificialities reign; it was not those danced Alexandrines, those declamatory springs, those antithetic capers, that noble emotion which pirouets round on one foot, so that one sees nothing except heaven and petticoats, ideality and lies! There is, indeed, nothing so odious to me as the ballet at the Paris Grand Opera, where the traditions of that classical dance are retained in their purest forms, while in the rest of the arts, in poetry, in music, and in painting, the French have overturned the classical system. It will be, however, difficult for them to bring about a similar revolution in the art of dancing; they will need, as in their political revolution, to have recourse to terrorism, and guillotine the legs of the obdurate dancers. Mademoiselle Laurence was no great dancer; the joints of her feet were not very supple, her legs were not exercised in all possible dislocations, she understood nothing of the art of dancing as Madame Vestris teaches it, but she danced as nature commands to dance: her whole being was in harmony with her *pas*; not only her feet but her whole body danced; her face danced—she was often pale, almost deathly pale, her eyes opened to an almost ghostly size, desire and pain quivered on her lips, and her black hair, which enclosed her brows in smooth oval, moved like a pair of fluttering wings. It was, indeed, no classical dance, but also no romantic dance, in the sense of a young Frenchman of the Eugène Renduel school. This dance had nothing mediæval, nor Venetian, nor hump-backed, nor Macabrian about it; there was neither moonshine nor incest in it. It was a dance which did not seek to answer by outward movements, but the outward movements seemed words of a strange speech which strove to express strange things. But what did this dance express? I could not understand, however passionately this speech uttered itself. I only guessed sometimes that it spoke of something intensely sorrowful. I, who so easily seized the meaning of all appearances, was nevertheless unable to solve this danced riddle; and that I groped in vain for the sense of it was partly the fault of the music, which certainly pointed intentionally to false roads, cunningly sought to lead me astray, and always disturbed me. Monsieur Turlutu's triangle often tittered maliciously. Madame, however, beat upon her drum so wrathfully, that her face glowed forth from the black cloud of cap like a blood-red northern light.

"Long after the troop had passed away, I remained standing at the same spot, considering what that dance might signify. Was it a national dance of the south of France or of Spain? In such a dance might appear the impetuosity with which the dancer swung her little body to and fro, and the wildness with which she often threw her head backward in the bold way of those Bacchantes whom we gaze at with amazement on ancient vases. There was an intoxicated absence of will about her dance, something gloomy and inevitable; it was like the dance of fate. Or was it a fragment of some venerable forgotten pantomime? Or was she dancing her personal history? Often the girl bent down to the earth with a listening ear, as though she heard a voice which spoke up to her. She trembled then like an aspen leaf, bent suddenly to another side, went through her maddest, most unrestrained leaps, then again bent her ear to the earth, listened more anxiously than before, nodded her head, became red and pale by turns, shuddered, stood for a while stiffly upright as if benumbed, and made finally a movement as one who washes his hands. Was it blood that so long and with such care, such horrible care, she was washing from her hands? She threw therewith a sideward glance so imploring, so full of entreaty, so soul-dissolving—and that glance fell by chance upon me.

"All the following night I was thinking of that glance, of that dance, of that strange accompaniment; and as, on the following day, I sauntered as usual through the streets of London, I longed to meet the pretty dancer again, and I constantly pricked my ears in case I might somewhere hear the music of the drum and the triangle. I had at last found something in London which interested me, and I no longer wandered aimless through its yawning streets.

"I had just come out of the Tower, after carefully examining the axe which cut off Anne Bullen's head, as well as the English crown-diamonds and the lions, when in front of the Tower I caught a glimpse, amid a crowd, of Madame with the great drum, and heard Monsieur Turlutu crowing like a cock. The learned dog again scraped together the heroism of the Duke of Wellington, the dwarf again showed his not-to-be-parried *tierces* and *quartes*, and Mademoiselle Laurence again began her wondrous dance. There were again the same enigmatic movements, the same speech which I could not understand, the same impetuous throwing back of the beautiful head, the same leaning down to the earth, the anguish which sought to soothe itself by ever madder leaps, and again the listening ear bent to the earth, the trembling, the pallor, the benumbed stiffness; then also the fearful mysterious washing of the hands, and at last the imploring side-glance, which rested upon me this time still longer than before.

130

"Yes, women, and young girls as well as women, immediately observe when they have excited the attention of a man. Although Mademoiselle Laurence, when she was not dancing, gazed immovable and ill-humouredly before her, and while she was dancing often cast only one glance on the public, it was now no mere chance that this glance fell upon me; and the oftener I saw her dance, the more significantly it gleamed, but also the more incomprehensibly. I was fascinated by this glance, and for three weeks, from morning till evening, I wandered about the streets of London, always remaining wherever Mademoiselle Laurence danced. In spite of the greatest confusion of sounds, I could catch the tones of the drum and the triangle at the farthest distance; and Monsieur Turlutu, as soon as he saw me hastening near, raised his most friendly crow. Although I never spoke a word to him or to Mademoiselle Laurence, or to madame, or to the learned dog, I seemed at last as if I belonged to the company. When Monsieur Turlutu made a collection, he always behaved with the most delicate tact as he drew near me, and looked in the opposite direction when I put a small coin in his little three-cornered hat. His demeanour was indeed most distinguished; he reminded one of the good manners of the past; one could tell that the little man had grown up with monarchs, and all the stranger was it when at times, altogether forgetting his dignity, he crowed like a cock.

"I cannot describe to you how vexed I became, when, after seeking for three days in vain for the little company through all the streets of London, I was forced to conclude that they had left the town. _Ennui_ again took me in its leaden arms, and again closed my heart. At last I could endure it no longer; I said farewell to the four estates of the realm—_i.e._, the mob, the blackguards, the gentlemen, and the fashionables—and travelled back again to civilised _terra firma_, where I knelt in adoration before the white apron of the first cook I met. Here once more I could sit down to dinner like a reasonable being, and refresh my soul by gazing at good-natured, unselfish faces. But I could not forget Mademoiselle Laurence; she danced in my memory for a long time; at solitary hours I often reflected over the lovely child's enigmatic pantomime, especially over the listening ear bent to the earth. It was a long time, too, before the romantic melodies of the triangle and drum died away in my memory."

"And is that the whole story?" cried out Maria, all at once, starting up eagerly.

Maximilian pressed her softly down, placed his finger significantly to his lips, and whispered, "Still! still! do not talk! Lie down, good and quiet, and I will tell you the rest of the story. Only on no account interrupt me."

Leaning slowly back in his chair, Maximilian pursued the story:—

"Five years afterwards I came for the first time to Paris, and at a very noteworthy period. The French had just performed their July revolution, and the whole world was applauding. This piece was not so horrible as the earlier tragedies of the Republic and the Empire. Only some thousand corpses remained upon the stage. The political Romanticists were not very contented, and announced a new piece in which more blood should flow, and the executioner have more to do.

131

"Paris delighted me by the cheerfulness which prevails there, and which exercises its influence over the most sombre minds. Singular! Paris is the stage on which the greatest tragedies of the world's history are performed—tragedies at the recollection of which hearts tremble and eyes become moist in the most distant lands; but to the spectator of these tragedies it happens as it happened to me once at the Porte Saint-Martin Theatre, when I went to see the *Tour de Nesle* performed. I found myself sitting behind a lady who wore a hat of rose-red gauze, and this hat was so broad that it obstructed the whole of my view of the stage, and I saw all the tragedy only through the red gauze of this hat, and all the horror of the *Tour de Nesle* appeared in the most cheerful rose-light. Yes, there is such a rose-light in Paris, which makes all tragedies cheerful to the near spectator, so that his enjoyment of life is not spoilt there. In the same way all the terrible things that one may bring in his own heart to Paris there lose their tormenting horror. Sorrows are singularly soothed. In this air of Paris all wounds are healed quicker than anywhere else; there is in this air something as generous, as kind, as amiable as in the people themselves.

"What most pleased me in the people of Paris was their polite bearing and distinguished air. Sweet pine-apple perfume of politeness! how beneficently thou refreshedst my sick soul, which had swallowed down in Germany so much tobacco smoke, sauerkraut odour, and coarseness! The simple words of apology of a Frenchman, who, on the day of my arrival, only gently pushed against me, rang in my ears like the melodies of Rossini. I was almost terrified at such sweet politeness, I, who was accustomed to German clownish digs in the ribs without apology. During the first week of my stay in Paris I several times deliberately sought to be jostled, simply to delight myself with this music of apology. But the French people has for me a certain touch of nobility, not only on account of its politeness, but also on account of its language. For, as you know, with us in the north the French language is one of the attributes of high birth; from childhood I had associated the idea of speaking French with nobility. And a Parisian market-woman spoke better French than a German canoness with sixty-four ancestors.

"On account of this language, which lends a distinguished bearing to it, the French people has in my eyes something delightfully fabulous. This originated in another reminiscence of my childhood. The first book in which I learnt French was the *Fables* of La Fontaine; its naïve, sensible manner of speech impressed itself on my recollection ineffaceably, and as I now came to Paris and heard French spoken everywhere, I was constantly reminded of La Fontaine's *Fables*, I constantly imagined I was hearing the well-known animal voices; now the lion spoke, then the wolf, then the lamb, or the stork, or the dove, not seldom, I thought, I caught the voice of the fox, and often the words awoke in my memory —'Eh! bonjour, Monsieur du Corbeau! Que vous êtes joli! que vous me semblez beau!'

"Such reminiscences, however, awoke in my soul still oftener when at Paris I ascended to that higher region which is called 'the world.' This was even that world which gave up to the happy La Fontaine the types of his animal characters. The winter season began soon after my arrival at Paris, and I took part in the *salon* life in which that world more or less joyfully moves. What struck me as most interesting in this world was not so much the equality of good manners which reigned there as the variety of its ingredients. Often when I gazed round at the people gathered peacefully together in a large drawing-room I thought I was in one of those curiosity shops where relics of all ages lie beside each other, a Greek Apollo, a Chinese pagoda, a Mexican Vizlipuzli by a Gothic Ecce-Homo, Egyptian idols with little dogs' heads, holy caricatures made of wood, of ivory, of metal, and so on. There I saw old mousquetaires who had danced with Marie Antoinette, republicans who were deified in the National Assembly, Montagnards without spot and without mercy, former men of the Directory who were throned in the Luxembourg, great dignitaries of the Empire, before whom all Europe had trembled, ruling Jesuits of the Restoration—in short, mere faded, mutilated deities of olden times, in whom nobody believed any longer. The names seem to recoil from each other, but the men one may see standing peaceful and friendly together like the antiquities in the shops of the Quai Voltaire. In German countries, where the passions are not so easily disciplined, for such a heterogeneous mass of persons to live together in society would be quite impossible. And with us in the cold north the vivacity of speech is not so strong as in warmer France, where the greatest enemies, if they meet one another in a *salon*, cannot long observe a gloomy silence. In France, also, the desire to please is so great that people zealously strive to please not only their friends, but also their enemies. There is constant drapery and affectation, and the women here have the delightful trouble of excelling the men in coquetry; but they succeed, nevertheless.

"I do not mean anything wicked by this observation, certainly not as regards the French ladies, and least of all as regards the Parisian ladies. I am their greatest adorer, and I adore them on account of their failings still more than on account of their virtues. I know nothing more excellent than the legend that the Parisian women come into the world with all possible failings, but that a kind fairy has mercy upon them and lends to each fault a spell by which it works as a charm. That kind fairy is Grace! Are the Parisian women beautiful? Who can say? Who can see through all the intrigues of the toilet? Who can decipher whether what the tulle betrays is genuine, or what the swelling silk displays, false? And when the eye succeeds in piercing the shell, and we are at the point of finding the kernel, we discover that it is enclosed in a new shell, and after this again in another, and with this ceaseless change of fashions they mock masculine acuteness. Are their faces beautiful? Even this is difficult to find out. For all their features are in constant movement; every Parisian woman has a thousand faces, each more laughing, *spirituel*, gracious than the other, and puts to confusion those who seek to choose the loveliest face among them, or at all events, who wishes to guess which is the true face. Are their eyes large? What do I know! We cease investigating the calibre of the canon when the ball carries off our heads. And when their eyes do not hit, they at least blind us with the flash, and we are glad enough to get out of range. Is the space between nose and mouth broad or narrow? It is often broad when they wrinkle up their noses; it is often narrow when they give their upper lips an insolent little pout. Have they large or small mouths? Who can say where the mouth leaves off and where the smile begins? In order to give a just opinion, both the observer and the object of observation must be in a state of rest. But who can be quiet near a Parisian, and what Parisian woman is ever quiet? There are people who think that they can observe a butterfly quite accurately when they have stuck it on to paper with a pin. That is as foolish as it is cruel. The motionless transfixed butterfly is a butterfly no longer. One must observe the butterfly in his antics round the flowers, and one must observe the Parisian woman, not at home, when she is made fast by a pin through her breast, but in the *salon*, at soirées, and balls, when she flutters about with her wings of gauze and silk beneath the gleaming chandeliers. Then is revealed in her an impetuous passion for life, a longing after a sweet stupor, a thirsting for intoxication, by which means she becomes almost horribly beautiful, and wins a charm which at the same time delights and terrifies our souls.

"This thirst to enjoy life, as if death was about to snatch them from the bubbling spring of enjoyment, or as if that spring was about to cease flowing, this haste, this fury, this madness of the Parisian women, especially as it shows itself at balls, reminds me always of the legend of the dead dancing-girls which we call Willis. These are young brides who died before the wedding-day, and the unsatisfied desire of dancing is preserved so powerfully in their hearts that they come every night out of their graves, assemble in bands on the high roads, and give themselves up at midnight to the wildest dances. Dressed in their wedding clothes, with garlands on their heads, and glittering rings on their pale hands, laughing horribly, irresistibly lovely, the Willis dance in the moonshine, and they dance ever more madly the more they feel that the hour of dancing, which has been granted them, is coming to an end, and that they must again descend to their cold graves.

"At a soirée once in the Chaussée d'Antin this idea moved my soul profoundly. It was a brilliant soirée, and none of the customary ingredients of social pleasure were wanting: enough light to illuminate us, enough mirrors to see ourselves in, enough people to heat us with the squeeze, enough *eau sucrée* to cool us. They began with music. Franz Liszt allowed himself to be drawn to the piano, pushed his hair over his genial brows, and waged one of his most brilliant battles. The keys seemed to bleed. If I am not mistaken, he played a passage from the *Palingenesis* of Ballanche, whose ideas he was translating into music, which was very useful for those who cannot read the works of that famous writer in the original. Afterwards he played Berlioz's *La Marche au Supplice*, that excellent piece which the young musician, if I am not mistaken, composed on the morning of his wedding-day. Throughout the room paled faces, heaving bosoms, highly-drawn breath during the pauses, were succeeded at last by stormy applause. The women are always as it were intoxicated when Liszt plays anything for them. The Willis of the *salon* now gave themselves up to dancing with frantic delight, and I had difficulty in getting out of this confusion and saving myself in the adjoining room. Here card-playing was going on, and several ladies were resting in large chairs, looking on at the players, or at all events pretending to interest themselves in the play. As I passed one of these ladies, and my arm touched her dress, I felt from hand to shoulder a slight quiver as from a very weak electric shock. A similar shock, but of the greatest force, went through my whole heart when I saw the lady's countenance. Was it she, or was it not? It was the same face, with the form and sunny colour of an antique, only it was no longer so marble pure and marble smooth as formerly. The acute observer might perceive on brow and cheeks several little flaws, perhaps small-pox marks, which here exactly resembled those delicate weather-flecks which may be seen on the faces of statues that have been standing some time in the rain. It was the same black hair which covered the brows in smooth oval like a raven's wings. As, however, her eyes met mine, and with that well-known side-glance, whose swift lightning had always shot so enigmatically through my soul, I doubted no longer—it was Mademoiselle Laurence.

"Stretched in a distinguished way on her chair, with a bouquet in one hand and the other placed on the arm of the chair, Mademoiselle Laurence sat not far from one of the tables, and seemed to devote her whole attention to the cards. Her dress of white satin was elegant and distinguished, but still quite simple. Except bracelets and breast-pins of pearl, she wore no jewels. An abundance of lace covered the youthful bosom, covered it almost puritanically up to the neck, and in this simplicity and modesty of clothing she formed a lovely and touching contrast with some elderly ladies, gaily adorned and glistening with diamonds, who sat near her, and displayed to view the ruins of former magnificence, the place where once Troy stood, in a state of melancholy nakedness. She had the same wondrous loveliness, the same enrapturing look of ill-humour, and I was irresistibly drawn towards her, till at last I stood behind her chair, burning with desire to speak to her, and yet held back by a trembling delicacy.

"I must have been standing silently behind her for some time, when she suddenly drew a flower from her bouquet and, without looking round, held it to me over her shoulder. The perfume of that flower was strong, and it exercised a peculiar enchantment over me. I felt myself freed from all social formality, and I seemed in a dream, where one does and says all kinds of things at which oneself wonders, and when one's words have an altogether childish, familiar, and simple character. Quiet, indifferent, negligent, as one does with old friends, I leant over the arm of the chair, and whispered in the youthful lady's ear, 'Mademoiselle Laurence, where is, then, the mother with the drum?'

'She is dead,' answered she, in just the same tone—as quiet, indifferent, negligent.

"After a short pause, I again leant over the arm of the chair, and whispered in the youthful lady's ear, 'Mademoiselle Laurence, where is the learned dog?'

"'He has run away into the wide world,' she answered, in the same quiet, indifferent, negligent tone.

"And again, after a short pause, I leant over the arm of the chair, and whispered in the youthful lady's ear, 'Mademoiselle Laurence, where, then, is Monsieur Turlutu, the dwarf?'

"'He is among the giants in the Boulevard du Temple,' she answered. She had hardly spoken these words, and in just the same quiet, indifferent, negligent tone, when a serious old man, with a tall military figure, came towards her and announced that her carriage was ready. Slowly rising from her seat, she leant upon his arm, and without casting one glance back to me, left the company.

"When I inquired of the lady of the house, who had been standing all the evening at the entrance of the principal saloon, presenting her smiles to those who came or went, the name of the young lady who had just gone out with the old man, she laughed gaily in my face, and exclaimed—'Mon Dieu! who can know everybody! I know her as little.'—She stopped, for she was about to say as little as myself, whom she had that evening seen for the first time. 'Perhaps,' I remarked, 'your husband can give me some information; where shall I find him?'

"'At the hunt at Saint Germain,' answered the lady, with a yet louder laugh; 'he went early yesterday morning, and will return to-morrow evening. But wait. I know somebody who has been talking a good deal with the lady you inquire after; I do not know his name, but you can easily find him out by inquiring after the young man whom M. Casimir Perrier kicked, I don't know where.'

"Although it is rather difficult to recognise anyone by the fact of his having received a kick from a minister, I soon discovered my man, and I desired from him a more intimate knowledge of the singular creature who had so interested me, and whom I could describe to him clearly enough. 'Yes,' said the young man, 'I know her very well; I have spoken to her at several soirées'—and he repeated to me a mass of meaningless things with which he had entertained her. What especially surprised him was her earnest look whenever he said anything complimentary to her. He also wondered not a little that she always declined his invitation to a *contre danse*, assuring him that she was unable to dance. Of name and condition he knew nothing. And nobody, as much as I inquired, could give me any more distinct information on the subject. In vain I ran through all possible soirées; nowhere could I find Mademoiselle Laurence."

"And that is the whole story?" exclaimed Maria, as she slowly turned round and yawned sleepily—"that is the whole memorable story? And you have never again seen either Mademoiselle Laurence, or the mother with the drum, or the dwarf Turlutu, or the learned dog?"

"Remain lying still," replied Maximilian. "I have seen them all again, even the learned dog. The poor rascal was certainly in a very sad state of necessity when I came across him at Paris. It was in the Quartier Latin. I had just passed the Sorbonne, when out of its gates rushed a dog, and behind him with sticks a dozen students, who were soon joined by two dozen old women, who all cried in chorus, 'The dog is mad!' The animal looked almost human in his death agony, tears flowed from his eyes, and as he ran panting by and lifted his moist glance towards me, I recognised my old friend the learned dog, the Duke of Wellington's panegyrist, who had once filled the people of England with wonderment. Was he really mad? Had he been driven mad by mere learning while pursuing his studies in the Quartier Latin? Or had he in the Sorbonne, by his growling and scratching, marked his disapprobation of the puffed-up charlatanry of some professor, who sought to free himself from his unfavourable hearer by proclaiming him to be mad? And, alas! the youths are not long investigating whether it is the wounded conceit of learning or envy that first called out, 'The dog is mad!' and they strike with their thoughtless sticks, and the old women are ready with their howling, and cry down the voice of innocence and reason. My poor friend must yield; before my eyes he was miserably struck to death, insulted, and at last thrown on a dunghill! Poor martyr of learning!

"Not much more pleasant was the condition of the dwarf, Monsieur Turlutu, when I found him on the Boulevard du Temple. Mademoiselle Laurence had certainly told me that he had gone there, but whether I had not thought of actually seeing him there, or that the crowd had hindered me, it was some time before I noted the place where the giants were to be seen. When I entered I found two tall fellows who lay idly on benches, and quickly sprang up and placed themselves in giant posture before me. They were, in truth, not as large as they boasted on the placards hanging outside. These two long fellows, who were dressed in pink *tricots*, had very black, perhaps false, whiskers, and brandished hollow wooden clubs over their heads. When I asked after the dwarf, whom the placards also announced, they replied that for four weeks he had not been exhibited on account of his increasing illness—that I could see him, however, on paying double the price of admission. How willingly one pays double admission-fee to see a friend again! And, alas, this was a friend who lay on his death-bed. This death-bed was properly a cradle, and the poor dwarf lay inside with his yellow shrivelled old face. A little girl of some fourteen years sat beside him, and rocked the cradle with her foot, and sang in a laughing, roguish tone—

"'Sleep, little Turlutu, sleep!'

"When the little fellow saw me, he opened his glassy pale eyes as wide as possible, and a melancholy smile played on his white lips; he seemed to recognise me again, stretched his shrunken little hand towards me, and gently rattled—'Old friend!'

"It was, in fact, a sad condition in which I found the man who, in his eighth year, had had a long conversation with Louis XVI., whom the Czar Alexander had fed with bon-bons, whom the Princess von Kyritz had taken on her lap, who had ridden on the Duke of Brunswick's dogs, whom the King of Bavaria had read his poems to, who had smoked out of the same pipe with German princes, whom the Pope had idolised, and Napoleon never loved! This last circumstance troubled him on his death-bed, or, as I said, in his death-cradle, and he wept over the tragic fate of the great Emperor, who had never loved him, but who died in such a sorrowful way at Saint Helena—'just as I am dying,' he added, 'solitary, misunderstood, forsaken by all kings and princes, a caricature of former magnificence!'

"Although I could not rightly understand how a dwarf who died among giants could compare himself with a giant who died among dwarfs, I was nevertheless moved by poor Turlutu's words and by his forsaken condition at the last moment.

137

I could not help expressing my astonishment that Mademoiselle Laurence, who was now so grand, gave herself no trouble about him. I had scarcely uttered this name than the dwarf in the cradle was seized by the most fearful spasms, and he whispered with his white lips—'Ungrateful child! that I brought up, that I would elevate to be my wife, that I taught to move and behave among the great of this world, how to smile, how to bow at court, how to act—you have used my instructions well, and you are now a great lady, and you have a coach and footmen, and plenty of money, and plenty of pride, and no heart. You leave me here to die—to die alone and in misery, as Napoleon died at Saint Helena! O Napoleon! you never loved me.' What he added I could not catch. He raised his head, made some movements with his hand, as if fighting against somebody, perhaps against death. But that is an opponent whose scythe neither a Napoleon nor a Turlutu can withstand. No skill in fencing avails here. Faint, as if overcome, the dwarf let his head sink down again, looked at me a long time with an indescribable, ghostly stare, suddenly crowed like a cock, and expired.

"His death troubled me the more since he had been unable to give me any more exact information about Mademoiselle Laurence. Where should I now find her again? I was not in love with her, nor did I feel my former inclination towards her; yet a mysterious desire spurred me to seek her everywhere. When I entered a drawing-room and examined the company, and could not find the well-known face, I soon lost all repose and was driven away. Reflecting over this feeling, I stood one day at a remote entrance to the Great Opera, waiting for a carriage, and waiting with considerable annoyance, for it was raining very fast. But no carriage came, or, rather, only carriages which belonged to other people, who placed themselves comfortably inside, and the place around me became gradually solitary. "Then you must come with me," said at last a lady, who, concealed in her black mantilla, had stood for a little time near me, and was now on the point of getting into a carriage. The voice sent a quiver through my heart, the well-known side-glance again exercised its charm, and I was again as in a dream on finding myself beside Mademoiselle Laurence in a cosy warm carriage. We did not speak, indeed we could not have understood each other, as the carriage rattled noisily through the streets of Paris for a long time, till it stopped at last before a great gateway.

"Servants in gorgeous livery lighted us up the steps and through a succession of rooms. A lady's-maid met us with sleepy face, and stammering many excuses, said that there was only a fire in the red room. Motioning to the woman to go away, Laurence said, with a laugh, 'Chance is leading you a long way to-night; there is only a fire in my bed-room.'

"In this bed-room, in which we soon found ourselves alone, blazed a large open fire, which was the pleasanter since the room was of immense size and height. This large sleeping-room, which rather deserved the name of a sleeping-hall, had a similarly desolate appearance. Furniture and decoration, all bore the impress of a time whose brilliance seems to us now so bedimmed, its sublimity so *jejune*, that its remains raise a certain dislike within us, if not indeed a smile. I speak of the time of the Empire, of the time of the golden eagle, of high-flying plumes, of

Greek coiffures, of glory, of great drum-majors, of military masses, of official immortality (conferred by the *Moniteur*), of continental coffee prepared from chickory, of bad sugar manufactured from beet root, and of princes and dukes made from nothing at all. But it had its charm, though, that time of pathetic materialism. Talma declaimed, Gros painted, Bigottini danced, Grassini sang, Maury preached, Rovigo had the police, the Emperor read Ossian, Pauline Borghese let herself be moulded as Venus, and quite naked too,[13] for the room was well warmed, like the bed-room in which I found myself with Mademoiselle Laurence.

"We sat by the fire chatting familiarly, and she told me with a sigh that she was married to a Buonopartist hero, who enlivened her every evening before going to bed with a description of one of his battles; a few days ago, before going away, he had fought for her the battle of Jena; he was very ill, and with difficulty survived the Prussian campaign. When I asked her how long her father had been dead, she laughed, and confessed that she had never known a father, and that her so-called mother had never been married.

"'Not married!' I exclaimed; 'I saw her myself in London in the deepest mourning on account of her husband's death!'

"'Oh,' replied Laurence, 'for twelve years she had always dressed herself in black, to excite people's compassion as an unhappy widow, as well as to allure any donkey desirous of marrying, for she hoped to reach the haven of marriage quicker under black flags. But only death had pity on her, and she died of a hæmorrhage. I never loved her, for she always, gave me plenty of beating and little to eat. I should have died of starvation if Monsieur Turlutu had not often given me a little piece of bread on the sly; but the dwarf wished to marry me on that account, and when his hopes were frustrated he made common cause with my mother—I say 'mother' from custom—and both agreed to torment me. They always said that I was a superfluous creature, and that the learned dog was worth a thousand times more than I with my bad dancing. And then they praised the dog at my expense, extolled him to the skies, caressed him, fed him with cakes, and threw me the crumbs. The dog, they said, was their best support; he delighted the public, who were not in the least interested in me; the dog must support me by his work. I ate the bread of the dog. The cursed dog!'

"'Oh, do not curse him any more,' I broke in upon her passion; 'he is dead now; I saw him die.'

"'Is the beast dead?' exclaimed Laurence, springing up with a red glow of joy over her face.

"'And the dwarf is also dead,' I added.

"'Monsieur Turlutu?' cried Laurence, also with joy. But this joy gradually died from her face, and in a milder, almost melancholy tone, she added, 'Poor Turlutu!'

"When I told her, without any concealment, that the dwarf had complained of her very bitterly on his death-bed, she became passionately disturbed, and assured me, with many protestations, that she had had the foresight to care for him as well as possible, that she had offered him a pension if he would go and live quietly somewhere in the country. 'But ambitious as he was,' Laurence pursued, "he wished to stay in Paris, and even to live at my house; he could then, he thought, through my interposition, renew his connections in the Faubourg Saint-Germain, and again take his former brilliant position in society. When I flatly refused him this, he told me that I was a cursed ghost, a vampyre, a death-child."

"Laurence suddenly stopped, shuddered violently, and said at last, with a deep sigh, 'Ah, I wish they had left me in the grave with my mother!' As I pressed her to explain these mysterious words, a stream of tears flowed from her eyes, and, trembling and sobbing, she confessed to me that the black woman with the drum, who gave herself out as her mother, had once herself told her that the rumour which went about concerning her birth was no mere story. 'For in the town where we lived,' pursued Laurence, 'they always called me the death-child! The old woman maintained that I was the daughter of a Count who lived there, and who constantly ill-treated his wife, and when she died buried her very magnificently; she was, however, near her confinement, and only apparently dead, and when some churchyard thieves opened the grave to strip the richly-adorned corpse, they found the countess alive and in child-birth; and as she expired immediately after delivery, the thieves placed her again quietly in her grave, took away the child, and gave it to the receiver of the stolen goods, the great ventriloquist's sweetheart, to be brought up. This poor child, who had been buried before it was born, was everywhere called the death-child. Ah! you cannot understand how much sorrow I felt even as a little girl when anyone called me by that name. While the great ventriloquist was alive, whenever he was discontented with me, he always called out, 'Cursed death-child, I wish you had never been taken out of the grave!' He was a skilful ventriloquist, and could so modulate his voice that it seemed to come up out of the earth, and he told me that that was the voice of my dead mother telling me her fate. He might well know that horrible fate, for he had been a valet of the Count's. He took a cruel pleasure in the horrible fright which I, poor little girl, received from the words which seemed to ascend from the earth. These words, which seemed to ascend from the earth, mingled together fearful tales—tales which I never understood in their connection, and which later on I gradually forgot; but when I danced they would again come into my mind with living power. Yes, when I danced a singular remembrance seized me; I forgot myself, and I seemed to be quite another person, and as if all the sorrows and secrets of this person were poisoning me, and as soon as I left off dancing it was all extinguished in my memory.'

"While Laurence said this, slowly and as if questioning, she stood before me at the fireplace, where the fire was burning pleasanter than ever; and I sat in the easy-chair, which was apparently the seat of her husband, where he told her his battles before going to bed of an evening. Laurence looked at me with her large eyes as if she was asking my advice; she moved her head to and fro in such a melancholy, reflective way; she filled me with such a sweet compassion; she was so slender, so young, so lovely, this lily that had sprung out of the grave, this daughter of death, this ghost with the face of an angel and the body of a bayadere! I do not know how it came to pass; perhaps it was the influence of the easy-chair on which I was sitting, but it suddenly came into my mind that I was the old general who had described the battle of Jena yesterday from this place, and as if I must go on with my narrative, and I said, 'After the battle of Jena all the Prussian fortresses yielded themselves up within a few weeks, almost without drawing a sword. First Magdeburg yielded; it was the strongest fortress, and had three hundred cannon. Was not that disgraceful?'

"But Mademoiselle Laurence allowed me to say no more; the troubled mood had vanished from her face; she laughed like a child, and cried, 'Yes, that was disgraceful, more than disgraceful! If I was a fortress and had three hundred guns, I would never yield myself!'

"But as Mademoiselle Laurence was not a fortress, and had not three hundred guns——"

At these words Maximilian suddenly stopped in his story, and, after a short pause, asked gently, "Are you asleep, Maria?"

"I'm asleep," answered Maria.

"So much the better," said Maximilian, with a smile; "then I need not be afraid of wearying you if I describe the furniture of the room in which I found myself, as novelists are accustomed to do rather at length now-a-days."

"Say what you like, dear friend; I'm asleep."

"It was," continued Maximilian, "a very magnificent bed. The feet, as in all the beds of the Empire, consisted of caryatides and sphinxes; it gleamed with richly-gilt eagles, billing like turtle doves, perhaps an emblem of love under the Empire. The curtains of the bed were of red silk, and as the flames from the fireplace shone brightly through them, I found myself with Laurence in a fiery red illumination, and I seemed to be the god Pluto with the flames of hell blazing round him as he held the sleeping Proserpine in his arms. She was asleep, and in this condition I gazed on her sweet face, and sought in her features a clue to that sympathy which my soul felt for her. What was the meaning of this woman? What sense lurked under the symbolism of that beautiful form? I held the charming enigma in my arms now as my own property, and yet I could not find the solution of it.

"But is it not folly to wish to sound the inner meaning of any phenomenon outside us, when we cannot even solve the enigma of our own souls? We hardly know even whether outside phenomena really exist! We are often unable to distinguish reality from mere dream-faces. Was it a shape of my fancy, or was it horrible reality that I heard and saw on that night? I know not. I only remember that as the wildest thoughts were flowing through my heart, a singular sound came to my ear. It was a crazy melody, peculiarly soft. It seemed known to me, and at last I distinguished the tones of a triangle and a drum. This music, whirring and humming, seemed to come from afar, and yet as I looked up I saw near me in the middle of the room a well-known performance. It was Monsieur Turlutu the

141

dwarf who played the triangle, and Madame beating the great drum, while the learned dog was scratching about on the floor, as if searching for his wooden letters. The dog appeared to move with difficulty, and his skin was spotted with blood. Madame still wore her black mourning, but her belly was no longer so spaciously protuberant, but repulsively pendant. Her face, too, was no longer red, but pale. The dwarf, who still wore the embroidered coat of an old French marquis and a powdered toupet, appeared to have grown somewhat, perhaps because he was so horribly lean. He again exhibited his skill in fencing, and seemed to be again spinning off his old vaunts; but he spoke so softly that I was unable to understand a word, and only by the movements of his lips could I sometimes observe that he was again crowing like a cock.

"While this ludicrous, horrible caricature moved like a magic lantern with confused haste before my eyes, I felt Mademoiselle Laurence breathing more and more uneasily. A cold paroxysm froze her whole body, and her sweet limbs writhed as if with unbearable agony. At last, however, supple as an eel, she glided from my arms, stood suddenly in the middle of the room, and began to dance, while the mother with the drum and the dwarf with the triangle continued their deadened soft music. She danced just as formerly on Waterloo Bridge and in the squares of London. There were the same mysterious pantomimes, the same outbreaks of passionate leaping, the same Bacchante-like throwing of the head backwards, often also the same leaning towards the earth, as if she wished to hear somebody speaking beneath, then also the trembling, the pallor, the benumbed stiffness, and again the listening with ear bent to the earth. Again also she rubbed her hands as if washing herself. At last she appeared again to cast her intense, sorrowful, imploring glance upon me, but now only in the features of her death-pale countenance could I recognise that glance—not in her eyes, for they were shut. In ever softer sounds the music died away; the mother with the drum and the dwarf, gradually growing pale and breaking like mist, vanished at last altogether; but Mademoiselle Laurence still stood and danced with closed eyes. This dance with closed eyes in the silent nocturnal chamber gave this sweet being so ghostly an appearance that a disagreeable feeling seized me; I shuddered, and was heartily glad when she finished her dance, and as easily as she had slipped away again glided into my arms.

"In truth, this scene was not pleasant to me. But we accustom ourselves to everything. And it is even possible that what was mysterious in this woman lent her a more peculiar charm, that an awful tenderness mingled with my emotions. In any case, after some weeks I ceased to wonder in the least when the low sounds of the drum and triangle were heard at night, and my dear Laurence suddenly started up and danced a solo with closed eyes. Her husband, the old Buonapartist, commanded in the neighbourhood of Paris, and his duties allowed him to pass the day only in the city. Of course he became my most intimate friend, and he wept when later on he bade me farewell. He travelled with his wife to Sicily, and I have seen neither of them again since."

When Maximilian had finished this narrative, he hastily seized his hat and slipped out of the room.

DON QUIXOTE.

[The following admirable account of *Don Quixote*—here given chiefly in Mr. Fleishman's translation—was written in 1837, as the introduction to an *edition de luxe* of Cervantes's masterpiece.]

THE first book that I read after I arrived at boyhood's years of discretion, and had tolerably mastered my letters, was *The Life and Deeds of the Sagacious Knight, Don Quixote de la Mancha*, written by Miguel Cervantes de Saavedra. Well do I remember the time, when, early in the morning, I stole away from home and hastened to the court-garden, that I might read Don Quixote without being disturbed. It was a beautiful day in May, the blooming Spring lay basking in the silent morning light, listening to the compliments of that sweet flatterer, the nightingale, who sang so softly and caressingly, with such a melting fervour, that even the shyest of buds burst into blossom, and the lusty grasses and the fragrant sunshine kissed more rapturously, and the trees and flowers trembled from very ecstasy. But I seated myself on an old moss-covered stone bench in the so-called Avenue of Sighs, not far from the water-fall, and feasted my little heart with the thrilling adventures of the valiant knight. In my childish simplicity I took everything in sober earnest; no matter how ridiculous the mishaps which fate visited upon the poor hero, I thought it must be just so, and imagined that to be laughed at was as much a part of heroism as to be wounded; and the former vexed me just as sorely as the latter grieved my heart. I was a child, and knew nothing of the irony God has interwoven into the world, and which the great poet has imitated in his miniature world;—and I wept most bitterly, when for all his chivalry and generosity the noble knight gained only ingratitude and cudgels. As I was unpracticed in reading, I spoke every word aloud, and so the birds and the trees, the brooks and the flowers, could hear all I read, and as these innocent beings know as little as children of the irony of the world, they too took it all for sober earnest, and wept with me over the sorrows of the unfortunate knight; an old worn-out oak sobbed even; and the water-fall shook more vehemently his white beard, and seemed to scold at the wickedness of the world. We felt that the heroism of the knight was none the less worthy of admiration because the lion turned tail without fighting, and that if his body was weak and withered, his armour rusty, his steed a miserable jade, his deeds were all the more worthy of praise. We despised the vulgar rabble who beat the poor hero so barbarously, and still more the rabble of higher rank, who were decked in silk attire, gay courtly phrases, and grand titles, and jeered at the man who was so far their superior in powers of mind and nobility of soul. Dulcinea's knight rose ever higher in my esteem, and my love for him grew stronger and stronger the longer I read in that wonderful book, which I continued to do daily in that same garden, so that when autumn came I had reached the end of the story,—and I shall never forget the day when I read the sorrowful combat, in which the knight came to so ignominious an end.

It was a gloomy day; dismal clouds swept over a leaden sky, the yellow leaves fell sorrowfully from the trees, heavy tear-drops hung on the last flowers that drooped down in a sad faded way their dying little heads, the nightingales had long since died away, from every side the image of transitoriness stared at me— and my heart was ready to break as I read how the noble knight lay on the ground, stunned and bruised, and through his closed visor said, in tones faint and feeble, as if he was speaking from the grave, "Dulcinea is the fairest lady in the world, and I the unhappiest knight on earth, but it is not meet that my weakness should disown this truth—strike with your lance, Sir Knight."

Ah me! that brilliant knight of the silver moon, who vanquished the bravest and noblest man in the world, was a disguised barber!

That was long ago. Many new springs have bloomed forth since then, yet their mightiest charm has always been wanting, for, alas! I no longer believe the sweet deceits of the nightingale, Spring's flatterer; I know how soon his magnificence fades, and when I look at the youngest rosebuds I see them in spirit bloom to a sorrowful red, grow pale, and be scattered by the winds. Everywhere I see a disguised Winter.

In my breast, however, still blooms that flaming love, which soared so ardently above the earth, to revel adventurously in the broad yawning spaces of heaven, and which, pushed back by the cold stars, and sinking home again to the little earth, was forced to confess, with sighing and triumph, that there is in all creation nothing fairer or better than the heart of man. This love is the inspiration that fills me, always divine, whether it does foolish or wise deeds.— And so the tears the little boy shed over the sorrows of the silly knight were in no wise spent in vain, any more than the later tears of the youth, as on many a night he wept in the study over the deaths of the holy heroes of freedom—over King Agis of Sparta, over Caius and Tiberius Gracchus of Rome, over Jesus of Jerusalem, and over Robespierre and Saint Just of Paris. Now that I have put on the *toga virilis*, and myself desire to be a man, the tears have come to an end, and it is necessary to act like a man, imitating my great predecessors; in the future, if God will, to be wept also by boys and youths. Yes, upon these one can still reckon in our cold age; for they can still be kindled by the breezes that blow to them from old books, and so they can comprehend the flaming hearts of the present. Youth is unselfish in its thoughts and feelings, and on that account it feels truth most deeply, and is not sparing, where a bold sympathy is wanted, with confession or deed. Older people are selfish and narrow-minded; they think more of the interest of their capital than of the interest of mankind; they let their little boat float quietly down the gutter of life, and trouble themselves little about the sailor who battles with the waves on the open sea; or they creep with clinging tenacity up to the heights of mayoralty or the presidency of their club, and shrug their shoulders over the heroic figures which the storm throws down from the columns of fame; and then they tell, perhaps, how they themselves also in their youth ran their heads against the wall, but that later on they reconciled themselves to the wall, for the wall was the absolute, existing by and for itself, which, because it was, was also reasonable, on which account he is unreasonable who will not endure a high, reasonable, inevitable, eternally-ordained

144

absolutism. Ah, these objectionable people, who wish to philosophise us into a gentle slavery, are yet more worthy of esteem than those depraved ones who do not even admit reasonable grounds for the defence of despotism, but being learned in history fight for it as a right of custom, to which men in the course of time have gradually accustomed themselves, and which has so become incontestably valid and lawful.

Ah, well! I will not, like Ham, lift up the garment of my fatherland's shame; but it is terrible how slavery has been made with us a matter for prating about, and how German philosophers and historians have tormented their brains to defend despotism, however silly or awkward, as reasonable and lawful. Silence is the honour of slaves, says Tacitus; these philosophers and historians maintain the contrary, and exhibit the badge of slavery in their button-holes.

Perhaps, after all, you are right, and I am only a Don Quixote, and the reading of all sorts of wonderful books has turned my head, as it was with the Knight of La Mancha, and Jean Jacques Rousseau was my Amadis of Gaul, Mirabeau my Roland or Agramanto; and I have studied too much the heroic deeds of the French Paladins and the round table of the National Convention. Indeed, my madness and the fixed ideas that I created out of books are of a quite opposite kind to the madness and the fixed ideas of him of La Mancha. He wished to establish again the expiring days of chivalry; I, on the contrary, wish to annihilate all that is yet remaining from that time, and so we work with altogether different views. My colleague saw windmills as giants; I, on the contrary, can see in our present giants only vaunting windmills. He took leather wine-skins for mighty enchanters, but I can see in the enchanters of to-day only leather wine-skins. He held beggarly pot-houses for castles, donkey-drivers for cavaliers, stable wenches for court ladies; I, on the contrary, hold our castles for beggarly pot-houses, our cavaliers for mere donkey-drivers, our court ladies for ordinary stable wenches. As he took a puppet-show for a state ceremony, so I hold our state ceremonies as sorry puppet-shows, yet as bravely as the brave Knight of La Mancha I strike out at the clumsy machinery. Alas! such heroic deeds often turn out as badly for me as for him, and like him I must suffer much for the honour of my lady. If I denied her from mere fear or base love of gain, I might live comfortably in this reasonably-constructed world, and I should lead a fair Maritorna to the altar, and let myself be blessed by fat enchanters, and banquet with noble donkey-drivers, and engender harmless romances as well as other little slaves! Instead of that, wearing the three colours of my lady, I must strike through unspeakable opposition, and fight battles, everyone of which costs me my heart's blood. Day and night I am in straits, for those enemies are so artful that many I struck to death still give themselves the appearance of being alive, changing themselves into all forms, and spoiling day and night for me. How many sorrows have I suffered by such fatal spectres! Where anything lovely bloomed for me then they crept in, those cunning ghosts, and broke even the most innocent buds. Everywhere, and when I should least suspect it, I discovered on the ground the traces of their silvery slime, and if I took no care, I might have a dangerous fall even in the house of my love. You may smile and hold such

145

anxieties for idle fancies like those of Don Quixote. But fancied pains hurt all the same; and if one fancies that he has drunk hemlock he may get into a consumption, and he certainly will not get fat. And the report that I have got fat is a calumny; at least I have not yet received any fat sinecure, even if I possess the requisite talents. I fancy that everything has been done to keep me lean; when I was hungry they fed me with snakes, when I was thirsty they gave me wormwood to drink; they poured hell into my heart, so that I wept poison and sighed fire; they crouched near me even in my dreams; and I see horrible spectres, noble lackey faces with gnashing teeth and threatening noses, and deadly eyes glaring from cowls, and white ruffled hands with gleaming knives.

And even the old woman who lives near me in the next room considers me to be mad, and says that I talk the maddest nonsense in my sleep; and the other night she plainly heard me calling out—"Dulcinea is the fairest woman in the world, and I the unhappiest knight on earth; but it is not meet that my weakness should disown this truth. Strike with your lance, Sir Knight!"

——

It is now eight years since I wrote the foregoing lines[14] for the Fourth Part of the *Reisebilder*, in which I described the impression which the reading of *Don Quixote* had made on my mind many years ago. Good Heavens! how swiftly time flies! It seems to me as if it were but yesterday that, in the Avenue of Sighs, in the court-garden at Düsseldorf, I finished reading the book, and my heart is still moved with admiration for the deeds and sufferings of the noble knight. Has my heart remained constant in this ever since, or has it, after passing through a wonderful cycle, returned to the emotions of childhood? The latter may well be the case, for I remember that during each lustrum of my life *Don Quixote* has made a different impression upon me. When I was blossoming into adolescence, and with inexperienced hands sought to pluck the roses of life, climbed the loftiest peaks in order to be nearer to the sun, and at night dreamed of naught else but eagles and chaste maidens, then Don Quixote was to me a very unsatisfactory book, and if it chanced to fall in my way I involuntarily shoved it aside. At a later period, when I had ripened into manhood, I became to a certain degree reconciled to Dulcinea's luckless champion, and I began to laugh at him. The fellow is a fool, said I. And yet, strange to say, the shadowy forms of the lean knight and his fat squire have ever followed me in all the journeyings of my life, particularly when I came to any critical turning-point. Thus I recollect that while making the journey to France, one morning in the post-chaise I awakened from a half-feverish slumber, and saw in the early morning mist two well-known figures riding by my side. The one on my right was Don Quixote de la Mancha, mounted on his lean, abstract Rosinante, the other on my left was Sancho Panza, on his substantial, positive grey donkey. We had just reached the French frontier. The noble Manchean bowed his head reverently before the tri-coloured flag, which fluttered towards us from the high post that marks the boundary line. Our good Sancho saluted with a somewhat less cordial nod the first French *gendarmes* whom we saw approaching near by. At last my two friends pushed on ahead, and I lost sight of them, only now and then I caught the sound of Rosinante's spirited

146

neighing, and the donkey's responsive bray.

At that time I was of the opinion that the ridiculousness of Don Quixotism consisted in the fact that the noble knight endeavoured to recall a long-perished past back to life, and his poor limbs and back came into painful contact with the harsh realities of the present. Alas! I have since learned that it is an equally ungrateful folly to endeavour to bring the future prematurely into the present, and that for such an assault upon the weighty interests of the day, one possesses but a very sorry steed, a brittle armour, and an equally frail body! And the wise man dubiously shakes his sage head at the one, as well as at the other, of these Quixotisms. But Dulcinea del Toboso is still the most beautiful woman in the world; although I lie stretched upon the earth, helpless and miserable, I will never take back that assertion, I cannot do otherwise—on with your lances, ye Knights of the Silver Moon, ye disguised barbers!

What leading idea guided Cervantes when he wrote his great book? Was his purpose merely the destruction of the romances of knight-errantry, the reading of which at that time was so much the rage in Spain that both clerical and secular ordinances against them were powerless? Or did he seek to hold up to ridicule all manifestations of human enthusiasm in general, military heroism in particular? Ostensibly he aimed only to satirise the romances above referred to, and through the exposition of their absurdities deliver them over to universal derision, and thus put an end to them. In this he succeeded most brilliantly; for that which neither the exhortations from the pulpit, nor the threats of the authorities could effect, that a poor writer accomplished with his pen. He destroyed the romances of chivalry so effectually that soon after the appearance of *Don Quixote* the taste for that class of literature wholly died out in Spain, and no more of that order were printed. But the pen of a man of genius is always greater than he himself; it extends far beyond his temporary purpose, and without being himself clearly conscious of it, Cervantes wrote the greatest satire against human enthusiasm. He had not the least presentiment of this, for he himself was a hero, who had spent the greater portion of his life in chivalrous conflicts, and who in his old age was wont to rejoice that he had participated in the battle of Lepanto, although he paid for this glory with the loss of his left hand.

The biographers can tell us but little concerning the person or private life of the poet who wrote *Don Quixote*. We do not lose much by the omission of such details, which are generally picked up from the female gossips of the neighbourhood. They see only the outer shell; but we see the man, his true, sincere, unslandered self.

He was a handsome, powerful man, Don Miguel Cervantes de Saavedra. He had a high forehead, and a large heart. His eyes possessed a wonderful magic; just as there are people who can look into the earth, and see the hidden treasures and the dead that lie buried there, so the eye of the great poet could penetrate the breasts of men, and see distinctly all that was concealed there. To the good his look was as a ray of sunlight gladdening and illuminating the heart; to the bad

147

his glance was a sword, sharply piercing their souls. His searching eyes penetrated to the very soul of a person, and questioned it, and if it refused to answer, he put it to the torture, and the soul lay stretched bleeding on the rack, while perhaps the body assumed an air of condescending superiority. Is it to be wondered at that many formed a dislike for him, and gave him but scant assistance in his journey through life? He never achieved rank or position, and from all his toilsome pilgrimages he brought back no pearls, but only empty shells. It is said that he could not appreciate the value of money, but I assure you he fully appreciated its worth when he had no more. But he never prized it as highly as he did his honour. He had debts, and in one of his writings, in which Apollo is supposed to grant to the poets a charter of privileges, the first paragraph declares: When a poet says he has no money, his simple assurance shall suffice, and no oath shall be required of him. He loved music, flowers, and women, but in his love for the latter he sometimes fared very badly, particularly in his younger days. Did the consciousness of future greatness console him, when pert young roses stung him with their thorns?—Once on a bright summer afternoon, while yet a young gallant, he walked along the banks of the Tagus in company with a pretty girl of sweet sixteen, who continually mocked at his tender speeches. The sun had not yet set, it still glowed with all its golden splendour, but high up in the heavens was the moon, pale and insignificant, like a little white cloud. "See'st thou," said the young poet to his sweetheart, "see'st thou yonder small pale disk? The river by our side in which it mirrors itself seems to receive its pitiful reflex on its proud bosom merely out of compassion, and the curling billows at times cast it disdainfully aside towards the shore. But wait until day fades into twilight; as soon as darkness descends, yonder pale orb will grow brighter and brighter, and will flood the whole stream with its silvery light, and the haughty billows that before were so scornful will then tremble with ecstasy at sight of the lovely moon, and roll rapturously towards it."

The history of poets must be sought for in their works, for there are to be found their most confidential confessions. In all his writings, in his dramas even more than in *Don Quixote*, we see, as I have before mentioned, that Cervantes had long been a soldier. In fact, the Roman proverb, "Living means fighting," finds a double application in his case. He took part as a common soldier in most of those fierce games of war which King Philip II. carried on in all countries for the honour of God and his own pleasure. The circumstance that Cervantes devoted his whole youth to the service of the greatest champion of Catholicism, and that he fought to advance Catholic interests, warrants the assumption that he had those interests at heart, and hence refutes the widely-spread opinion that only the fear of the Inquisition withheld him from discussing in *Don Quixote* the great Protestant questions of the time. No, Cervantes was a faithful son of the Roman church, and he not only bled physically in knightly combats for her blessed banner, but his whole soul suffered a most painful martyrdom during his many years of captivity among the Unbelievers.

We are indebted to accident for most of the details of Cervantes's doings while in Algiers, and here we recognise in the great poet an equally great hero. The history of his captivity gives a most emphatic contradiction to the melodious lie of that polished man of the world, who made Augustus and the German pedants believe that he was a poet, and that poets are cowards. No, the true poet is also a true hero, and in his breast dwells that God-like patience, which, as the Spaniards say, is a second fount of courage. There is no more elevating spectacle than that of the noble Castilian who serves the Dey of Algiers as a slave, constantly meditating an escape, with unflagging energy preparing his bold plans, composedly facing all dangers, and when the enterprise miscarries, is ready to submit to torture and death rather than betray his accomplices. The blood-thirsty master of his body becomes disarmed by such grand magnanimity and virtue. The tiger spares the fettered lion, and trembles before the terrible "One-Arm," whom with but a single word he could dispatch to his death. Cervantes is known in all Algiers as "One-Arm," and the Dey confesses that only when he knows that the one-armed Spaniard is in safe-keeping can he sleep soundly at night, assured of the safety of his city, his army, and his slaves.

I have referred to the fact that Cervantes was always a common soldier, but even in so subordinate a position he succeeded in distinguishing himself to such a degree as to attract the notice of the great general, Don John of Austria, and on his return from Italy to Spain he was furnished with the most complimentary letters of recommendation to the king, in which his advancement was most emphatically urged. When the Algerine corsairs, who captured him on the Mediterranean Sea, beheld these letters, they took him to be a person of the highest rank and importance, and hence demanded so large a ransom that notwithstanding all their efforts and sacrifices his family were not able to purchase his freedom, and the unfortunate poet's captivity was thereby prolonged and embittered. Thus the recognition of his merits became an additional source of misfortune, and thus to the very end of his days was he mocked by that cruel dame, the Goddess Fortuna, who never forgives genius for having achieved fame and honour without her assistance.

But are the misfortunes of a man of genius always the work of blind chance, or do they necessarily follow from his inner nature and environment? Does his soul enter into strife with the world of reality, or do the coarse realities begin the unequal conflict with his noble soul?

Society is a republic. When an individual strives to rise, the collective masses press him back through ridicule and abuse. No one shall be wiser or better than the rest. But against him, who by the invincible power of genius towers above the vulgar masses, society launches its ostracism, and persecutes him so mercilessly with scoffing and slander, that he is finally compelled to withdraw into the solitude of his own thoughts.

Verily, society is republican in its very essence. Every sovereignty, intellectual as well as material, is hated by it. The latter oftener gives aid to the former than is generally imagined. We ourselves came to this conclusion soon after the revolution of July, when the spirit of republicanism manifested itself in all social relations. Our republicans hated the laurels of a great poet even as they hated

149

the purple of a great king. They sought to level the intellectual inequalities of mankind, and in as much as they regarded all ideas that had been produced on the soil of the state as general property, nothing remained to be done but to decree an equality of style also. In sooth, a good style was decried as something aristocratic, and we heard manifold assertions: "A true democrat must write in the style of the people—sincere, natural, crude." Most of the Party of Action succeeded easily in doing this, but not every one possesses the gift of writing badly, especially if one has previously formed the habit of writing well, and then it was at once said, "That is an aristocrat, a lover of style, a friend of art, an enemy of the people." They were surely honest in their views, like Saint Hieronymus, who considered his good style a sin, and gave himself sound scourgings for it.

Just as little as we find anti-Catholic, so also do we fail to discover anti-absolutist strains in *Don Quixote*. The critics who think that they scent such sentiments therein are clearly in error. Cervantes was the son of a school which went so far as to poetically idealise the idea of unquestioning obedience to the sovereign. And that sovereign was the King of Spain at a time when its majesty dazzled the whole world. The common soldier felt himself a ray in that halo of glory, and willingly sacrificed his individual freedom to gratify the national pride of the Castilian.

The political grandeur of Spain at that time contributed not a little to exalt and enlarge the hearts of her poets. In the mind of a Spanish poet, as in the realm of Charles V., the sun never set. The fierce wars against the Moors were ended, and as after a storm the flowers are most fragrant, so poesy ever blooms most grandly after a civil war. We witness the same phenomenon in England at the time of Elizabeth, and at the same time as in Spain there arose a galaxy of poets, which invites the most remarkable parallelisms. There we see Shakespeare, here Cervantes, as the flower of the school.

Like the Spanish poets under the three Philips, so also the English poets under Elizabeth present a certain family likeness, and neither Shakespeare nor Cervantes have claim to originality in our sense of the word. They by no means differ from their contemporaries through peculiar modes of thought or feeling, or by an especial manner of portrayal, but only through greater depth, fervour, tenderness, and power. Their creations are more infused and penetrated with the divine spark of poetry.

But both poets were not only the flowers of their time, but they were also the germs of the future. As Shakespeare, by the influence of his works, particularly on Germany and the France of to-day, is to be regarded as the creator of the later dramatic art, so must we honour in Cervantes the author of the modern novel. I shall allow myself a few passing observations on the subject.

The older novels, the so-called romances of chivalry sprang from the poetry of the middle ages. They were at first prose versions of those epic poems whose heroes are derived from the mythical traditions of Charlemagne and the Holy Grail. The subject was always knightly adventures. It was the romance of the

150

nobility, and the personages that figured therein were either fabulous, fantastic beings, or knights with golden spurs; nowhere an allusion to the people. These romances of knighthood, which degenerated into the most ridiculous absurdities, Cervantes overthrew by his *Don Quixote*. But while by his satire he destroyed the earlier romances, he also furnished a model for a new school of fiction, which we call the Modern Novel. Such is always the wont of great poets; while they tear down the old, they at the same time build up the new; they never destroy without replacing. Cervantes created the modern novel by introducing into his romances of knighthood a faithful description of the lower classes, by intermingling with it phases of folk-life. This partiality for describing the doings of the common rabble, of the vilest tatterdemalions, is not only found in Cervantes, but in all his literary contemporaries, and among the Spanish painters as well as among the poets of that period. A Murillo, who stole heaven's loveliest tints with which to paint his beautiful Madonnas, painted with the same love the filthiest creatures of this earth. It was perhaps the enthusiasm for art itself that made these noble Spaniards find equal pleasure in the faithful portrayal of a beggar lad scratching his head as in the representation of the Blessed Virgin. Or, perhaps, it was the charm of contrast that led noblemen of the highest rank, a dapper courtier like Quevedo, or a powerful minister like Mendoza, to fill their romances with ragged beggars and vagabonds. They perhaps sought to relieve the monotony of their lofty rank by putting themselves in imagination into a quite different sphere of life, just as we find a similar tendency among some of our German authors, whose novels contain naught else but descriptions of the nobility, and who always make their heroes counts and barons. We do not find in Cervantes this one-sided tendency to portray the vulgar only; he intermingles the ideal and the common; one serves as light or as shade to the other, and the aristocratic element is as prominent in it as the popular. But this noble, chivalrous, aristocratic element disappears entirely from the novels of the English, who were the first to imitate Cervantes, and to this day always keep him in view as a model. These English novelists since Richardson's reign are prosaic natures; to the prudish spirit of their time even pithy descriptions of the life of the common people are repugnant, and we see on yonder side of the channel those *bourgeois* novels arise, wherein the petty, humdrum life of the middle classes is depicted. The public were surfeited with this deplorable class of literature until recently, when appeared the great Scot, who effected a revolution, or rather a restoration, in novel-writing. As Cervantes introduced the democratic element into romance, at a time when one-sided knight-errantry ruled supreme, so Walter Scott restored the aristocratic element to romance when it had wholly disappeared, and only a prosaic bourgeoisie was to be found there. By an opposite course Walter Scott again restored to romance that beautiful symmetry which we admire in Cervantes's *Don Quixote*.

I believe that the merits of England's second great poet have never in this respect been recognised. His Tory proclivities, his partiality for the past, were wholesome for literature, and for those masterpieces of his genius that everywhere found favour and imitators, and which drove into the darkest corners of the circulating libraries those ashen-grey, ghostly remains of the *bourgeoisie* romances. It is an error not to recognise Walter Scott as the founder of the so-called Historical Romance, and to endeavour to trace the latter to German initiative. This error arises from the failure to perceive that the characteristic feature of the Historical Romance consists just in the harmony between the aristocratic and democratic elements, and that Walter Scott, through the re-introduction of the aristocratic element, most beautifully restored that harmony which had been overthrown during the absolutism of the democratic element, whereas our German romanticists eliminated the democratic element entirely from their novels, and returned again to the ruts of those crazy romances of knight-errantry that flourished before Cervantes. Our De la Motte-Fouqué is only a straggler from the ranks of those poets who gave to the world *Amadis de Gaul*, and similar extravagant absurdities. I admire not only the talent, but also the courage of the noble Baron who, two centuries after the appearance of *Don Quixote*, has written his romances of chivalry. It was a peculiar period in Germany when the latter appeared and found favour with the public. What was the significance in literature of that partiality for knight-errantry, and for those pictures of the old feudal times? I believe that the German people desired to bid an eternal farewell to the middle ages, but moved with emotion as we Germans are so apt to be, we took our leave with a kiss. For the last time we pressed our lips to the old tombstone. True, some of us behaved in a very silly manner on that occasion. Ludwig Tieck, the smallest boy in school, dug the dead ancestors out of their grave, rocked the coffin as if it were a cradle, and in childish, lisping accents sang, "Sleep, little grandsire, sleep."

I have called Walter Scott England's second great poet, and his novels masterpieces; but it is to his genius only that I would give the highest praise. His novels I can by no means place on an equality with the great romance of Cervantes. The latter surpasses him in epic spirit. Cervantes was, as I have already stated, a Catholic poet, and it is perhaps to this circumstance that he is indebted for that grand epic composure of soul, which, like a crystalline firmament, overarches those picturesque and poetical creations; nowhere is there a rift of scepticism. Added to this is the calm dignity which is the national characteristic of the Spaniard. But Walter Scott belongs to a church which subjects even divine matters to a sharp examination; as an advocate and as a Scotchman he is accustomed to action and to debate, and we find the dramatic element most prominent in his novels, as well as in his life and his temperament. Hence his works can never be regarded as the pure model of that style of fiction which we denominate the Romance. To the Spaniards is due the honour of having produced the best novel, as England is entitled to the credit of having achieved the highest rank in the drama.

And the Germans, what palm remains for them? Well, then, we are the best lyric poets on earth. No people possesses such beautiful songs as the Germans. At present the nations are too much occupied with political affairs, but when these are once laid aside, then let us Germans, English, Spaniards, French, Italians, all go out into the green forests and chant our lays, and the nightingale shall be umpire. I am convinced that in this tournament of minstrelsy the songs of

Wolfgang Goethe will win the prize.

Cervantes, Shakespeare, and Goethe form the triumvirate of poets, who, in the three great divisions of poetry, epic, dramatic, and lyric, have achieved the greatest success. The writer of these pages is perhaps peculiarly fitted to sound the praises of our great countryman as the most perfect of lyric poets. Goethe stands midway between the two classes of song-writers, between those two schools, of which one, alas! is known by my own name, the other as the Suabian school. Both have their merits; they have indirectly promoted the welfare of German poetry. The first effected a wholesome reaction against the one-sided idealism of German poetry, it led the intellect back to stern realities, and uprooted that sentimental Petrarchism that has always seemed to us as a Quixotism in verse. The Suabian school also contributed indirectly to the weal of German poetry. If in Northern Germany strong and healthy poetical productions came to light, thanks are perhaps due to the Suabian school, which attracted to itself all the sickly chlorotic, mawkishly-pious, clumsy votaries of the German muse. Stuttgart was the fontanel, as it were, for the German muse.

While I ascribe the highest achievements in drama, in romance, and in lyric poetry to this great triumvirate, far be it from me to depreciate the poetical merits of other great poets. Nothing is more foolish than the query, "Which poet is greater than the other?" Flame is flame, and its weight cannot be determined in pounds and ounces. Only a narrow shopkeeper mind will attempt to weigh genius in its miserable cheese scales. Not only the ancients, but some of the moderns, have written works in which the fire of poetry burns with a splendour equal to that of the masterpieces of Shakespeare, Cervantes, and Goethe. Nevertheless, these names hold together as if through some secret bond. A kindred spirit shines forth from their creations, an immortal tenderness exhales from them like the breath of God, the modesty of nature blooms in them. Goethe not only constantly reminds one of Shakespeare, but also of Cervantes, and he resembles the latter even in the details of style, and in that charming prose diction which is tinged with a vein of the sweetest and most harmless irony. Cervantes and Goethe resemble each other even in their faults, in diffusiveness of style, in those long sentences that we occasionally find in their writings, and which may be compared to a procession of royal equipages. Not infrequently but a single thought sits in one of those long, wide-spreading sentences that rolls majestically along like a great, gilded court-chariot, drawn by six plumed steeds. But that single idea is always something exalted, perhaps even royal.

My remarks concerning the genius of Cervantes and the influence of his book have been necessarily scant. Concerning the true value of his romance from an artistic standpoint, I must express myself still more briefly, as otherwise questions might arise which would lead to wide digressions into the sphere of æsthetics. I may only call attention in a general way to the form of the romance, and to the two figures that constitute its central point. The form is that of a description of travels which has ever been the most natural for this class of writings. I am reminded of The Golden Ass of Apuleius, the first romance of antiquity. Later poets sought to relieve the monotony of this form through what

153

we to-day call *fabliaux*. But on account of poverty of invention the majority of romance writers have borrowed each other's fables; at least, part have always used the same tales, making but slight variations. Hence, through the resulting sameness of characters, situations, and complications, the public became at last somewhat wearied of romance-reading. To escape from the tediousness of hackneyed tales and fables, they sought refuge in the ancient, original form of narratives of travels. But this form will again be wholly supplanted just as soon as some creative genius shall arise with a new and original style of romance. In literature, as well as in politics, all things are subject to the law of action and reaction.

As regards the two figures that are called Don Quixote and Sancho Panza, that so constantly burlesque, and yet so wonderfully complement each other, so that together they form the one true hero of the romance,—these two figures give evidence equally of the poet's artistic taste and of his intellectual profundity. If other authors, in whose romances the hero journeys solitary and alone through the world, are compelled to have recourse to monologues, letters, or diaries in order to communicate the thoughts and emotions of their heroes, Cervantes can always let a natural dialogue arise; and, inasmuch as the one figure always parodies the other, the author's purpose is the more clearly shown. Manifold have been the imitations of this double figure which lends to the romance of Cervantes such an artistic naturalness, and out of which, as from a single seed, has grown the whole novel, with all its wild foliage, its fragrant blossoms, its glowing fruits, its apes and marvellous birds that cluster amid its branches, resembling one of those giant trees of India.

But it would be unjust to charge all this to a servile imitation; on the surface, as it were, lay the introduction of two such figures as Don Quixote and Sancho Panza, of which the one, the poetical nature, seeks adventures, and the other, half out of affection, half out of selfish motives, follows through sunshine and rain, as we often meet them in real life. In order to recognise this couple anywhere, under the most varied disguises, in art as well as in life, one must keep in view only the essential, the spiritual characteristics, not the incidental or external. I could offer innumerable instances of this. Do we not find Don Quixote and Sancho Panza clearly repeated in Don Juan and Leporello, and to a certain degree also in the persons of Lord Byron and his servant Fletcher? Do we not recognise these two types and their changed relations in the figures of the Knight von Waldsee and his Caspar Larifari, as also in the form of many an author and his publisher? The latter clearly discerns his author's follies, but in order to reap pecuniary profit out of them, faithfully accompanies him in all his ideal vagaries. And Master Publisher Sancho, even if at times he gains only buffets in the transaction, yet always remains fat, while the noble knight grows daily more and more emaciated. But not only among men, but also among women, have I often met the counterparts of Don Quixote and his henchman. I particularly remember a beautiful English lady, an impulsive, enthusiastic blonde, who, accompanied by her friend, had run away from a London boarding-school, to roam the wide world over in search of a noble, true-hearted lover, such as she had dreamed of on soft moonlight nights. Her friend, a short, plump brunette, also hoped through this opportunity to gain, if not so rare and high an ideal, at least a husband of good appearance. Still do I see her, with her slender figure, and blue, love-longing eyes, standing on the beach at Brighton, casting wistful glances over the billowy sea towards the French coast; meanwhile her companion cracked hazel-nuts, munched the sweet kernels with relish, and threw the shells into the water.

And yet neither in the masterpieces of other artists, nor in nature herself, do we find these two types in their varying relations so minutely elaborated as in Cervantes. Every trait in the character and appearance of the one answers to a contrasting, and yet kindred, trait in the other. Here every detail has a burlesque signification; yes, even between Rosinante and Sancho's grey donkey there exists the same ironic parallelism as between the squire and the knight, and the two beasts are made to convey symbolically the same idea. As in their modes of thought, so also in their speech, do master and servant reveal a most marvellous contrast, and I cannot here omit to refer to the difficulties with which the translator has had to contend in order to reproduce in German the homely, gnarled dialect of our good Sancho. Through his blunt, frequently vulgar speeches, and his fondness for proverbialising, our good Sancho reminds us of King Solomon's fool, and of Marculfe, who, also, in opposition to a somewhat pathetic idealism, expresses in short and pithy sayings the practical wisdom of the common people. Don Quixote, on the contrary, speaks the language of culture, of the higher classes, and in the solemn gravity of his well-rounded periods, he fairly represents the high-born Hidalgo. At times his sentences are spun out too broadly, and the knight's language resembles a haughty court dame, attired in a much bepuffed silken robe, with a long rustling train. But the graces, disguised as pages, laughingly carry the tips of this train, and the long sentences end with the most charming turns.

The character of Don Quixote's language and that of Sancho Panza may be briefly summarised in the words: the former, when he speaks, seems always mounted on his high horse; the latter, as if seated on his humble donkey.

It is remarkable that a book which is so rich as *Don* Quixote in picturesque matter has as yet found no painter who has taken from it subjects for a series of independent art works. Is the spirit of the book so volatile and fanciful that the variegated colours elude the artist's skill? I do not think so, for *Don Quixote*, light and fanciful as it is, is still based on rude, earthly realities, as must necessarily be the case to make it a book of the people. Is it, perhaps, because behind the figures brought before us by the poet, deeper ideas lie hidden, which the artist cannot produce again, so that he can give only the outward features, salient though they be, but fails to grasp and reproduce the deeper meaning?

GODS IN EXILE.

[*Gods in Exile*, in which Heine has gathered up some of the mediæval legends concerning the later history of the Greek and Roman gods, was written in the early spring of 1853 (a few pages, however, had been written so long before as 1836), and published in the *Revue des Deux Mondes* for that year. The translation, by Mr. Fleishman, here used, has been carefully revised, and in part rewritten.

It will be observed that the years between 1837 and 1853 are unrepresented in this volume. During that period—with the exception of the fragment of *The Rabbi of Bacharach* (which was, however, written earlier) and his book on Börne, both published in 1840—Heine produced very little prose.]

...I AM speaking here of that metamorphosis into demons which the Greek and Roman gods underwent when Christianity achieved supreme control of the world. The superstition of the people ascribed to those gods a real but cursed existence, coinciding entirely in this respect with the teaching of the Church. The latter by no means declared the ancient gods to be myths, inventions of falsehood and error, as did the philosophers, but held them to be evil spirits, who, through the victory of Christ, had been hurled from the summit of their power, and now dragged along their miserable existences in the obscurity of dismantled temples or in enchanted groves, and by their diabolic arts, through lust and beauty, particularly through dancing and singing, lured to apostasy unsteadfast Christians who had lost their way in the forest.... I will remind the reader that the perplexities into which the poor old gods fell at the time of the final triumph of Christendom—that is, in the third century—offer striking analogies to former sorrowful events in their god-lives; for they found themselves plunged into the same sad predicament in which they had once before been placed in that most ancient time, in that revolutionary epoch when the Titans broke loose from their confinement in Orcus and, piling Pelion on Ossa, scaled high Olympus. At that time the poor gods were compelled to flee ignominiously and conceal themselves under various disguises on earth. Most of them repaired to Egypt, where, as is well known, for greater safety, they assumed the forms of animals. And in a like manner, when the true Lord of the universe planted the banner of the cross on the heavenly heights, and those iconoclastic zealots, the black band of monks, hunted down the gods with fire and malediction and razed their temples, then these unfortunate heathen divinities were again compelled to take to flight, seeking safety under the most varied disguises and in the most retired hiding-places. Many of these poor refugees, deprived of shelter and ambrosia, were now forced to work at some plebeian trade in order to earn a livelihood. Under these circumstances several, whose shrines had been confiscated, became wood-choppers and day-labourers in Germany, and were compelled to drink beer instead of nectar. It appears that Apollo was reduced to this dire plight, and stooped so low as to accept service with cattle-breeders, and as once before he had tended the cows of Admetus, so now he lived as a shepherd in Lower Austria. Here, however, he aroused suspicion through the marvellous sweetness of his singing and, being recognised by a learned monk as one of the ancient magic-working heathen gods, he was delivered over to the ecclesiastical courts. On the rack he confessed that he was the god Apollo. Before his execution he begged that he might be permitted for the last time to play the zither and sing to its accompaniment. But he played so touchingly and sang so enchantingly, and was so handsome in face and form, that all the women wept; and many of them indeed afterwards sickened. After some lapse of time, it was decided to remove his body from the grave under the impression that he was a vampire, and impale it upon a stake, this being an approved domestic remedy certain to effect the cure of the sick women; but the grave was found empty.

I have but little to communicate concerning the fate of Mars, the ancient god of war. I am not disinclined to believe that during the feudal ages he availed himself of the then prevailing doctrine that might makes right. Lank Schimmelpennig, nephew of the executioner of Münster, once met Mars at Bologna, and conversed with him. Shortly before he had served as a peasant under Froudsberg, and was present at the storming of Rome. Bitter thoughts must have filled his breast when he saw his ancient, favourite city, and the temples wherein he and his brother gods had been so revered, now ignominiously laid waste.

Better than either Mars or Apollo fared the god Bacchus at the great stampede, and the legends relate the following:—In Tyrol there are very large lakes, surrounded by magnificent trees that are mirrored in the blue waters. Trees and water murmur so that one experiences strange feelings of awe when one wanders there alone. On the bank of such a lake stood the hut of a young fisherman, who lived by fishing, and who also acted as ferryman to any travellers who wished to cross the lake. He had a large boat, that was fastened to the trunk of an old tree not far from his dwelling. Here he lived quite alone. Once, about the time of the autumnal equinox, towards midnight, he heard a knocking at his window, and on opening the door he saw three monks, with their heads deeply muffled in their cowls, who seemed to be in great haste. One of them hurriedly asked him for the boat, promising to return it within a few hours. The monks were three, and the fisherman could not hesitate; so he unfastened the boat, and when they had embarked and departed, he went back to his hut and lay down. He was young, and soon fell asleep; but in a few hours he was awakened by the returning monks. When he went out to them, one of them pressed a silver coin into his hand, and then all three hastened away. The fisherman went to look at his boat, which he found made fast. Then he shivered, but not from the night-air. A peculiarly chilling sensation had passed through his limbs, and his heart seemed almost frozen, when the monk who paid the fare touched his hand; the monk's fingers were cold as ice. For some days the fisherman could not forget this circumstance; but youth will soon shake off mysterious influences, and the fisherman thought no more of the occurrence until the following year, when, again just at the time of the autumnal equinoxes, towards midnight, there was a knocking at the window of the hut, and again the three cowled monks appeared, and again demanded the boat. The fisherman delivered up the boat with less anxiety this time, but when after a few hours they returned, and one of the monks again hastily pressed a coin into his hand, he again shuddered at the touch of the icy cold fingers. This happened every year at the same time and in the same manner. At last, as the seventh year drew near, an irresistible desire seized on the fisherman to learn, at all costs, the secret that was hidden under these three cowls. He piled a mass of nets into the boat, so as to form a hiding-place into which he could slip while the monks were preparing to embark. The sombre expected travellers came at the accustomed time, and the fisherman succeeded in hiding himself under the nets unobserved. To his astonishment, the voyage lasted but a short time, whereas it usually took him over an hour to reach the opposite shore; and greater yet was his surprise when here, in a locality with which he had been quite familiar, he beheld a wide forest-glade which he had never before seen, and which was covered with flowers that, to him, were of quite strange kind. Innumerable lamps hung from the trees, and vases filled with blazing rosin stood on high pedestals; the moon, too, was so bright that the fisherman could see all that took place, as distinctly as if it had been mid-day. There were many hundreds of young men and young women, most of them beautiful as pictures, although their faces were all as white as marble, and this circumstance, together with their garments, which consisted of white, very white, tunics with purple borders, girt up, gave them the appearance of moving statues. The women wore on their heads wreaths of vine leaves, either natural or wrought of gold and silver, and their hair was partly plaited over the brow into the shape of a crown, and partly fell in wild locks on their necks. The young men also wore wreaths of vine leaves. Both men and women swinging in their hands golden staffs covered with vine leaves, hastened joyously to greet the new-comers. One of the latter threw aside his cowl, revealing an impertinent fellow of middle age, with a repulsive, libidinous face, and pointed goat-ears, and scandalously extravagant sexuality. The second monk also threw aside his cowl, and there came to view a big-bellied fellow, not less naked, whose bald pate the mischievous women crowned with a wreath of roses. The faces of the two monks, like those of the rest of the assemblage, were white as snow. White as snow also was the face of the third monk, who laughingly brushed the cowl from his head. As he unbound the girdle of his robe, and with a gesture of disgust flung off from him the pious and dirty garment, together with crucifix and rosary, lo! there stood, robed in a tunic brilliant as a diamond, a marvellously beautiful youth with a form of noble symmetry, save that there was something feminine in the rounded hips and the slender waist. His delicately-curved lips, also, and soft, mobile features gave him a somewhat feminine appearance; but his face expressed also a certain daring, almost reckless heroism. The women caressed him with wild enthusiasm, placed an ivy-wreath upon his head, and threw a magnificent leopard-skin over his shoulders. At this moment came swiftly dashing along, drawn by two lions, a golden two-wheeled triumphal chariot. Majestically, yet with a merry glance, the youth leaped on the chariot, guiding the wild steeds with purple reins. At the right of the chariot strode one of his uncassocked companions, whose lewd gestures and unseemly form delighted the beholders, while his comrade, with the bald pate and fat paunch, whom the merry women had placed on an ass, rode at the left of the chariot, carrying in his hand a golden drinking-cup, which was constantly refilled with wine. On moved the chariot, and behind it whirled the romping, dancing, vine-crowned men and women. At the head of the triumphal procession marched the orchestra; the pretty, chubby-cheeked youth, playing the double flute; then the nymph with the high-girt tunic, striking the jingling tambourine with her knuckles; then the equally gracious beauty, with the triangle; then the goat-footed trumpeters, with handsome but lascivious faces, who blew their fanfares on curious sea-shells and fantastically-shaped horns; then the lute-players.

But, dear reader, I forgot that you are a most cultured and well-informed reader, and have long since observed that I have been describing a Bacchanalia and a feast of Dionysius. You have often seen on ancient bas-reliefs, or in the engravings of archæological works, pictures of the triumphal processions held in honour of the god Bacchus; and surely, with your cultivated and classic tastes, you would not be frightened even if at dead of night, in the depths of a lonely forest, the lonely spectres of such a Bacchanalian procession, together with the customary tipsy personnel, should appear bodily before your eyes. At the most you would only give way to a slight voluptuous shudder, an æsthetic awe, at sight of this pale assemblage of graceful phantoms, who have risen from their monumental sarcophagi, or from their hiding-places amid the ruins of ancient temples, to perform once more their ancient, joyous, divine service; once more, with sport and merry-making, to celebrate the triumphal march of the divine liberator, the Saviour of the senses; to dance once more the merry dance of paganism, the *can-can* of the antique world—to dance it without any hypocritical disguise, without fear of the interference of the police of a spiritualistic morality, with the wild abandonment of the old days, shouting, exulting, rapturous. Evoe Bacche!

But alas, dear reader, the poor fisherman was not, like yourself, versed in mythology; he had never made archæological studies; and terror and fear seized upon him when he beheld the Triumphator and his two wonderful acolytes emerge from their monks' garb. He shuddered at the immodest gestures and leaps of the Bacchantes, Fauns, and Satyrs, who, with their goats' feet and horns, seemed to him peculiarly diabolical, and he regarded the whole assemblage as a congress of spectres and demons, who were seeking by their mysterious rites to bring ruin on all Christians. His hair stood on end at sight of the reckless impossible posture of a Mænad, who, with flowing hair and head thrown back, only balanced herself by the weight of her thyrsus. His own brain seemed to reel as he saw the Corybantes in mad frenzy wounding their own bodies with short swords, seeking voluptuousness in pain itself. The soft and tender, yet so terrible, tones of the music seemed to penetrate to his very soul, like a burning, consuming, excruciating flame. But when he saw that defamed Egyptian symbol, of exaggerated size and crowned with flowers, borne upon a tall pole by an unashamed woman, then sight and hearing forsook the poor fisherman—and he darted back to the boat, and crept under the nets, with chattering teeth and trembling limbs, as though Satan already held him fast by the foot. Soon after, the three monks also returned to the boat and shoved off. When they had disembarked at the original starting-place, the fisherman managed to escape unobserved from his hiding-place, so that they supposed he had merely been behind the willows awaiting their return. One of the monks, as usual, with icy-cold fingers pressed the fare into the fisherman's hand, then all three hurried away.

For the salvation of his own soul, which he believed to be endangered, and also to guard other good Christians from ruin, the fisherman held it his duty to communicate a full account of the mysterious occurrence to the Church authorities; and as the superior of a neighbouring Franciscan monastery was in great repute as a learned exorcist, the fisherman determined to go to him without delay. The rising sun found him on his way to the monastery, where, with modest demeanour, he soon stood before his excellency the superior, who received him seated in an easy-chair in the library, and with hood drawn closely over his face, listened meditatively while the fisherman told his tale of horror. When the recital was finished, the superior raised his head, and as the hood fell back, the fisherman saw, to his dismay, that his excellency was one of the three monks who annually sailed over the lake—the very one, indeed, whom he had the previous night seen as a heathen demon riding in the golden chariot drawn by lions. It was the same marble-white face, the same regular, beautiful features, the same mouth with its delicately-curved lips. And these lips now wore a kindly smile, and from that mouth now issued the gracious and melodious words, "Beloved son in Christ, we willingly believe that you have spent the night in company of the god Bacchus. Your fantastic ghost-story gives ample proof of that. Not that we would say aught unpleasant of this god: at times he is undoubtedly a care-dispeller, and gladdens the heart of man. But he is very dangerous for those who cannot bear much; and to this class you seem to belong. We advise you to partake in future very sparingly of the golden juice of the grape, and not again to trouble the spiritual authorities with the fantasies of a drunken brain. Concerning this last vision of yours, you had better keep a very quiet tongue in your head; otherwise the secular arm of our beadle shall measure out to you twenty-five lashes. And now, beloved son in Christ, go to the monastery kitchen, where brother butler and brother cook will set before you a slight repast."

With this, the reverend father bestowed the customary benediction on the fisherman, and when the latter, bewildered, took himself off to the kitchen and suddenly came face to face with brother cook and brother butler, he almost fell to the earth in affright, for they were the same monks who had accompanied the superior on his midnight excursions across the lake. He recognised one by his fat paunch and bald head, and the other by his lascivious grin and goat-ears. But he held his tongue, and only in later years did he relate his strange story.

Several old chronicles which contain similar legends locate the scene near the city of Speyer, on the Rhine.

Along the coast of East Friesland an analogous tradition is found, in which the ancient conception of the transportation of the dead to the realm of Hades, which underlies all those legends, is most distinctly seen. It is true that none of them contain any mention of Charon, the steersman of the boat: this old fellow seems to have entirely disappeared from folk-lore, and is to be met with only in puppet-shows. But a far more notable mythological personage is to be recognised in the so-called forwarding agent, or dispatcher, who makes arrangements for the transportation of the dead, and pays the customary passage-money into the hands of the boatman; the latter is generally a common fisherman, who officiates as Charon. Notwithstanding his quaint disguise, the true name of this dispatcher may readily be guessed, and I shall therefore relate the legend as faithfully as possible.

The shores of East Friesland that border on the North Sea abound with bays, which are used as harbours, and are called fiords. On the farthest projecting promontory of land generally stands the solitary hut of some fisherman, who here lives, peaceful and contented, with his family. Here nature wears a sad and melancholy aspect. Not even the chirping of a bird is to be heard, only now and then the shrill screech of a sea-gull flying up from its nest among the sand-hills, that announces the coming storm. The monotonous plashings of the restless sea harmonise with the sombre, shifting shadows of the passing clouds. Even the human inhabitants do not sing here, and on these melancholy coasts the strain of a *volkslied* is never heard. The people who live here are an earnest, honest, matter-of-fact race, proud of their bold spirit and of the liberties which they have inherited from their ancestors. Such a people are not imaginative, and are little given to metaphysical speculations. Fishing is their principal support, added to which is an occasional pittance of passage-money for transporting some traveller to one of the adjacent islands.

It is said that at a certain period of the year, just at mid-day, when the fisherman and his family are seated at table eating their noonday meal, a traveller enters and asks the master of the house to vouchsafe him an audience for a few minutes to speak with him on a matter of business. The fisherman, after vainly inviting the stranger to partake of the meal, grants his request, and they both step aside to a little table. I shall not describe the personal appearance of the stranger in detail, after the tedious manner of novel-writers: a brief enumeration of the salient points will suffice. He is a little man, advanced in years, but well preserved. He is, so to say, a youthful greybeard: plump, but not corpulent; cheeks ruddy as an apple; small eyes, which blink merrily and continually, and on his powdered little head is set a three-cornered little hat. Under his flaming yellow cloak, with its many collars, he wears the old-fashioned dress of a well-to-do Dutch merchant, such as we see depicted in old portraits—namely, a short silk coat of a parrot-green colour, a vest embroidered with flowers, short black trousers, striped stockings, and shoes ornamented with buckles. The latter are so brightly polished that it is hard to understand how the wearer could trudge a-foot through the slimy mud of the coast and yet keep them so clean. His voice is a thin, asthmatic treble, sometimes inclining to be rather lachrymose; but the address and bearing of the little man are as grave and measured as beseem a Dutch merchant. This gravity, however, appears to be more assumed than natural, and is in marked contrast with the searching, roving, swift-darting glances of the eye, and with the ill-repressed fidgettiness of the legs and arms.

161

That the stranger is a Dutch merchant is evidenced not only by his apparel, but also by the mercantile exactitude and caution with which he endeavours to effect as favourable a bargain as possible for his employers. He is, as he says, a forwarding agent, and has received from some of his mercantile friends a commission to transport a certain number of souls, as many as can find room in an ordinary boat, from the coast of East Friesland to the White Island. In fulfilment of this commission, he adds, he wishes to know if the fisherman will this night convey in his boat the aforesaid cargo to the aforesaid island; in which case he is authorised to pay the passage-money in advance, confidently hoping that, in Christian fairness, the fisherman will make his price very moderate. The Dutch merchant (which term is, in fact, a pleonasm, since every Dutchman is a merchant) makes this proposition with the utmost nonchalance, as if it referred to a cargo of cheeses, and not to the souls of the dead. The fisherman is startled at the word "souls," and a cold chill creeps down his back, for he immediately comprehends that the souls of the dead are here meant, and that the stranger is none other than the phantom Dutchman, who has already intrusted several of his fellow-fishermen with the transportation of the souls of the dead, and paid them well for it, too.

These East Frieslanders are, as I have already remarked, a brave, healthy, practical people; in them is lacking that morbid imagination which makes us so impressible to the ghostly and supernatural. Our fisherman's weird dismay lasts but a moment; suppressing the uncanny sensation that is stealing over him, he soon regains his composure, and, intent on securing as high a sum as possible, he assumes an air of supreme indifference. But after a little chaffering the two come to an understanding, and shake hands to seal the bargain. The Dutchman draws forth a dirty leather pouch, filled entirely with little silver pennies of the smallest denomination ever coined in Holland, and in these tiny coins counts out the whole amount of the fare. With instructions to the fisherman to be ready with his boat at the appointed place about the midnight hour when the moon becomes visible, the Dutchman takes leave of the whole family, and, declining their repeated invitations to dine, the grave little figure, dignified as ever, trips lightly away.

At the time agreed upon the fisherman appears at the appointed place. At first the boat is rocked lightly to and fro by the waves; but by the time the full moon has risen above the horizon the fisherman notices that his bark is less easily swayed, and so it gradually sinks deeper and deeper in the stream, until finally the water comes within a hand's-breadth of the boat's bow. This circumstance apprises him that his passengers, the souls, are now aboard, and he pushes off from shore with his cargo. Although he strains his eyes to the utmost, he can distinguish nothing but a few vapoury streaks that seem to be swayed hither and thither, and to intermingle with one another, but assume no definite forms. Listen intently as he may, he hears nothing but an indescribably-faint chirping and rustling. Only now and then a sea-gull with a shrill scream flies swiftly over his head; or near him a fish leaps up from out the stream, and for a moment stares at him with a vacuous look. The night-winds sigh, and the sea-breezes grow more chilly. Everywhere only water, moonlight, and silence! and silent as all around him is the fisherman, who finally reaches the White Island and moors his boat. He sees no one on the strand, but he hears a shrill, asthmatic, wheezy, lachrymose voice, which he recognises as that of the Dutchman. The latter seems to be reading off a list of proper names, with a peculiar, monotonous intonation, as if rehearsing a roll-call. Among the names are some which are known to the fisherman as belonging to persons who have died that year. During the reading of the list, the boat is evidently being gradually lightened of its load, and as soon as the last name is called it rises suddenly and floats free, although but a moment before it was deeply imbedded in the sand of the sea-shore. To the fisherman this is a token that his cargo has been properly delivered, and he calmly rows back to his wife and child, to his beloved home on the fiord.

...Notwithstanding this clever disguise, I have ventured to guess who the important mythological personage is that figures in this tradition. It is none other than the god Mercury, Hermes Psychopompos, the whilom conductor of the dead to Hades. Verily, under that shabby yellow cloak and prosaic tradesman's figure is concealed the youthful and most accomplished god of heathendom, the cunning son of Maia. On his little three-cornered hat not the slightest tuft of a feather is to be seen which might remind the beholder of the winged cap, and the clumsy shoes with steel buckles fail to give the least hint of the winged sandals. This grave and heavy Dutch lead is quite different from the mobile quicksilver, from which the god derived his very name. But the contrast is so exceedingly striking as to betray the god's design, which is the more effectually to disguise himself. Perhaps this mask was not chosen out of mere caprice. Mercury was, as you know, the patron god of thieves and merchants, and, in all probability, in choosing a disguise that should conceal him, and a trade by which to earn his livelihood, he took into consideration his talents and his antecedents.

...And thus it came to pass that the shrewdest and most cunning of the gods became a merchant, and, to adapt himself most thoroughly to his rôle, became the *ne plus ultra* of merchants—a Dutch merchant. His long practice in the olden time as Psychopompos, as conveyor of the dead to Hades, marks him out as particularly fitted to conduct the transportation of the souls of the dead to the White Island, in the manner just described.

The White Island is occasionally also called Brea, or Britannia. Does this perhaps refer to White Albion, to the chalky cliffs of the English coast? It would be a very humorous idea if England was designated as the land of the dead, as the Plutonian realm, as hell. In such a form, in truth, England has appeared to many a stranger.

In my essay on the Faust legend I discussed at full length the popular superstition concerning Pluto and his dominion. I showed how the old realm of shadows became hell, and how its old gloomy ruler became more and more diabolical. Neither Pluto, god of the nether regions, nor his brother, Neptune, god of the sea, emigrated like the other gods. Even after the final triumph of Christendom they remained in their domains, their respective elements. No matter what silly fables concerning him were invented here above on earth, old Pluto sat by his Proserpine, warm and cosey down below.

Neptune suffered less from calumny than his brother Pluto, and neither church-bell chimes nor organ-strains could offend his ears in the depths of old ocean, where he sat peacefully by the side of his white-bosomed wife, Dame Amphitrite, surrounded by his court of dripping nereids and tritons. Only now and then, when a young sailor crossed the equator, he would dart up from the briny deep, in his hand brandishing the trident, his head crowned with sea-weed, and his flowing, silvery beard reaching down to the navel. Then he would confer on the neophyte the terrible sea-water baptism, accompanying it with a long unctuous harangue, interspersed with coarse sailor jests, to the great delight of the jolly tars. The harangue was frequently interrupted by the spitting of amber quids of chewed tobacco, which Neptune so freely scattered around him. A friend, who gave me a detailed description of the manner in which such a sea-miracle is performed, assured me that the very sailors that laughed most heartily at the droll antics of Neptune never for a moment doubted the existence of such a god, and sometimes when in great danger they even prayed to him.

Neptune, as we have seen, remained monarch of the watery realm; and Pluto, notwithstanding his metamorphosis into Satan, still continued to be prince of the lower regions. They fared better than did their brother Jupiter, who, after the overthrow of their father, Saturn, became ruler of heaven, and as sovereign of the universe resided at Olympus, where, surrounded by his merry troop of gods, goddesses, and nymphs-of-honour, he carried on his ambrosial rule of joy. But when the great catastrophe occurred,—when the rule of the cross, that symbol of suffering, was proclaimed,—then the great Kronides fled, and disappeared amid the tumults and confusion of the transmigration of races. All traces of him were lost, and I have in vain consulted old chronicles and old women: none could give me the least information concerning his fate. With the same purpose in view, I have ransacked many libraries, where I was shown the magnificent codices ornamented with gold and precious stones, true odalisques in the harem of science. To the learned eunuchs who, with such affability, unlocked for me those brilliant treasures, I here return the customary thanks. It appears as if no popular tradition of a medieval Jupiter exists; and all that I could gather concerning him consists of a story told me by my friend, Niels Andersen.

...The events that I am about to relate, said Niels Andersen, occurred on an island, the exact situation of which I cannot tell. Since its discovery no one has been able again to reach it, being prevented by the immense icebergs that tower like a high wall around the island, and seldom, probably, permit a near approach. Only the crew of a Russian whaling-vessel, which a storm had driven so far to the north, ever trod its soil; and since then over a hundred years have elapsed. When the sailors had, by means of a small boat, effected a landing, they found the island to be wild and desolate. Sadly waved the blades of tall sedgy grass over the quicksands; here and there grew a few stunted fir-trees, or barren shrubs. They saw a multitude of rabbits springing around, on which account they named it the Island of Rabbits. Only one miserable hut gave evidence that a human being dwelt there. As the sailors entered the hut they saw an old, very old man, wretchedly clad in a garment of rabbit skins rudely stitched together. He was seated in a stone chair in front of the hearth, trying to warm his emaciated hands and trembling knees by the flaring brushwood fire. At his right side stood an immense bird, evidently an eagle, but which had been roughly treated by time, and shorn of all its plumage save the long bristly quills of its wings, that gave it a highly grotesque, and, at the same time, hideous appearance. At the old man's left, squatted on the earth, was an extraordinarily large hairless goat, which seemed to be very old; although full milky udders, with fresh, rosy nipples, hung at its belly.

Among the sailors were several Greeks, one of whom, not thinking that his words would be understood by the aged inhabitant of the hut, remarked in the Greek language to a comrade, "This old fellow is either a spectre or an evil demon." But at these words the old man suddenly arose from his seat, and to their great surprise the sailors beheld a stately figure, which, in spite of its advanced age, raised itself erect with commanding, yes, with king-like dignity, his head almost touching the rafters. The features, too, although rugged and weather-beaten, showed traces of original beauty, they were so noble and well-proportioned. A few silvery locks fell over his brow, which was furrowed by pride and age. His eyes had a dim and fixed look, but occasionally they would still gleam piercingly; and from his mouth were heard in the melodious and sonorous words of the ancient Greek language, "You are mistaken, young man; I am neither a spectre nor an evil demon; I am an unhappy old man, who once knew better days. But who are ye?"

The sailors explained the accident which had befallen them, and then inquired concerning the island. The information, however, was very meagre. The old man told them that since time immemorial he had inhabited this island, whose bulwark of ice served him as a secure asylum against his inexorable foes. He subsisted principally by catching rabbits, and every year, when the floating icebergs had settled, a few bands of savages crossed over on sleds, and to them he sold rabbit-skins, receiving in exchange various articles of indispensable necessity. The whales, which sometimes came swimming close to the island, were his favourite company. But it gave him pleasure to hear again his native tongue, for he too was a Greek. He entreated his countrymen to give him an account of the present condition of Greece. That the cross had been torn down from the battlements of Grecian cities apparently caused the old man a malicious satisfaction; but it did not altogether please him when he heard that the crescent had been planted there instead. It was strange that none of the sailors knew the names of the cities concerning which the old man inquired, and which, as he assured them, had flourished in his time. In like manner the names of the present cities and villages in Greece, which were mentioned by the sailors, were unknown to him; at this the old man would shake his head sadly, and the sailors looked at one another perplexed. They noticed that he knew exactly all the localities and geographical peculiarities of Greece; and he described so accurately and vividly the bays, the peninsulas, the mountain-ridges, even the knolls and most trifling rocky elevations, that his ignorance of these localities was all the more surprising. With especial interest, with a certain anxiety even, he questioned them concerning an ancient temple, which in his time, he assured them, had been the most beautiful in all Greece; but none of his hearers knew the name, which he pronounced with a loving tenderness. But finally, when the old man had again described the site of the temple, with the utmost particularity, a young sailor recognised the place by the description.

The village wherein he was born, said the young man, was situated hard by, and when a boy he had often tended his father's swine at the very place where there had been found ruins of an ancient structure, indicating a magnificent grandeur in the past. Now, only a few large marble pillars remained standing; some were plain, unadorned columns, others were surmounted by the square stones of a gable. From the cracks of the masonry the blooming honeysuckle-vines and red bell-flowers trailed downwards. Other pillars—among the number some of rose-coloured marble—lay shattered on the ground, and the costly marble head-pieces, ornamented with beautiful sculpture, representing foliage and flowers, were overgrown by rank creepers and grasses. Half buried in the earth lay huge marble blocks, some of which were squares, such as were used for the walls; others were three-cornered slabs for roof-pieces. Over them waved a large, wild fig-tree, which had grown up out of the ruins. Under the shadow of that tree, continued the young man, he had passed whole hours in examining the strange figures carved on the large marble blocks; they seemed to be pictorial representations of all sorts of sports and combats, and were very pleasing to look at, but, alas! much injured by exposure, and overgrown with moss and ivy. His father, whom he had questioned in regard to the mysterious signification of these pillars and sculptures, told him that these were the ruins of an ancient pagan temple, and had once been the abode of a wicked heathen god, who had here wantoned in lewd debauchery, incest, and unnatural vices. Notwithstanding this, the unenlightened heathen were accustomed to slaughter in his honour a hundred oxen at a time, and the hollowed marble block into which was gathered the blood of the sacrifices was yet in existence. It was, in fact, the very trough which they were in the habit of using as a receptacle for refuse wherewith to feed the swine.

So spoke the young sailor. But the old man heaved a sigh that betrayed the most terrible anguish. Tottering, he sank into his stone chair, covered his face with his hands, and wept like a child. The great, gaunt bird, with a shrill screech, flapped its immense wings, and menaced the strangers with claws and beak. The old goat licked its master's hands, and bleated mournfully as in consolation.

At this strange sight, an uncanny terror seized upon the sailors: they hurriedly left the hut, and were glad when they could no longer hear the sobbing of the old man, the screaming of the bird, and the bleating of the goat. When they were safely on board the boat, they narrated their adventure. Among the crew was a learned Russian, professor of philosophy at the university of Kazan; and he declared the matter to be highly important. With his forefinger held knowingly to the side of his nose, he assured the sailors that the old man of the island was undoubtedly the ancient god Jupiter, son of Saturn and Rhea. The bird at his side was clearly the eagle that once carried in its claws the terrible thunderbolts. And the old goat was, in all probability, none other than Althea, Jupiter's old nurse, who had suckled him in Crete, and now in exile again nourished him with her milk.

This is the story as told to me by Niels Andersen; and I must confess that it filled my soul with a profound melancholy. Decay is secretly undermining all that is great in the universe, and the gods themselves must finally succumb to the same miserable destiny. The iron law of fate so wills it, and even the greatest of the immortals must submissively bow his head. He of whom Homer sang, and whom Phidias sculptured in gold and ivory, he at whose glance earth trembled, he, the lover of Leda, Alcmena, Semele, Danaë, Callisto, Io, Leto, Europa, etc.—even he is compelled to hide himself behind the icebergs of the North Pole, and in order to prolong his wretched existence must deal in rabbit-skins, like a shabby Savoyard!

I do not doubt that there are people who will derive a malicious pleasure from such a spectacle. They are, perhaps, the descendants of those unfortunate oxen who, in hecatombs, were slaughtered on the altars of Jupiter. Rejoice! avenged is the blood of your ancestors, those poor martyrs of superstition. But we, who have no hereditary grudge rankling in us, we are touched at the sight of fallen greatness, and withhold not our holiest compassion.

CONFESSIONS.

[Heine wrote these *Confessions*, which form one of his most characteristic works, in the winter of 1853-4. They were originally intended to form part of the book on Germany. The translation here given is Mr. Fleishman's, revised by collation with the original.]

A WITTY Frenchman—a few years ago these words would have been a pleonasm— once dubbed me an unfrocked Romanticist. I have a weakness for all that is witty; and spiteful as was this appellation, it nevertheless delighted me highly. Notwithstanding the war of extermination that I had waged against Romanticism, I always remained a Romanticist at heart, and that in a higher degree than I myself realised. After I had delivered the most deadly blows against the taste for Romantic poetry in Germany, there stole over me an inexpressible yearning for the blue flower in the fairy-land of Romanticism, and I grasped the magic lyre and sang a song wherein I gave full sway to all the sweet extravagances, to all the intoxication of moonlight, to all the blooming, nightingale-like fancies once so fondly loved. I know it was "the last free-forest song of Romanticism,"[15] and I am its last poet. With me the old German lyric school ends; while with me, at the same time, the modern lyric school of Germany begins. Writers on German literature will assign to me this double rôle. It would be unseemly for me to speak at length on this subject, but I may with justice claim a liberal space in the history of German Romanticism. For this reason I ought to have included in my account of the Romantic school a review of my own writings. By my omission to do this, a gap has been left which I cannot easily fill. To write a criticism of one's self is an embarrassing, even an impossible task. I should be a conceited coxcomb to obtrude the good I might be able to say of myself, and I should be a great fool to proclaim to the whole world the defects of which I might also be conscious. And even with the most honest desire to be sincere, one cannot tell the truth about oneself. No one has as yet succeeded in doing it, neither Saint Augustine, the pious bishop of Hippo, nor the Genevese Jean Jacques Rousseau—least of all the latter, who proclaimed himself the man of truth and nature, but was really much more untruthful and unnatural than his contemporaries.

...Rousseau, who in his own person also slandered human nature, was yet true to it in respect to our primitive weakness, which consists in always wishing to appear in the eyes of the world as something different from what we really are. His self-portraiture is a lie, admirably executed, but still only a brilliant lie.

I recently read an anecdote concerning the King of Ashantee, which illustrates in a very amusing manner this weakness of human nature. When Major Bowditch was despatched by the English Governor of the Cape of Good Hope as resident ambassador to the court of that powerful African monarch, he sought to ingratiate himself with the courtiers, especially with the court-ladies, by taking their portraits. The king, who was astonished at the accuracy of the likenesses, requested that he also might be painted, and had already had several sittings, when the artist noticed in the features of the king, who had often sprung up to observe the progress of the picture, the peculiar restlessness and embarrassment of one who has a request on the tip of his tongue and yet hesitates to express it. The painter pressed his majesty to tell his wish, until at last the poor African king inquired, in a low voice, if he could not be painted white.

And so it is. The swarthy negro king wishes to be painted white. But do not laugh at the poor African: every human being is such another negro king, and all of us would like to appear before the public in a different colour from that which fate has given us. Fully realising this, I took heed not to draw my own portrait in my review of the Romantic school. But in the following pages I shall have ample occasion to speak of myself, and this will to a certain extent fill up the gap caused by the lacking portrait; for I have here undertaken to describe, for the reader's benefit and enlightenment, the philosophical and religious changes which have taken place in the author's mind since my book on Germany was written.

Fear not that I shall paint myself too white and my fellow-beings too black. I shall always give my own colours with exact fidelity, so that it may be known how far my judgment is to be trusted when I draw the portraits of others.

...Madame de Staël's hate of the Emperor is the soul of her book, *De l'Allemagne*, and, although his name is nowhere mentioned, one can see at every line how the writer squints at the Tuilleries. I doubt not that the book annoyed the Emperor more than the most direct attack; for nothing so much irritates a man as a woman's petty needle-pricks. We are prepared for great sabre-strokes, and instead we are tickled at the most sensitive spots.

Oh, the women! we must forgive them much, for they love much—and many. Their hate is, in fact, only love turned the wrong way. At times they try to injure us, but only because they hope thereby to please some other man. When they write, they have one eye on the paper and the other on a man. This rule applies to all authoresses, with the exception of Countess Hahn-Hahn, who only has one eye. We male authors have also our prejudices. We write for or against something, for or against an idea, for or against a party; but women always write for or against one particular man, or, to express it more correctly, on account of one particular man. We men will sometimes lie outright; women, like all passive creatures, seldom invent, but can so distort a fact that they can thereby injure us more surely than by a downright lie. I verily believe my friend Balzac was right when he once said to me, in a sorrowful tone, *"La femme est un être dangereux."*

Yes, women are dangerous; but I must admit that beautiful women are not so dangerous as those whose attractions are intellectual rather than physical; for the former are accustomed to have men pay court to them, while the latter meet the vanity of men half-way, and through the bait of flattery acquire a more powerful influence than the beautiful women. I by no means intend to insinuate that Madame de Staël was ugly; but beauty is something quite different. She had single points which were pleasing; but the effect as a whole was anything but pleasing. To nervous persons, like the sainted Schiller, her custom of continually twirling between her fingers some fragment of paper or similar small article was particularly annoying. This habit made poor Schiller dizzy, and in desperation he grasped her pretty hand to hold it quiet. This innocent action led Madame de Staël to believe that the tender-hearted poet was overpowered by the magic of her personal charms. I am told that she really had very pretty hands and beautiful arms, which she always displayed. Surely the Venus of Milo could not show such beautiful arms! Her teeth surpassed in whiteness those of the finest steed of Araby. She had very large, beautiful eyes, a dozen amorets would have found room on her lips, and her smile is said to have been very sweet: therefore she could not have been ugly,—no woman is ugly. But I venture to say that had fair Helen of Sparta looked so, the Trojan War would not have occurred, and the strongholds of Priam would not have been burned, and Homer would never have sung the wrath of Pelidean Achilles.

...In my Memoirs I relate with more detail than is admissible here how, after the French Revolution of July 1830, I emigrated to Paris, where I have ever since lived quiet and contented. What I did and suffered during the Restoration will be told when the disinterestedness of such a publication is no longer liable to doubt or suspicion. I worked much and suffered much; and about the time that the sun of the July revolution arose in France, I had gradually become very weary, and needed recreation. Moreover, the air of my native land was daily becoming more unwholesome for me, and I was compelled to contemplate seriously a change of climate. I had visions: in the clouds I saw all sorts of horrible, grotesque faces, that annoyed me with their grimaces. It sometimes seemed to me as if the sun were a Prussian cockade. At night I dreamed of a hideous black vulture that preyed on my liver; and became very melancholy. In addition to all this, I had become acquainted with an old magistrate from Berlin who had spent many years in the fortress of Spandau, and who described to me how unpleasant it was in winter to wear iron manacles. I thought it very un-Christian not to warm the irons a little, for if our chains were only warmed somewhat, they would not seem so very unpleasant, and cold natures could even endure them very well. The chains ought also to be perfumed with the essence of roses and laurels, as is the custom in France. I asked my magistrate if oysters were often served at Spandau. He answered, no; Spandau was too far distant from the sea. Meat, also, he said, was seldom to be had, and the only fowls were the flies which fell into one's soup. About the same time I became acquainted with a commercial traveller of a French wine establishment, who was never tired of praising the merry life of Paris,—how the air was full of music, how from morning until night one heard the singing of the "Marseillaise" and "En avant, marchons!" and "Lafayette aux cheveux blancs." He told me that at every street-corner was the inscription, "Liberty, Equality, Fraternity." He likewise recommended the champagne of his firm, and gave me a large number of business cards. He also promised to furnish me with letters of introduction to the best Parisian restaurants, in case I should visit Paris. As I really did need recreation, and as Spandau was at too great a distance from the sea to procure oysters, and as the fowl-soup of Spandau was not to my taste, and as, moreover, the Prussian chains were very cold in winter and could not be conducive to my health, I determined to go to Paris, the fatherland of champagne and the "Marseillaise," there to drink the former, and to hear the latter sung, together with "En avant, marchons!" and "Lafayette aux cheveux blancs."

I crossed the Rhine on May 1st, 1831. I did not see the old river-god, father Rhine, so I contented myself with dropping my visiting card into the water. I am told that he was sitting down below, conning his French grammar; for during the Prussian rule his French had grown rusty from long disuse, and now he wished to practice it anew, in order to be prepared for contingencies. I thought I could hear him, conjugating, "J'aime, tu aimes, il aime; nous aimons"—but what does he love? Surely not the Prussians!

I awoke at St. Denis from a sweet morning sleep, and heard for the first time the shout of the driver, "Paris! Paris!" Here we already inhaled the atmosphere of the capital, now visible on the horizon. A rascally lackey tried to persuade me to visit the royal sepulchre at St. Denis; but I had not come to France to see dead kings.... In twenty minutes I was in Paris, entering through the triumphal arch of the Boulevard St. Denis, which was originally erected in honour of Louis XIV., but now served to grace my entry into Paris. I was surprised at meeting such multitudes of well-dressed people, tastefully arrayed like the pictures of a fashion-journal. I was also impressed by the fact that they all spoke French, which, in Germany, is the distinguishing mark of the higher classes; the whole nation are as noble as the nobility with us. The men were all so polite, and the pretty women all smiled so graciously. If some one accidentally jostled me without immediately asking pardon, I could safely wager that it was a fellow-countryman. And if a pretty woman looked a little sour, she had either eaten sauerkraut or could read Klopstock in the original. I found everything quite charming. The skies were so blue, the air so balmy, and here and there the rays of the sun of July were still glimmering. The cheeks of the beauteous Lutetea were still flushed from the burning kisses of that sun, and the bridal flowers on her bosom were not yet wilted. But at the street-corners the words, "Liberté, égalité, fraternité," had already been erased. Honeymoons fly so quickly!

I immediately visited the restaurants to which I had been recommended. The landlords assured me that they would have made me welcome even without letters of introduction, for I had an honest and distinguished appearance, which in itself was a sufficient recommendation. Never did a German landlord so address me, even if he thought it. Such a churlish fellow feels himself in duty bound to suppress all pleasant speeches, and his German bluntness demands that he shall tell only the most disagreeable things to our faces. In the manner, and even in the language, of the French, there is so much delicious flattery, which costs so little, and is yet so gratifying. My poor sensitive soul, which had shrunk with shyness from the rudeness of the fatherland, again expanded under the genial influence of French urbanity. God has given us tongues that we may say something pleasant to our fellow-men.

My French had grown rusty since the battle of Waterloo, but after half-an-hour's conversation with a pretty flower-girl in the Passage de l'Opéra it soon flowed fluently again. I managed to stammer forth gallant phrases in broken French, and explained to the little charmer the Linnæan system, in which flowers are classified according to their stamens. The little one practised a different system, and divided flowers into those which smelled pleasantly and those which smelled unpleasantly. I believe that she applied a similar classification to men. She was surprised that, notwithstanding my youth, I was so learned, and spread the fame of my erudition through the whole Passage de l'Opéra. I inhaled with rapturous delight the delicious aroma of flattery, and amused myself charmingly. I walked on flowers, and many a roasted pigeon came flying into my gaping mouth.

...Among the notabilities whom I met soon after my arrival in Paris was Victor Bohain; and I love to recall to memory the jovial, intellectual form of him who did so much to dispel the clouds from the brow of the German dreamer, and to initiate his sorrow-laden heart into the gaieties of French life. He had at that time already founded the *Europe Littéraire*, and, as editor, solicited me to write for his journal several articles on Germany, after the *genre* of Madame de Staël. I promised to furnish the articles, particularly mentioning, however, that I should write them in a style quite different from that of Madame de Staël. "That is a matter of indifference to me," was the laughing answer; "like Voltaire, I tolerate every *genre*, excepting only the *genre ennuyeux*." And in order that I, poor German, should not fall into the *genre ennuyeux*, friend Bohain often invited me to dine with him, and stimulated my brain with champagne. No one knew better

171

than he how to arrange a dinner at which one should not only enjoy the best *cuisine*, but be most pleasantly entertained. No one could do the honours of host as well as he; and he was certainly justified in charging the stockholders of the *Europe Littéraire* with one hundred thousand francs as the expense of these banquets. Even his wooden leg contributed to the humour of the man, and when he hobbled around the table, serving out champagne to his guests, he resembled Vulcan performing the duties of Hebe's office amidst the uproarious mirth of the assembled gods. Where is Victor Bohain now? I have heard nothing of him for a long period. The last I saw of him was about ten years ago, at an inn at Granville. He had just come over from England, where he had been studying the colossal English national debt, in this occupation smothering the recollection of his own little personal debts, to this little town on the coast of Normandy, and here I found him seated at a table with a bottle of champagne and an open-mouthed, stupid-looking citizen, to whom he was earnestly explaining a business project by which, as Bohain eloquently demonstrated, a million could be realised. Bohain always had a great fondness for speculation, and in all his projects there was always a million in progress—never less than a million. His friends nicknamed him, on this account, Messer Millione.

...The founding of the *Europe Littéraire* was an excellent idea. Its success seemed assured, and I have never been able to understand why it failed. Only one evening before the day on which the suspension occurred, Victor Bohain gave a brilliant ball in the editorial *salons* of the journal, at which he danced with his three hundred stockholders, just like Leonidas with his three hundred Spartans the day before the battle of Thermopylæ. Every time that I behold in the gallery of the Louvre the painting by David which portrays that scene of antique heroism, I am reminded of the last ball of Victor Bohain. Just like the death-defying king in David's picture, so stood Victor Bohain on his solitary leg; it was the same classic pose. Stranger, when thou strollest in Paris through the Chaussée d'Antin towards the Boulevards, and findest thyself in the low-lying, filthy street that was once called the Rue Basse du Rempart, know that thou standest at the Thermopylæ of the *Europe Littéraire*, where Victor Bohain with his three hundred stockholders so heroically fell.

...In my articles on German philosophy I blabbed without reserve the secrets of the schools, which, draped in scholastic formulas, were previously known only to the initiated. My revelations excited the greatest surprise in France, and I remember that leading French thinkers naively confessed to me that they had always believed German philosophy to be a peculiar mystic fog, behind which divinity lay hidden as in a cloud, and that German philosophers were ecstatic seers, filled with piety and the fear of God. It is not my fault that German philosophy is just the reverse of that which until now we have called piety and fear of God, and that our latest philosophers have proclaimed absolute atheism to be the last word of German philosophy. Relentlessly and with bacchantic recklessness they tore aside the blue curtain from the German heavens, and cried, "Behold! all the gods have flown, and there above sits only an old spinster with leaden hands and sorrowful heart—Necessity."

172

Alas! what then sounded so strange is now being preached from all the house-tops in Germany, and the fanatic zeal of many of these propagandists is terrible! We have now bigoted monks of atheism, grand-inquisitors of infidelity, who would have bound Voltaire to the stake because he was at heart an obstinate deist. So long as such doctrines remained the secret possession of an intellectual aristocracy, and were discussed in a select coterie-dialect which was incomprehensible to the lackeys in attendance, while we at our philosophical *petit-soupers* were blaspheming, so long did I continue to be one of the thoughtless free-thinkers, of whom the majority resembled those grand-seigneurs who, shortly before the Revolution, sought by means of the new revolutionary ideas to dispel the tedium of their indolent court-life. But as soon as I saw that the rabble began to discuss the same themes at their unclean symposiums, where instead of wax-candles and chandeliers gleamed tallow-dips and oil-lamps; when I perceived that greasy cobblers and tailors presumed in their blunt mechanics' speech to deny the existence of God; when atheism began to stink of cheese, brandy, and tobacco—then my eyes were suddenly opened, and that which I had not comprehended through reason, I now learned through my olfactory organs and through my loathing and disgust. Heaven be praised! my atheism was at an end.

To be candid, it was perhaps not alone disgust that made the principles of the godless obnoxious to me, and induced me to abandon their ranks. I was oppressed by a certain worldly apprehension which I could not overcome, for I saw that atheism had entered into a more or less secret compact with the most terribly naked, quite fig-leafless, communistic communism. My dread of the latter has nothing in common with that of the parvenu, who trembles for his wealth, or with that of well-to-do tradesmen, who fear an interruption of their profitable business. No; that which disquiets me is the secret dread of the artist and scholar, who sees our whole modern civilisation, the laboriously-achieved product of so many centuries of effort, and the fruit of the noblest works of our ancestors, jeopardised by the triumph of communism. Swept along by the resistless current of generous emotions, we may perhaps sacrifice the cause of art and science, even all our own individual interests, for the general welfare of the suffering and oppressed people. But we can no longer disguise from ourselves what we have to expect when the great, rude masses, which by some are called the people, by others the rabble, and whose legitimate sovereignty was proclaimed long ago, shall obtain actual dominion. The poet, in particular, experiences a mysterious dread in contemplating the advent to power of this uncouth sovereign. We will gladly sacrifice ourselves for the people, for self-sacrifice constitutes one of our most exquisite enjoyments—the emancipation of the people has been the great task of our lives; we have toiled for it, and in its cause endured indescribable misery, at home as in exile—but the poet's refined and sensitive nature revolts at every near personal contact with the people, and still more repugnant is the mere thought of its caresses, from which may Heaven preserve us! A great democrat once remarked that if a king had taken him by the hand, he would immediately have thrust it into the fire to purify it. In the same manner I would say, if the sovereign people vouchsafed to press my hand, I would hasten to wash it. The poor people is not beautiful, but very ugly; only that ugliness simply comes from dirt, and will disappear as soon as we open public baths, in which His Majesty may gratuitously bathe himself.

...It required no great foresight to foretell these terrible events so long before their occurrence. I could easily prophesy what songs would one day be whistled and chirped in Germany, for I saw the birds hatching that in after-days gave tone to the new school of song. I saw Hegel, with his almost comically serious face, like a setting hen, brooding over the fatal eggs; and I heard his cackling; to tell the truth, I seldom understood him, and only through later reflection did I arrive at an understanding of his works. I believe he did not wish to be understood.

...One beautiful starlight night, Hegel stood with me at an open window. I, being a young man of twenty-two, and having just eaten well and drunk coffee, naturally spoke with enthusiasm of the stars, and called them abodes of the blest. But the master muttered to himself, "The stars! Hm! hm! the stars are only a brilliant eruption on the firmament." "What!" cried I; "then there is no blissful spot above, where virtue is rewarded after death?" But he, glaring at me with his dim eyes, remarked, sneering, "So you want a *pourboire* because you have supported your sick mother and not poisoned your brother?" At these words he looked anxiously around, but was reassured when he saw that it was only Henry Beer.

...I was never an abstract thinker, and I accepted the synthesis of the Hegelian philosophy without examination, because its deductions flattered my vanity. I was young and arrogant, and it gratified my self-conceit when I was informed by Hegel that not, as my grandmother had supposed, He who dwelt in the heavens, but I myself, here on earth, was God. This silly pride had, however, by no means an evil influence on me. On the contrary, it awoke in me the heroic spirit, and at that period I practiced a generosity and self-sacrifice which completely cast into the shade the most virtuous and distinguished deeds of the good *bourgeoisie* of virtue, who did good merely from a sense of duty and in obedience to the laws of morality. I was myself the living moral law, and the fountain-head of all right and all authority. I myself was morality personified; I was incapable of sin, I was incarnated purity.... I was all love, and incapable of hate. I no longer revenged myself on my enemies; for, rightly considered, I had no enemies; at least, I recognised none as such. For me there now existed only unbelievers who questioned my divinity. Every indignity that they offered me was a sacrilege, and their contumely was blasphemy. Such godlessness, of course, I could not always let pass unpunished; but in those cases it was not human revenge, but divine judgment upon sinners. Absorbed in this exalted practice of justice, I would repress with more or less difficulty all ordinary pity. As I had no enemies, so also there existed for me no friends, but only worshippers, who believed in my greatness, and adored me, and praised my works, those written in verse as well as those in prose. Towards this congregation of truly devout and pious ones I was particularly gracious, especially towards the young-lady devotees.

But the expense of playing the rôle of a God, for whom it were unseemly to go in

174

tatters, and who is sparing neither of body nor of purse, is immense. To play such a rôle respectably, two things are above all requisite—much money and robust health. Alas! it happened that one day [in February 1848] both these essentials failed me, and my divinity was at an end. Luckily, the highly-respected public was at that time occupied with events so dramatic, so grand, so fabulous and unprecedented, that the change in the affairs of so unimportant a personage as myself attracted but little attention. Unprecedented and fabulous were indeed the events of those crazy February days, when the wisdom of the wisest was brought to naught, and the chosen ones of imbecility were raised aloft in triumph. The last became the first, and the lowliest became the highest. Matter, like thought, was turned upside down, and the world was topsy-turvy. If in those mad days I had been sane, those events would surely have cost me my wits; but, lunatic as I then was, the contrary necessarily came to pass, and, strange to say, just in the days of universal madness I regained my reason! Like many other divinities of that revolutionary period, I was compelled to abdicate ignominiously, and to return to the lowly life of humanity. I came back into the humble fold of God's creatures. I again bowed in homage to the almighty power of a Supreme Being, who directs the destinies of this world, and who for the future shall also regulate my earthly affairs. The latter, during the time I had been my own Providence, had drifted into sad confusion, and I was glad to turn them over to a celestial superintendent, who with his omniscience really manages them much better. The belief in God has since then been to me not only a source of happiness, but it has also relieved me from all those annoying business cares which are so distasteful to me. This belief has also enabled me to practice great economies; for I need no longer provide either for myself or for others, and since I have joined the ranks of the pious I contribute almost nothing to the support of the poor. I am too modest to meddle, as formerly, with the business of Divine Providence. I am no longer careful for the general good; I no longer ape the Deity; and with pious humility I have notified my former dependants that I am only a miserable human being, a wretched creature that has naught more to do with governing the universe, and that in future, when in need and affliction, they must apply to the Supreme Ruler, who dwells in heaven, and whose budget is as inexhaustible as His goodness—whereas I, a poor ex-god, was often compelled, even in the days of my godhead, to seek the assistance of the devil. It was certainly very humiliating for a god to have to apply to the devil for aid, and I am heartily thankful to be relieved from my usurped glory. No philosopher shall ever again persuade me that I am a god. I am only a poor human creature, that is not over well; that is, indeed, very ill. In this pitiable condition it is a true comfort to me that there is some one in the heavens above to whom I can incessantly wail out the litany of my sufferings, especially after midnight, when Mathilde has sought the repose that she oft sadly needs. Thank God! in such hours I am not alone, and I can pray and weep without restraint; I can pour out my whole heart before the Almighty, and confide to Him some things which one is wont to conceal even from one's own wife.

After the above confession, the kindly-disposed reader will easily understand why I no longer found pleasure in my work on the Hegelian philosophy. I saw clearly that its publication would benefit neither the public nor the author. I comprehended that there is more nourishment for famishing humanity in the most watery and insipid broth of Christian charity than in the dry and musty spider-web of the Hegelian philosophy. I will confess all. Of a sudden I was seized with a mortal terror of the eternal flames. I know it is a mere superstition; but I was frightened. And so, on a quiet winter's night, when a glowing fire was burning on my hearth, I availed myself of the good opportunity, and cast the manuscript of my work on the Hegelian philosophy into the flames. The burning leaves flew up the chimney with a strange and hissing sound.

Thank God! I was rid of it! Alas! would that I could destroy in the same manner all that I have ever published concerning German philosophy! But that is impossible, and since I cannot prevent their republication, as I lately learned to my great regret, no other course remains but to confess publicly that my exposition of German philosophy contains the most erroneous and pernicious doctrines.

...It is strange! during my whole life I have been strolling through the various festive halls of philosophy, I have participated in all the orgies of the intellect, I have coquetted with every possible system, without being satisfied, like Messalina after a riotous night; and now, after all this, I suddenly find myself on the same platform whereon stands Uncle Tom. That platform is the Bible, and I kneel by the side of my dusky brother in faith with the same devotion.

What humiliation! With all my learning, I have got no farther than the poor ignorant negro who can hardly spell! It is even true that poor Uncle Tom appears to see in the holy book more profound things than I, who am not yet quite clear, especially in regard to the second part.

...But, on the other hand, I think I may flatter myself that I can better comprehend, in the first part of the holy book, the character of Moses. His grand figure has impressed me not a little. What a colossal form! I cannot imagine that Og, King of Bashan, could have looked more giant-like. How insignificant does Sinai appear when Moses stands thereon! That mountain is merely a pedestal for the feet of the man whose head towers in the heavens and there holds converse with God. May God forgive the sacrilegious thought! but sometimes it appears to me as if this Mosaic God were only the reflected radiance of Moses himself, whom he so strongly represents in wrath and in love. It were a sin, it were anthropomorphism, to assume such an identity of God and his prophet; but the resemblance is most striking.

I had not previously much admired the character of Moses, probably because the Hellenic spirit was predominant in me, and I could not pardon the lawgiver of the Jews for his hate of the plastic arts. I failed to perceive that Moses, notwithstanding his enmity to art, was nevertheless himself a great artist, and possessed the true artistic spirit. Only, this artistic spirit with him, as with his Egyptian countrymen, was applied to the colossal and the imperishable. But not, like the Egyptians, did he construct his works of art from bricks and granite, but he built human pyramids and carved human obelisks. He took a poor shepherd tribe and from it created a nation which should defy centuries; a great, an immortal, a consecrated race, a God-serving people, who to all other nations should be as a model and prototype: he created Israel.

I have never spoken with proper reverence either of the artist or of his work, the Jews; and for the same reason—namely, my Hellenic temperament, which was opposed to Jewish asceticism. My prejudice in favour of Hellas has declined since then. I see now that the Greeks were only beautiful youths, but that the Jews were always men, strong, unyielding men, not only in the past, but to this very day, in spite of eighteen centuries of persecution and suffering. Since that time I have learned to appreciate them better, and, were not all pride of ancestry a silly inconsistency in a champion of the revolution and its democratic principles, the writer of these pages would be proud that his ancestors belonged to the noble house of Israel, that he is a descendant of those martyrs who gave the world a God and a morality, and who have fought and suffered on all the battle-fields of thought.

The histories of the middle ages, and even those of modern times, have seldom enrolled on their records the names of such knights of the Holy Spirit, for they generally fought with closed visors. The deeds of the Jews are just as little known to the world as is their real character. Some think they know the Jews because they can recognise their beards, which is all they have ever revealed of themselves. Now, as during the middle ages, they remain a wandering mystery, a mystery that may perhaps be solved on the day which the prophet foretells, when there shall be but one shepherd and one flock, and the righteous who have suffered for the good of humanity shall then receive a glorious reward.

You see that I, who in the past was wont to quote Homer, now quote the Bible, like Uncle Tom. In truth, I owe it much. It again awoke in me the religious feeling; and this new birth of religious emotion suffices for the poet, for he can dispense far more easily than other mortals with positive religious dogmas.

...The silliest and most contradictory reports are in circulation concerning me. Very pious but not very wise men of Protestant Germany have urgently inquired if, now that I am ill and in a religious frame of mind, I cling with more devotion than heretofore to the Lutheran evangelic faith, which, until now, I have only professed after a luke-warm, official fashion. No, dear friends, in that respect no change has taken place in me, and if I continue to adhere to the evangelic faith at all, it is because now, as in the past, that faith does not at all inconvenience me. I will frankly avow that when I resided in Berlin, like several of my friends, I would have preferred to separate myself from the bonds of all denominations, had not the rulers there refused a residence in Prussia, and especially in Berlin, to any who did not profess one of the positive religions recognised by the State. As Henry IV. once laughingly said, "Paris vaut bien une messe," so could I say, with equal justice, "Berlin is well worth a sermon." Both before and after, I could easily tolerate the very enlightened Christianity which at that time was preached in some of the churches of Berlin. It was a Christianity filtered from all superstition, even from the doctrine of the divinity of Christ, like mock-turtle soup without turtle. At that time I myself was still a god, and no one of the positive religions had more value for me than another. I could wear any of their uniforms out of courtesy, after the manner of the Russian Emperor, who, when he vouchsafes the King of Prussia the honour to attend a review at Potsdam, appears uniformed as a Prussian officer of the guard.

Now that my physical sufferings, and the reawakening of my religious nature, have effected in me many changes, does the uniform of Lutheranism in some measure express my true sentiments? How far has the formal profession become a reality? I do not propose to give direct answers to these questions, but I shall avail myself of the opportunity to explain the services which, according to my present views, Protestantism has rendered to civilisation. From this may be inferred how much more I am now in sympathy with this creed.

At an earlier period, when philosophy possessed for me a paramount interest, I prized Protestantism only for its services in winning freedom of thought, which, after all, is the foundation on which in later times Leibnitz, Kant, and Hegel could build. Luther, the strong man with the axe, must, in the very nature of things, have preceded these warriors, to open a path for them. For this service I have honoured the Reformation as being the beginning of German philosophy, which justified my polemical defence of Protestantism. Now, in my later and more mature days, when the religious feeling again surges up in me, and the shipwrecked metaphysician clings fast to the Bible,—now I chiefly honour Protestantism for its services in the discovery and propagation of the Bible. I say "discovery," for the Jews, who had preserved the Bible from the great conflagration of the sacred temple, and all through the middle ages carried it about with them like a portable fatherland, kept their treasure carefully concealed in their ghettos. Here came by stealth German scholars, the predecessors and originators of the Reformation, to study the Hebrew language and thus acquire the key to the casket wherein the precious treasure was enclosed. Such a scholar was the worthy Reuchlinus; and his enemies, the Hochstraaten, in Cologne, who are represented as the party of darkness and ignorance, were by no means such simpletons. On the contrary, they were far-sighted Inquisitors, who foresaw clearly the disasters which a familiar acquaintance with the Holy Scriptures would bring on the Church. Hence the persecuting zeal with which they sought to destroy the Hebrew writings, at the same time inciting the rabble to exterminate the Jews, the interpreters of these writings. Now that the motives of their actions are known, we see that, properly considered, each was in the right. This reactionary party believed that the spiritual salvation of the world was endangered, and that all means, falsehood as well as murder, were justifiable, especially against the Jews. The lower classes, pinched by poverty, and heirs of the primeval curse, were embittered against the Jews because of the wealth they had amassed; and what to-day is called the hate of the proletariate against the rich, was then called hate against the Jews. In fact, as the latter were excluded from all ownership of land and from every trade, and relegated to dealing in money and merchandise, they were condemned by law to be rich, hated, and murdered. Such murders, it is true, were in these days committed under the mantle of religion, and the cry was, "We must kill those who once killed our God." How strange! The very people who had given the world a God, and whose whole life was inspired by the worship of God, were stigmatised as deicides! The bloody parody of such madness was witnessed at the outbreak of the revolution in San Domingo, where a negro mob devastated the plantations with murder and fire, led by a negro fanatic who carried an immense crucifix, amid bloodthirsty cries of "The whites killed Christ; let us slay all whites!"

Yes, to the Jews the world is indebted for its God and His word. They rescued the Bible from the bankruptcy of the Roman empire, and preserved the precious volume intact during all the wild tumults of the migration of races, until Protestantism came to seek it and translated it into the language of the land and spread it broadcast over the whole world. This extensive circulation of the Bible has produced the most beneficent fruits, and continues to do so to this very day. The propaganda of the Bible Society have fulfilled a providential mission, which will bring forth quite different results from those anticipated by the pious gentlemen of the British Christian Missionary Society. They expect to elevate a petty, narrow dogma to supremacy, and to monopolise heaven as they do the sea, making it a British Church domain—and see, without knowing it, they are demanding the overthrow of all Protestant sects; for, as they all draw their life from the Bible, when the knowledge of the Bible becomes universal, all sectarian distinctions will be obliterated.

While by tricks of trade, smuggling, and commerce the British gain footholds in many lands, with them they bring the Bible, that grand democracy wherein each man shall not only be king in his own house, but also bishop. They are demanding, they are founding, the great kingdom of the spirit, the kingdom of the religious emotions, and the love of humanity, of purity, of true morality, which cannot be taught by dogmatic formulas, but by parable and example, such as are contained in that beautiful, sacred, educational book for young and old—the Bible.

To the observant thinker it is a wonderful spectacle to view the countries where the Bible, since the Reformation, has been exerting its elevating influence on the inhabitants, and has impressed on them the customs, modes of thought, and temperaments which formerly prevailed in Palestine, as portrayed both in the Old and in the New Testament. In the Scandinavian and Anglo-Saxon sections of Europe and America, especially among the Germanic races, and also to a certain extent in Celtic countries, the customs of Palestine have been reproduced in so marked a degree that we seem to be in the midst of the ancient Judean life. Take, for example, the Scotch Protestants: are not they Hebrews, whose names even are biblical, whose very cant smacks of the Phariseeism of ancient Jerusalem, and whose religion is naught else than a pork-eating Judaism? It is the same in Denmark and in certain provinces of North Germany, not to mention the majority of the new sects of the United States, among whom the life depicted in the Old Testament is pedantically aped. In the latter, that life appears as if daguerreotyped: the outlines are studiously correct, but all is depicted in sad, sombre colours; the golden tints and harmonising colours of the promised land

179

are lacking. But the caricature will disappear sooner or later. The zeal, the imperishable and the true—that is to say, the morality—of ancient Judaism will in those countries bloom forth just as acceptably to God as in the old time it blossomed on the banks of Jordan and on the heights of Lebanon. One needs neither palm-trees nor camels to be good; and goodness is better than beauty.

The readiness with which these races have adopted the Judaic life, customs, and modes of thought is, perhaps, not entirely attributable to their susceptibility of culture. The cause of this phenomenon is, perhaps, to be sought in the character of the Jewish people, which always had a marked elective affinity with the character of the Germanic, and also to a certain extent with that of the Celtic races. Judea has always seemed to me like a fragment of the Occident misplaced in the Orient. In fact, with its spiritual faith, its severe, chaste, even ascetic customs,—in short, with its abstract inner life,—this land and its people always offered the most marked contrasts to the population of neighbouring countries, who, with their luxuriantly varied and fervent nature of worship, passed their existence in a Bacchantic dance of the senses.

At a time when, in the temples of Babylon, Nineveh, Sidon, and Tyre, bloody and unchaste rites were celebrated, the description of which, even now, makes our hair stand on end, Israel sat under its fig-trees, piously chanting the praises of the invisible God, and exercised virtue and righteousness. When we think of these surroundings we cannot sufficiently admire the early greatness of Israel. Of Israel's love of liberty, at a time when not only in its immediate vicinity, but also among all the nations of antiquity, even among the philosophical Greeks, the practice of slavery was justified and in full sway,—of this I will not speak, for fear of compromising the Bible in the eyes of the powers that be. No Socialist was more of a terrorist than our Lord and Saviour. Even Moses was such a Socialist; although, like a practical man, he attempted only to reform existing usages concerning property. Instead of striving to effect the impossible, and rashly decreeing the abolition of private property, he only sought for its moralisation by bringing the rights of property into harmony with the laws of morality and reason. This he accomplished by instituting the jubilee, at which period every alienated heritage, which among an agricultural people always consisted of land, would revert to the original owner, no matter in what manner it had been alienated. This institution offers the most marked contrast to the Roman statute of limitations, by which, after the expiration of a certain period, the actual holder of an estate could no longer be compelled to restore the estate to the true owner, unless the latter should be able to show that within the prescribed time he had, with all the prescribed formalities, demanded restitution. This last condition opened wide the door for chicanery, particularly in a state where despotism and jurisprudence were at their zenith, and where the unjust possessor had at command all means of intimidation, especially against the poor who might be unable to defray the expense of litigation. The Roman was both soldier and lawyer, and that which he conquered with the strong arm he knew how to defend by the tricks of law. Only a nation of robbers and casuists could have invented the law of prescription, the statute of limitations, and consecrated it in that detestable book which may be called the bible of the Devil—I mean the codex of Roman civil law, which, unfortunately, still holds sway.

I have spoken of the affinity which exists between the Jews and the Germans, whom I once designated as the two pre-eminently moral nations. While on this subject, I desire to direct attention to the ethical disapprobation with which the ancient German law stigmatises the statute of limitations: this I consider a noteworthy fact. To this very day the Saxon peasant uses the beautiful and touching aphorism, "A hundred years of wrong do not make a single year of right."

The Mosaic law, through the institution of the jubilee year, protests still more decidedly. Moses did not seek to abolish the right of property; on the contrary, it was his wish that everyone should possess property, so that no one might be tempted by poverty to become a bondsman and thus acquire slavish propensities. Liberty was always the great emancipator's leading thought, and it breathes and glows in all his statutes concerning pauperism. Slavery itself he bitterly, almost fiercely, hated; but even this barbarous institution he could not entirely destroy. It was rooted so deeply in the customs of that ancient time that he was compelled to confine his efforts to ameliorating by law the condition of the slaves, rendering self-purchase by the bondsman less difficult, and shortening the period of bondage.

But if a slave thus eventually freed by process of law declined to depart from the house of bondage, then, according to the command of Moses, the incorrigibly servile, worthless scamp was to be nailed by the ear to the gate of his master's house, and after being thus publicly exposed in this disgraceful manner, he was condemned to life-long slavery. Oh, Moses! our teacher, Rabbi Moses! exalted foe of all slavishness! give me hammer and nails that I may nail to the gate of Brandenburg our complacent, long-eared slaves in liveries of black-red-and-gold.

I leave the ocean of universal religious, moral, and historical reflections, and modestly guide my bark of thought back again into the quiet inland waters of autobiography, in which the author's features are so faithfully reflected.

In the preceding pages I have mentioned how Protestant voices from home, in very indiscreet questions, have taken for granted that with the reawakening in me of the religious feeling my sympathy for the Church had also grown stronger. I know not how clearly I have shown that I am not particularly enthusiastic for any dogma or for any creed; and in this respect I have remained the same that I always was. I repeat this statement in order to remove an error in regard to my present views, into which several of my friends who are zealous Catholics have fallen. How strange! at the same time that in Germany Protestantism bestowed on me the undeserved honour of crediting me with a conversion to the evangelic faith, another report was circulating that I had gone over to Catholicism. Some good souls went so far as to assert that this latter conversion had occurred many years ago, and they supported this statement by definitely naming time and place. They even mentioned the exact date; they designated by name the church in which I had abjured the heresy of Protestantism, and adopted the only true and saving faith, that of the Roman Catholic Apostolic Church. The only detail that was lacking was how many peals of the bell had been sounded at this ceremony.

From the newspapers and letters that reach me I learn how widely this report has won credence; and I fall into a painful embarrassment when I think of the sincere, loving joy which is so touchingly expressed in some of these epistles. Travellers tell me that the salvation of my soul has even furnished a theme for pulpit eloquence. Young Catholic priests seek permission to dedicate to me the first fruits of their pen. I am regarded as a shining light—that is to be—of the Church. This pious folly is so well meant and sincere that I cannot laugh at it. Whatever may be said of the zealots of Catholicism, one thing is certain: they are no egotists; they take a warm interest in their fellow-men—alas! often a little too warm an interest. I cannot ascribe that false report to malice, but only to mistake. The innocent facts were in this case surely distorted by accident only. The statement of time and place is quite correct. I was really in the designated church on the designated day, and I did there undergo a religious ceremony; but this ceremony was no hateful abjuration, but a very innocent conjugation. In short, after being married according to the civil law, I also invoked the sanction of the Church, because my wife, who is a strict Catholic, would not have considered herself properly married in the eyes of God without such a ceremony; and for no consideration would I shake this dear being's belief in the religion which she has inherited.

It is well, moreover, that women should have a positive religion. Whether there is more fidelity among wives of the evangelic faith, I shall not attempt to discuss. But the Catholicism of the wife certainly saves the husband from many annoyances. When Catholic women have committed a fault, they do not secretly brood over it, but confess to the priest, and as soon as they have received absolution they are again as merry and light-hearted as before. This is much pleasanter than spoiling the husband's good spirits or his soup by downcast looks or grieving over a sin for which they hold themselves in duty bound to atone during their whole lives by shrewish prudery and quarrelsome excess of virtue. The confessional is likewise useful in another respect. The sinner does not keep her terrible secret preying on her mind; and since women are sure, sooner or later, to babble all they know, it is better that they should confide certain matters to their confessor than that they should, in some moment of overpowering tenderness, talkativeness, or remorse, blurt out to the poor husband the fatal confession.

Scepticism is certainly dangerous in the married state, and, although I myself was a free-thinker, I permitted no word derogatory to religion to be spoken in my house. In the midst of Paris I lived like a steady, commonplace townsman; and therefore when I married I desired to be wedded under the sanction of the Church, although in this country the civil marriage is fully recognised by society. My free-thinking friends were vexed at me for this, and overwhelmed me with reproaches, claiming that I had made too great concessions to the clergy. Their chagrin at my weakness would have been still greater had they known the other

182

concessions that I had made to the hated priesthood. As I was a Protestant wedding a Catholic, in order to have the ceremony performed by a Catholic priest it was necessary to obtain a special dispensation from the archbishop, who in these cases exacts from the husband a written pledge that the offspring of the marriage shall be educated in the religion of the mother. But, between ourselves, I could sign this pledge with the lighter conscience since I knew the rearing of children is not my specialty, and as I laid down my pen the words of the beautiful Ninon de L'Enclos came into my mind—"O, le beau billet qu' a Lechastre!"

...I will crown my confessions by admitting that, if at that time it had been necessary in order to obtain the dispensation of the archbishop, I would have bound over not only the children but myself. But the ogre of Rome, who, like the monster in the fairy tales, stipulates that he shall have for his services the future births, was content with the poor children who were never born. And so I remained a Protestant, as before—a protesting Protestant; and I protest against reports which, without being intended to be defamatory, may yet be magnified so as to injure my good name.

...There is not a particle of unkindly feeling in my breast against the poor ogre of Rome. I have long since abandoned all feuds with Catholicism, and the sword which I once drew in the service of an idea, and not from private grudge, has long rested in its scabbard. In that contest I resembled a soldier of fortune, who fights bravely, but after the battle bears no malice either against the defeated cause or against its champions.

Fanatical enmity towards the Catholic Church cannot be charged against me, for there was always lacking in me the self-conceit which is necessary to sustain such an animosity. I know too well my own intellectual calibre not to be aware that with my most furious onslaughts I could inflict but little injury on a colossus such as the Church of St. Peter. I could only be a humble worker at the slow removal of its foundation stones, a task which may yet require centuries. I was too familiar with history not to recognise the gigantic nature of that granite structure. Call it, if you will, the bastile of intellect; assert, if you choose, that it is now defended only by invalids; but it is therefore not the less true that the bastile is not to be easily captured, and many a young recruit will break his head against its walls.

As a thinker and as a metaphysician, I was always forced to pay the homage of my admiration to the logical consistency of the doctrines of the Roman Catholic Church, and I may also take credit to myself that I have never by witticism or ridicule attacked its dogmas or its public worship. Too much and too little honour has been vouchsafed me in calling me an intellectual kinsman of Voltaire. I was always a poet; and hence the poesy which blossoms and glows in the symbolism of Catholic dogma and culture must have revealed itself more profoundly to me than to ordinary observers, and in my youthful days I was often touched by the infinite sweetness, the mysterious, blissful ecstasy and awe-inspiring grandeur of that poetry. There was a time when I went into raptures over the blessed Queen of Heaven, and in dainty verse told the story of her grace and goodness. My first collection of poems shows traces of this beautiful Madonna period, which in later editions I weeded out with laughable anxiety.

The time for vanity has passed, and everyone is at liberty to smile at this confession.

It will be unnecessary for me to say that, as no blind hate against the Catholic Church exists in me, so also no petty spite against its priests rankles in my heart. Whoever knows my satirical vein will surely bear witness that I was always lenient and forbearing in speaking of the human weaknesses of the clergy, although by their attacks they often provoked in me a spirit of retaliation. But even at the height of my wrath I was always respectful to the true priesthood; for, looking back into the past, I remembered benefits which they had once rendered me; for it is Catholic priests whom I must thank for my first instruction; it was they who guided the first steps of my intellect.

Pedagogy was the specialty of the Jesuits, and although they sought to pursue it in the interest of their order, yet sometimes the passion for pedagogy itself, the only human passion that was left in them, gained the mastery; they forgot their aim, the repression of reason and the exaltation of faith, and, instead of reducing men to a state of childhood, as was their purpose, out of the children they involuntarily made men by their instruction. The greatest men of the Revolution were educated in Jesuit schools. Without the training there acquired, that great intellectual agitation would perhaps not have broken out till a century later.

Poor Jesuit fathers! You have been the bugbear and the scapegoat of the liberals. The danger that was in you was understood, but not your merits. I could never join in the denunciations of my comrades, who at the mere mention of Loyola's name would always become furious, like bulls when a red cloth is held before them. It is certainly noteworthy, and may perhaps at the assizes in the valley of Jehoshaphat be set down as an extenuating circumstance, that even as a lad I was permitted to attend lectures on philosophy. This unusual favour was exceptional in my case, because the rector Schallmeyer was a particular friend of our family. This venerable man often consulted with my mother in regard to my education and future career, and once advised her, as she afterwards related to me, to devote me to the service of the Catholic Church, and send me to Rome to study theology. He assured her that through his influential friends in Rome he could advance me to an important position in the Church. But at that time my mother dreamed of the highest worldly honours for me. Moreover, she was a disciple of Rousseau, and a strict deist. Besides, she did not like the thought of her son being robed in one of those long black cassocks, such as are worn by Catholic priests, and in which they look so plump and awkward. She knew not how differently, how gracefully, a Roman *abbate* wears such a cassock, and how jauntily he flings over his shoulders the black silk mantle, which in Rome, the ever-beautiful, is the uniform of gallantry and wit.

Oh, what a happy mortal is such a Roman *abbate*! He serves not only the Church of Christ, but also Apollo and the Muses, whose favourite he is. The Graces hold his inkstand for him when he indites the sonnets which, with such delicate cadences, he reads in the Accademia degli Arcadi. He is a connoisseur of art, and needs only to taste the lips of a young songstress in order to be able to foretell whether she will some day be a celeberrima cantatrice, a diva, a world-renowned prima-donna. He understands antiquities, and will write a treatise in the choicest Ciceronian Latin concerning some newly-unearthed torso of a Grecian Bacchante, reverentially dedicating it to the supreme head of Christendom, to the Pontifex Maximus, for so he addresses him. And what a judge of painting is the Signor *Abbate*, who visits the painters in their ateliers and directs their attention to the fine points of their female models! The writer of these pages had in him just the material for such an *abbate*, and was just suited for strolling in delightful *dolce far niente* through the libraries, art galleries, churches, and ruins of the Eternal City, studying among pleasures, and seeking pleasure while studying. I would have read mass before the most select audiences, and during Holy Week I would have mounted the pulpit as a preacher of strict morality,—of course even then never degenerating into ascetic rudeness. The Roman ladies, in particular, would have been greatly edified, and through their favour and my own merit I would, perhaps, have risen eventually to high rank in the hierarchy of the Church. I would, perhaps, have become a monsignore, a violet-stocking; perhaps even a cardinal's red hat might have fallen on my head. The proverb says—

"There is no priestling, how small soe'er he be,
That does not wish himself a Pope to be."

And so it might have come to pass that I should attain the most exalted position of all, for, although I am not naturally ambitious, I would yet not have refused the nomination for Pope, had the choice of the conclave fallen on me. It is, at all events, a very respectable office, and has a good income attached to it; and I do not doubt that I could have discharged the duties of my position with the requisite address. I would have seated myself composedly on the throne of St. Peter, presenting my toe for the kisses of all good Christians, the priests as well as the laity. With a becoming dignity I would have let myself be carried in triumph through the pillared halls of the great basilica, and only when it tottered very threateningly would I have clung to the arms of the golden throne, which is borne on the shoulders of six stalwart camerieri in crimson uniform. By their side walk bald-headed monks of the Capuchin order, carrying burning torches. Then follow lackeys in gala dress, bearing aloft immense fans of peacocks' feathers, with which they gently fan the Prince of the Church. It is all just like Horace Vernet's beautiful painting of such a procession. With a like imperturbable sacerdotal gravity—for I can be very serious if it be absolutely necessary—from the lofty Lateran I would have pronounced the annual benediction over all Christendom. Here, standing on the balcony, *in pontificalibus* and with the triple crown upon my head, surrounded by my scarlet-hatted cardinals and mitred bishops, priests in suits of gold brocade and monks of every hue, I would have presented my holiness to the view of the swarming multitudes below, who, kneeling and with bowed heads, extended farther than the eye could reach; and I could composedly have stretched out my hands and blessed the city and the world.

185

But, as thou well knowest, gentle reader, I have not become a Pope, nor a cardinal, nor even a papal nuncio. In the spiritual as well as in the worldly hierarchy I have attained neither office nor rank; I have accomplished nothing in this beautiful world; nothing has become of me—nothing but a poet.

But no, I will not feign a hypocritical humility, I will not depreciate that name. It is much to be a poet, especially to be a great lyric poet, in Germany, among a people who in two things—in philosophy and in poetry—have surpassed all other nations. I will not with a sham modesty—the invention of worthless vagabonds—depreciate my fame as a poet. None of my countrymen have won the laurel at so early an age; and if my colleague, Wolfgang Goethe, complacently writes that "the Chinese with trembling hand paints Werther and Lotte on porcelain," I can, if boasting is to be in order, match his Chinese fame with one still more legendary, for I have recently learned that my poems have been translated into the Japanese language.

...But at this moment I am as indifferent to my Japanese fame as to my renown in Finland. Alas! fame, once sweet as sugared pine-apple and flattery, has for a long time been nauseous to me; it tastes as bitter to me now as wormwood. With Romeo, I can say, "I am the fool of fortune." The bowl stands filled before me, but I lack a spoon. What does it avail me that at banquets my health is pledged in the choicest wines, and drunk from golden goblets, when I, myself, severed from all that makes life pleasant, may only wet my lips with an insipid potion? What does it avail me that enthusiastic youths and maidens crown my marble bust with laurel-wreaths, if meanwhile the shrivelled fingers of an aged nurse press a blister of Spanish flies behind the ears of my actual body. What does it avail me that all the roses of Shiraz so tenderly glow and bloom for me? Alas! Shiraz is two thousand miles away from the Rue d'Amsterdam, where, in the dreary solitude of my sick-room, I have nothing to smell, unless it be the perfume of warmed napkins. Alas! the irony of God weighs heavily upon me! the great Author of the universe, the Aristophanes of Heaven, wished to show the petty, earthly, so-called German Aristophanes that his mightiest sarcasms are but feeble banter compared with His, and how immeasurably he excels me in humour and in colossal wit.

Yes, the mockery which the Master has poured out over me is terrible, and horribly cruel is His sport. Humbly do I acknowledge His superiority, and I prostrate myself in the dust before Him. But, although I lack such supreme creative powers, yet in my spirit also the eternal reason flames brightly, and I may summon even the wit of God before its forum, and subject it to a respectful criticism. And here I venture to offer most submissively the suggestion that the sport which the Master has inflicted on the poor pupil is rather too long drawn out: it has already lasted over six years, and after a time becomes monotonous. Moreover, if I may take the liberty to say it, in my humble opinion the jest is not new, and the great Aristophanes of Heaven has already used it on a former occasion, and has, therefore, been guilty of plagiarism on His own exalted self. In order to prove this assertion, I will quote a passage from the Chronicle of Lüneberg. This chronicle is very interesting for those who seek information concerning the manners and customs of Germany during the middle ages. As in a fashion-journal, it describes the wearing-apparel of both sexes which was in vogue at each particular period. It also imparts information concerning the popular ballads of the day, and quotes the opening lines of several of them. Among others, it records that during the year 1480 there were whistled and sung throughout all Germany certain songs, which for sweetness and tenderness surpassed any previously known in German lands. Young and old, and the women in particular, were quite bewitched by these ballads, which might be heard the livelong day. But these songs, so the chronicle goes on to say, were composed by a young priest who was afflicted with leprosy, and lived a forlorn, solitary life, secluded from all the world. You are surely aware, dear reader, what a horrible disease leprosy was during the middle ages, and how the wretched beings afflicted with this incurable malady were driven out from all society and from the abodes of men, and were forbidden to approach any human being. Living corpses, they wandered to and fro, muffled from head to foot, a hood drawn over the face, and carrying in the hand a bell, the Lazarus-bell, as it was called, through which they were to give timely warning of their approach, so that every one could get out of the way in time. The poor priest whose fame as a lyric poet the chronicle praised so highly was such a leper; and while all Germany, shouting and jubilant, sang and whistled his songs, he, a wretched outcast, in the desolation of his misery sat sorrowful and alone.

Oh, that fame was the old, familiar scorn, the cruel jest of God, the same as in my case, although there it appears in the romantic garb of the middle ages. The *blasé* king of Judea said rightly, There is no new thing under the sun. Perhaps that sun itself, which now beams so imposingly, is only an old warmed-up jest.

Sometimes among the gloomy phantasms that visit me at night I seem to see before me the poor priest of the Lüneberg Chronicle, my brother in Apollo, and his sorrowful eyes stare strangely out of his hood; but almost at the same moment it vanishes, and, faintly dying away, like the echo of a dream, I hear the jarring tones of the Lazarus-bell.

FOOTNOTES:

[1] There are three German biographies of Heine, those of Strodtmann, Karpeles, and Proelss; a new edition of his works in six volumes, with a biography and notes by Dr. Elster, has lately been announced. Mr. Matthew Arnold, by his well-known essay and poem, has done much to stimulate English interest in Heine. A careful critical estimate by Mr. Charles Grant (*Contemporary*, Sept. 1880) may be mentioned with praise.

[2] He lodged at 32, Craven Street, Strand.

[3] "C'est le Bible, plus que tout autre livre," a distinguished French critic wrote lately, "qui a façonné le génie poétique de Heine, en lui donnant sa forme et sa couleur. Ses véritables maîtres, ses vrais inspirateurs sont les glorieux inconnus qui ont écrit l'Ecclesiaste et les Proverbes, le Cantique des cantiques, le livre de Job et ce chez d'œuvre d'ironie discrète intitulé: le livre du prophète Jonas. Celui qui s'appelait un rossignol Allemand niché dans la perruque de Voltaire fut à la fois le moins évangélique des hommes et le plus vraiment biblique des poètes modernes."

[4] He committed suicide.—Ed.

[5] Or in English.

[6] Heine at this period was never tired of laughing at Göttingen, and here couples it with six particularly insignificant towns.—Ed.

[7] *Dumm* in German means stupid.

[8] In the French edition Heine rightly substituted "The Emperor Maximilian."

[9] *i.e.* Ariosto.—Ed.

[10] Michel corresponds to John Bull.—Ed.

[11] This is a common error. Faust the printer is quite a distinct person.—Ed.

[12] It must be remembered that Heine visited England in 1827.

[13] This is said to have been the response of Princess Borghese to a friend who asked her how she had felt when sitting as a model to Canova.—Ed.

[14] Heine only quotes the first part of the passage from the *Reisebilder*, which has here been given in full.—Ed.

[15] Heine here alludes to *Atta Troll*.—Ed.

45593903R00107

Made in the USA
San Bernardino, CA
12 February 2017